Redesign Your Life in Modern Age

Redesign Your Life in Modern Age

Balvinder Kumar

PRABHAT PRAKASHAN

ISO 9001: 2015 Publishers

Published by
PRABHAT PRAKASHAN
4/19 Asaf Ali Road,
New Delhi-110 002 (INDIA)
e-mail: prabhatbooks@gmail.com

ISBN 978-93-5322-976-4
REDESIGN YOUR LIFE IN MODERN AGE
by Shri Balvinder Kumar

First Edition
2020

Price
₹ 500.00 (Rupees Five Hundred only)

Printed at
R-Tech Offset Printers, Delhi

Contents

Acknowledgements

First and the foremost, I would like to express my gratitude to my loving family - Neha, Ankita, Akshay and Ishan, who all have supported and contributed in making this book a reality. Special thanks to Amit Slathia, the artist and painter in getting making many illustrations done. Special appreciation goes to my niece Ishani Anand, a young artist, designer and illustrator who also helped me in converting many ideas and concepts into illustrations. I am further thankful to Ms Jo-Ann Langseth, USA for editing the book in a timely manner. Last but surely not the least; I am grateful to my close friend Ashutosh Sharma, USA who facilitated me in conceptualizing many core ideas that form part of the book – thank you Ashu.

Foreword

Balvinder and I studied together at the University of Delhi, and upon meeting after over 35 years in August 2017, and getting over all the lame excuses and the complains of not keeping in touch with each other, he suggested we write a book together, perhaps around the controversial topic of "Destiny". His enthusiasm was commendable, and I could not refuse. This venture also brought old memories back. Balvinder, then a student of the Botany Department, and I used to often go for lunch or a cup of tea/coffee together. His only connection to Physics (where I was a student) was his friendship with me. He would start a discussion and ask questions, and I would respond with a lot of quantum and classical physics and science explanations. As friends we had a strong bonding and we could discuss all types of issues from the problems of the education system and academia to the government and the society and the future both of mankind and ours. At the top of the list was the worry of finding a respectable and well-paying job. This was a normal and usual concern any Post graduate student in India had at that time. We would sip coffee and talk about the open job competitions and what it would take to make it to the selection list. He was always a very dedicated student, but initially not as determined, and I used to give him endless lectures about the importance of having a definite goal and to be determined, and how to achieve this goal by defining clear objectives and taking coherent actions (as if I knew it all!!).

Over time, Balvinder gained confidence and became more determined by each day to make it to the top, and in the end, we both achieved the goals we set for ourselves: he got selected to the Indian Forest Services and then to The Indian Administrative Service (retiring as the Secretary of the Department of the Government of India), and as my goal was simply to learn the subject and how to use knowledge for the betterment of mankind thus I continued my research work in engineering and sciences abroad and in due course was awarded Professorships in European, Indian and US Universities, and later became CEO of my own Engineering and Science Centre.

What followed our meeting in 2017, was a concerted effort to produce the book we agreed to write. Over the next couple of years, we discussed the topic and its scope in depth, and continued to talk about many specific issues and discussed our philosophies about life and destiny, and of course, the making of the book. It was like reliving our old times together, but this time over the phone and with a lot more of practical life experiences that helped us to focus on the content of the book! Due to unavoidable circumstances, we experienced some hiccups and delays and although the material for the book had been produced, it was not cohesive and not yet ready for publication. We agreed that instead of delaying this work any further it would be more productive to share the ideas with the readers in a different format and in the form of an independent book. Balvinder rose to the challenge, and he produced this book.

In "Redesign Your Life in Modern Age", Balvinder has presented multiple aspects of living well and to the fullest by discussing the essentials of the individual and the environment. The book with over 70 illustrations has an Indian flair, but it should serve the global readers as well. It is like a delicious meal served as beautifully presented "Indian Thali". Overall, an uninitiated reader will enjoy the aroma of the experience and the taste of knowledge that the book has, and an involved reader will in addition have the delight of discussing the flavours, taste and the ingredients of this thali's items both individually and collectively. A reader will find this book useful in revisiting his or her current lifestyle and living, and help initiate himself or herself to start discovering the meaning and purpose of his goals and daily acts. In the end, in "Life's Journey" Balvinder has, through his own views, attempted to take the reader to a well laid path to living a satisfactory life.

When Balvinder asked me to write a foreword for this book, I happily accepted it as I knew that in this book, not only I have seen the reflection of many of our discussions on human life, habits, destiny and religion and spiritualism, but also with his nature and vast experience, he is deemed to be the right person to present these thoughts in a book form for the benefit of a greater audience.

In his introduction, Balvinder is able to expand on the conclusion about the elements that affect an individual's life that I have reached and discussed with him on several occasions.: "human, human and human" – He neatly explains these three prime determinants that make up a human journey. Some other excellent quotes from the book are:

Humans, Nature and Destruction: In the 1960s quote by scientist Dr James Lovelock "The nature and life co-exist or more accurately, the life is part of nature and vice versa."

"Most of the time, the main problem is that we are not aware that we are in overthinking mode due to strong identification with our mind."

The book presents a brief but an up to date knowledge of the brain and body relationship: "The most straightforward scientific evidence of a strong relationship between the physical brain and the mind is the impact that physical alterations have on the functioning of the mind. On this basis, there is a broad understanding among the medical community that our brain, the visible structure is located inside our head, while our mind is part of the invisible, transcendent world of thought, feeling, attitude, belief, imagination etc. To understand the mind, it is essential to have a deeper knowledge of our brain." The book goes on to explain the mind both conscious and subconscious and its role and actions in the decision making and acts of an individual.

Balvinder has done justice to Nature by discussing the human acceptance of the existence of God and spirituality. The book goes on to discuss the human suffering, illness and pain and the ultimate journey to death. In this context, the comments on the state of the mind and the reality versus the imagination of the mind and Balvinder's research on studies that have shown the need of focus as a prerequisite to happiness. In this context, the mind and hence thoughts are linked to the immune system thus the health of the body becomes an important factor in achieving happiness. In the end, the book presents the inevitable death of living (not just human) in a very acceptable and welcoming way. A good work will never be without some flaws and "Man's Spiritual Journey" is no different as it has some disconnects and the explanations and situational examples assumes that readers are familiar with Indian culture.

In the past Balvinder has succeeded in taking the readers through 'Man's Spiritual Journey' and then interesting them in 'Awakening the Thinking Mind', and now when the mind is up and running, he has succeeded in helping the reader complete their quest for a happy life in the book "Redesign Your Life in Modern Age". In summary, "Redesign Your Life in Modern Age" is written by a person of highest integrity, vast experience and knowledge and is a complete "thali", offering every reader a plenty to choose from, and overall this book is a great feast for the reader's mind.

Professor Ashutosh Sharma "Bhraguvanshi"
December 1, 2019
Town of Gilbert, Arizona, USA

Just a Human who has been fortunate to be in the company of Educators, Philosophers, Inventors, Scientists, Technologists, Authors, Thinkers.....

Chief Executive Officer and President, Bishanti Corp, Oregon, USA
Distinguished Visiting Professor, IIT, Kanpur, India
Founder, Institute of National Development and Individual Advancement, Oregon, USA
Founding Director, Arizona Vedic Cultural Center of Swaminarayan Gurukul USA, Phoenix, USA
Former Director of Molecular Measurement Technology Centre, Cranfield, UK

List of Illustrations

1

Introduction

1.1 Human Journey

Every one's life ends the same way. What really matters is how we design our life.

Human, human and human -- these are the three prime determinants that make up a human journey. The first one is comprised of our biological parents and forebears. The second is the set of people who nurture the new-born and influence his or her early childhood experiences. Last is the set of people who cross paths with us and make a contribution to our upbringing. This may include influencing our thoughts, behaviours, actions, and pivotal events. We undertake our journey from birth to death deeply intertwined with these three sets of people. Directly and indirectly, they assist us in reaching our final destination in life. In this way, the complex and undulating journey through innumerable experiences leads us to our destiny.

The first set of humans, those who have determined our genetic blueprint, have set the stage on which the mind is exposed to the outer world. The genetic material in every cell carries the blueprint for every aspect of our physical body, from our height and complexion to the risks of critical illnesses, such as cancer. No two humans are genetically identical -- yet we are all 99.9 percent the same! The genes we carry from our parents and ancestors make every individual unique. There are estimated to be around 20,000 to 25,000 human genes. This estimate has been repeatedly revised, starting from one hundred and extending to over one thousand. The genes we are born with don't change, but their expression can vary substantially, especially during one's formative years. How genes work is a highly complex process. Experiences leave a chemical 'signature' on the genes which determine whether and how the genes are expressed.

The debate over the role of genetic blueprint versus environmental factors that impact us throughout our lives is one of the oldest philosophical issues within psychology. In the past, there was a widespread view suggesting that our genes determine our life to a significant extent, but later medical science suggested that nurture – the environment in which we all grow – is far more important than the genes we inherit from our parents. Today, however, most experts recognize that both nature and nurture play a significant role in determining our lives. They also realize that nature and nurture interact in important ways all throughout life.

Figure 1.1: Life Journey – We all undertake different routes and modes to reach the same destination in life.

The second set of influential humans, the parents and other caregivers, deeply affect the infant and establish a close link with his or her mind. Neurological research shows that the early childhood years play a key role in children's brain development. Leaving deep imprints on the child's mind, some of those early experiences may overshadow some aspects of genetic constitution written by the biological parents. The interaction of genes and experience determines childhood mental health. The physical, emotional, and social development of young children has a direct effect on their overall development and on the adult they become. The emotional well-being of young children is directly tied to the functioning of their parents and the families in which they live. When these relationships are mentally adverse, harmful, or stressed, children are at high risk of developing mental health problems at later stages.

Numerous studies and simple observation show that adverse and traumatic experiences during childhood often lead to violent and criminal behaviour in adolescence and adulthood. Young children who experience recurrent abuse or neglect, domestic violence, or an addicted parent are particularly vulnerable. The quality of care and nurturing that is provided by the parents has greatest impact on the future of their children. Recent studies confirm that the first five years are particularly critical for the development of the child's brain. They are especially important in the development of learning skills, as well as social and emotional abilities.

Now the last set of people enters the new person's life, establishing connections as the child undertakes his or her journey into adulthood. As self-awareness grows, and with it an independent understanding of the world, the individual now establishes a place on the path leading to destiny. By exercising varying degrees of "free will," we start writing our story, portraying ourselves as the central figure. The greater the free will we exercise while interacting with the surrounding world, the more conscious our choices become. We are then better equipped to realize the opportunities that we all come across.

We now design the map by which our journey proceeds through events that take place in life. Our individual world starts spinning, and the creation and fulfilment of destiny begins. Desires, aspirations, ambitions, and goals drive us forward along the path. Sometimes we make a quantum jump; other times we're forced to go back. Often we stumble and get up promptly, while other times we remain stationary or "stuck." Our response to circumstances determines the pace of our journey toward destiny. Our capacity to make conscious decisions and the degree of self-awareness about oneself and the world around us affects our pace as well.

As we proceed towards our destination, we taste a cocktail of success and failure, pain and suffering, satisfaction and disappointments. How we react and cope with those situations also influences the speed of our life's journey. Control over inner self, mind, and body, all connected and deeply intermingled, shape the lessons we learn in life. On some occasions, we surrender ourselves to circumstances, while at other times we graciously and wisely prevail. All situations, pleasant or unpleasant, are necessary parts of our journey. As we grow, our understanding of life evolves, and so does our idea of destiny. All the while, we are designing our destiny and traveling to our destination.

If we see things from a broad perspective, we find three kinds of people around us. First are those who are born lucky. It means they're born with a silver spoon in their mouths, having a strong support system by way of wealth normally coupled with social status. They are not required to struggle; their future course of events is mostly scripted by their families. In a way, their destiny runs along mostly predictable lines. In the second category are those who have grown up well-nurtured and in excellent overall circumstances. Thanks to their parents' loving ministrations and close guidance, they generally have a robust belief system. For them, to create their destiny is a comparatively easy task. Here we again have a lucky group of people who can steer their destiny without much difficulty. Theirs is an especially conducive environment to fulfilling their dreams.

The last category into which the population falls is far more numerous and less fortunate. Because of their circumstances, they are compelled to lead a repetitive, habitual, and more or less purposeless life. There may be dozens of convincing reasons for them to lead such a life, including poverty, backwardness, and adverse experiences during early years. Those so afflicted flow with the current, like water. They know of no other way to live than in their own self-made prisons. Lacking confidence, they fear the unknown that awaits them outside of their comfort zone and strenuously resist change. They may, however, stumble upon opportunities which may change the course of their life. Such "unfortunates" make very little effort to create their destiny. They justify their existence on the basis of the Hindu concept of karma. They are there because of their old karmas (thoughts, words, and deeds) from previous incarnations. They do, however, try to help their children or very close ones in fulling their dreams. That's the main driving force behind their life. For them, there is just about no possibility of "creating destiny" but rather meekly following a predetermined path to a set destination. They are unaware that in venturing out from their self-defined little world they could refashion their destiny.

There is a huge variation in our physical and mental attributes when we land in this world. The reason is the genetic material that we inherit from our biological parents. Though 99.9% of the genetic blueprint is identical among humans, the unique environmental conditions in which we all grow up amplify our differences. As we age, each one of us becomes more and more "unique" – older, but newer! Within that uniqueness we continue to make choices and decisions that keep on scripting the roadmap of our journey. Many stagnate, some move faster, some bound forward and some walk backward. Uncertainty plays a major role as we move ahead on the path. That's how we keep on scripting our destiny.

Those who pursue destiny must possess a fair degree of self-awareness and practice mindfulness. Not only must they be aware of their own strengths, weaknesses, behaviour patterns, mind-set, and other traits, but also free of habitual, addictive, and compulsive/impulsive behaviour. Self-awareness enables them to understand other people -- their feelings, emotions, and behaviour -- in kind and helpful ways. It is also advantageous to have a robust and sound belief system, coupled with purpose. It is the power of beliefs that cause things to happen in our lives. Rooted deeply within us, most of us hold them dear. Without positive and progressive beliefs about ourselves and our fellows, it's extremely difficult to succeed and create our own destiny.

We all have been gifted with the power of neuroplasticity. Our brain is so plastic that it keeps on changing throughout our lifetime, responding to new situations and challenges with the creation of fresh neural pathways and connections. Whenever we experience anything new, including injury and disease, the brain engages in synaptic pruning, eliminating the connections that are no longer useful and building new ones. Right up till the last day of our life, we can form new neural pathways in our head while also strengthening our existing connections. At any stage of life, strengthening occurs by way of practice, repetition, and reinforcement.

Our mind is hugely flexible and adaptable. We can transform ourselves whenever need arises. However, the inhibitor is emotional inertia -- we resist change, and don't want to take risks or venture out from our habitual life. Despite our unawareness of this fact, most of us love the way we live! We spend years and years following the same routines. There may off course be, and generally are, genuine reasons to come out from those stale and difficult life situations, but we surrender and give up struggle very easily. That's the majority of people keep on living a meaningless life.

Although most people are not in a position to script their own destiny due to a host of reasons, we are all collectively contributing to Human Destiny in the Making. On the one hand, humanity is facing many crises, such as global warming, increasing inequality, drug-resistant diseases, warfare and mass destruction, and physical and spiritual poverty. There may be many other potential threats, like asteroid impact and cosmic threats. On the other hand, humanity is witnessing technological revolutions at breakneck speed. Given these challenges and opportunities, we predict that humans will reach a point at which they consciously create their own destiny. Technology should certainly assist humans, in the long run, to overcome the challenges that we encounter today in managing our internal and external worlds. However, all suppositions are hypothetical presumptions that may go totally wrong.

To reach our desired destination requires the right mix of conditions and circumstances. We can equate creation or shaping of destiny with the Goldilocks principle, which states that out of the vast range of all possible conditions on Earth, the "just right" combinations of chemicals, elements, temperature, etc., all miraculously emerged in order to support life. Life could not have evolved if prevailing conditions were even slightly different. Likewise, we can design our destiny to the degree that there is a right mix of conditions, such as the favourable genetic blueprint we get from our parents, inspiring and supportive childhood experiences, encountering the right opportunities at the most opportune moments, stable temperament and mind-set, a robust belief system, and so on. The list is exhaustive. If at any stage something goes wrong, then the journey gets disrupted. The direction gets changed. An extremely small variation in any prevailing condition can have wider ramifications on the outcome. The butterfly effect is not rare to observe in our lives.

2

Understanding the Outer World –with legacy of the past, journey to modern age and beyond

Most ancient civilizations are known to have existed for thousands of years B.C., and there is plenty of evidence that many of them were highly developed. One commonality that may be seen from their ruins and whatever archaeological evidence is available today is that the people of these civilisations firmly believed in supernatural phenomena, in life after death, and a supreme power controlling all earthly happenings (and, more precisely, those of their own local world). Crusaders, whether religious or simply bloodthirsty, held the common belief that they were destined and commanded by God to do what they were doing. The trend was seen among people of less standing and power as well. The weaker segment of society thus accepted atrocities and injustice as the inevitable result of destiny.

Today's citizen increasingly believes in global citizenship, but remains extremely protective of his own local way of living, often to the point of xenophobia. In such a situation it is likely that as new technologies emerge and further development happens, the human race will increasingly look outwards to unexplored frontiers, both on earth and on other planets, where they may live with like-minded individuals. These explorations and developments lack coherence with the old belief of "destiny" by nature. Furthermore, such explorations cannot be made just by accident, as a tremendous amount of time and effort must go into planning, resource development, and implementation of these plans. Emergence of androids, artificial intelligence, and eventually self-sufficient and most likely self-reproducing or replicating humanoids seems inevitable.

On the one side, we are progressing at lightning speed in this century. We have entered into a fourth industrial revolution, in which disruptive technologies and trends such as the Internet of Things (IoT), robotics, virtual reality (VR), 3D printing, and artificial intelligence (AI) are changing the way we live and work. On the other side, large parts of countries like India are still living in the early 20th century. Radically different worlds exist simultaneously. Progressive societies look eagerly to having control over their destiny, but the remaining population still sees their destiny as completely in the hands of God. This seeming chasm between believers and nonbelievers will continue to exist. Religion is still deeply embedded in our collective psyche. A large section of the population strongly believes in the existence of God, and they think of God as the sole driving force behind the actions they take.

Thanks to technological innovation and the sharp surge in social media, all minds becoming linked. Almost the whole world has become one global society, connected though the digital world. Mobile internet has also rapidly increased the number of people who are actively participating in social media and the digital economy. From GPS navigation to ride-sharing platforms like Uber and Ola, to mobile-payment systems, there is huge impact on people's lives and livelihoods. Our collective awareness is rising exponentially. People share their feelings among both their intimates and cyber "friends" the world over. This was never seen a decade earlier. We can see clear signs of a major shift or change in collective consciousness.

Over the centuries, humanity has been becoming less and less violent and aggressive, as more and more people have started adopting a more spiritual way of life. Spiritual practices like meditation and yoga are increasingly embraced, not only in the Western world but throughout the entire world. As organized religion declines, spirituality rises. These changes are, however, very slow, so it's difficult to perceive noticeable changes around us. On certain fronts, such as climate change, internal conflicts, and terrorism, we see deterioration. But in many areas, progressive and transformational changes are taking place. The average citizen across globe is becoming richer, healthier, smarter, and more connected with others through technology.

While it's extremely difficult, if not impossible, to conceptualize human destiny in its nascent state, it's certain that humanity will transcend from a collective of individuals to a synchronized Global Society. It will be a sustainable and cooperative society, including all nations. This Global Society should, by its very nature, be incompatible with internal conflicts, nationalism, terrorism, etc. As we increasingly connect through technology and quality of life improves sharply, the emergence of a Global Society seems certain. Brain-to-brain communication through direct transmission of thoughts will soon become commonplace. We are gradually moving to create a singular mind.

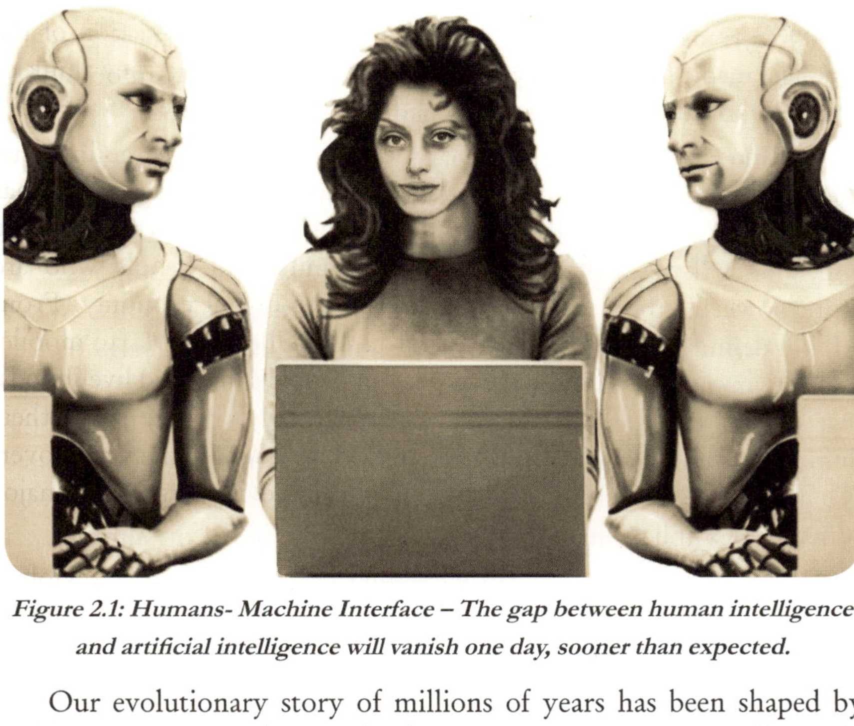

Figure 2.1: Humans- Machine Interface – The gap between human intelligence and artificial intelligence will vanish one day, sooner than expected.

Our evolutionary story of millions of years has been shaped by genetic mutation and natural selection. We continue to collectively evolve through these processes. Laurence Daniel Hurst, Professor of Evolutionary Genetics in the Department of Biology and Biochemistry at the University of Bath and Director of the Milner Centre for Evolution, shares this view. He is of the opinion that human evolution may be accelerating. His studies suggest that "by looking at global studies of our DNA, we can see evidence that natural selection has recently made changes and continues to do so. Though modern healthcare frees us from many causes of death, in countries without access to good healthcare, populations are continuing to evolve."

On the one hand, humans are continuing to evolve naturally ; on the other hand, technology is progressing at a much faster rate. The way we live, think, and work is changing rapidly. Every year sees the emergence of new technologies and inventions. It also seems certain that humans will act as a bridge between biological life and technology. Our bodies, our brains, and machines may all one day merge, predict scientists. A mind-controlled robotic exoskeleton was dramatically demonstrated when a paraplegic man made the first kick at the 2014 World Cup. The ability to translate neurological information into hard data is growing fast. The medical community is poised to download neural information. These and other wonders await humanity in the near future.

Another component that will greatly influence human destiny is the advent of superior-to-human artificial intelligence (AI), with huge implications on human life. Among the possibilities are that humans will, sooner than we think, be able to create giant supercomputers, far more powerful than the composite of all human intelligence. While AI will definitely and radically improve human life, it will also replace humans in many traditional areas of employment. Experts predict that AI will not only enhance human effectiveness, but also threaten human autonomy and capabilities. Serious concerns have been raised about human-AI evolution and AI's impact on the future of humanity. Whether it will be able to design human destiny in the distant future is a debatable point, but again, the possibility exists.

Modern humans are left with no choice but to continue along this 400-year-old path of science and technology development and utilization. Clearly, the slow death of "destiny" orchestrated by nature or "God" began with the observations and discoveries of ground breaking thinkers and philosophers. There were no scientists in the early days, as only the privileged and near-privileged were free to express their thoughts in the courts and public. They had no clear scientific method to follow and no systematic pathway to achieve results or arrive at conclusions. These great minds of their time were brave and different from the general crowd, but they were, of course, "way off" on many of their conclusions.

The time has come when we have started doubting our own abilities to imagine what our future will hold. Not so long ago, generation after generation lived in more or less the same world. Now the speed of change is increasing exponentially. The generation gap is rising sharply. We can still imagine how our grandparents must have lived, but now we can't simply foresee how our great-grandchildren will be living. Their lives will be fundamentally different from ours. Maybe, thousands of years down the road, we would have conquered at least the Milky Way galaxy, if not farther. Humans would certainly be living on many others planets, like Venus and Mars. We lack the knowledge to make assumptions about human destiny beyond, say, a hundred years.

Dr. Michio Kaku, an American theoretical physicist and futurist, presents a compelling vision of how humanity may develop a sustainable civilization in outer space. He reveals the developments in robotics, nanotechnology and biotechnology that may allow us to terraform and build habitable cities on Mars and beyond. He then journeys out of our solar system and discusses how new technologies such as Nano ships, laser sails. and fusion rockets may actually make interstellar travel a possibility. Ultimately, he predicts that humans may someday achieve a form of immortality and be able to leave their bodies entirely, laser porting to new havens in space. What fascinating future scenarios! Is this the destiny we are making, or is something else destined for humanity? Only wild guesses can be made.

Today, more than ever before, humans appear to be moving away from traditions in all aspects of life. Dogmas, assumptions, and traditional values are being challenged, reviewed, refined, and changed. Modern humans' consideration of destiny is no different. It is in our DNA to seek change, and this cannot be done unless we challenge what we know. Indeed, we want our destiny to be written by our own hand, a kind of "Designer Destiny," as it were.

2.1 Humans, Nature and Destruction – we are on the verge of a tipping point of nature's destruction

Given Earth's perfect conditions for life, it is no coincidence that life in such astonishing variety and abundance has flourished here. Cosmologists have not been, so far, able to detect life on any other planet in the universe. In the 1960s, scientist Dr James Lovelock proposed the Gaia hypothesis, which says that living organisms interact with their inorganic surroundings on Earth to form a synergistic, self-regulating system that helps to maintain and perpetuate the conditions for life. Lovelock named the idea after Gaia, the goddess who personified the Earth in Greek mythology. The Gaia theory further explains that the composition of the Earth's atmosphere is kept in a dynamically steady state by the presence of life. The theory maintains that this system as a whole seeks a physical and chemical environment optimal for contemporary life. Later this theory has been researched further especially in view of our current climate crisis. Lovelock argues that humans have now pushed Gaia to her limit.

Lovelock thought that we are heading for a very warm world, where only Polar Regions will be comfortable for most life forms. Eventually, he suspected, Gaia would pull things back into check, but it might be too late for the human race. His prediction appears to be coming true. There is no denying the fact that Mother Nature is associated with each and every act and breath of humans, and life in general. Where then does destiny fit into this equation of nature and mankind (assuming that no life other than human life has a destiny!!)? In order to see through this seeming life-nature duality (like the quantum mechanical wave particle duality), we find that it is impossible to separate nature from human life!

One can argue that when life ends into nature, nature comes back to life! The fruits of human development have brought upon nature many unforeseen and unfortunate outcomes. This was not planned by nature (obviously) or by humans who, most certainly, due to their ignorance, short sightedness, laziness, mismanagement, and corporate greed have individually and collectively impacted environment. In our constant reach for growth and development, the ecological systems on which not just humanity but all life forms depend have been adversely impacted. Advancing at an exponential rate, science and technology have gradually changed the relationship we earlier had.

Our treatment of Mother Earth has radically changed. We never thought nature could be so deeply intertwined with our existence and so essential for our physical and psychological well-being. According to a study conducted by researchers at the University of California, Berkeley, and Princeton University, USA, in the year 2013, shifts in climate were strongly linked to human violence around the world ; even relatively minor departures from normal temperatures or rainfall can substantially increase the risk of conflict. We'd never before imagined that climate change could be related to human conflicts.

Figure 2.1A: Nature that nurtures humans is being systematically destroyed by humans themselves.

The degradation/ exploitation of nature has led to climate change, which in turn poses existential threat to almost all ecosystems. An ecosystem is a geographic area like a forest, lake, desert, or mountain range, wherein a community of plants, animals, and other living organisms cooperatively exist. If one component is adversely affected, the equilibrium of the entire system is disturbed. Because of changing conditions owing to climate change, wildlife is disappearing at an alarming rate. According to the World Wildlife Federation, the Earth has lost half of its wild animal population over the past 40 years. Everywhere, from Pole to Pole, the impact of global warming can be felt. It's one sign of a destiny-in-the-making for the human race.

Some believe that mankind and Earth as a whole have reached an environmental tipping point which will be hard, if not impossible, to stabilize and reverse. Glaciers, oceans, forests, mountains, and deserts showcase the sad results of these changes. Even the planets and moon of our solar system have been showing remarkable changes.

According to a 2019 report from the Intergovernmental Science-Policy Platform on Biodiversity and Ecosystem Services, nature is being eroded at rates unprecedented in human history. The IPBES assessment has shown the strong interrelationship between climate change, the loss of biodiversity and human well-being. Climate change has been identified as a primary driver of biodiversity loss, already altering every part of nature. Sir Robert Watson, who chaired this study, warns, "We have all assumed that nature would always be here for us and our children. However, our boundless consumption, short-sighted reliance on fossil fuels, and our unsustainable use of nature now seriously threaten our future."

More than 11,000 scientists from 153 countries have warned that 'untold suffering' is inevitable without deep and lasting shifts in human activities that contribute to greenhouse gas emissions and other factors related to climate change. They declared clearly and unequivocally that planet Earth is facing a climate emergency. In fact, they presented a suite of graphical vital signs of climate change over the last 40 years for human activities which led change the climate. In November 2019, in a paper published in BioScience, 11,258 signatories including 69 from India, present trends in climate change and provide a set of effective mitigating actions. They noted that the climate crisis was closely linked to excessive consumption of the wealthy lifestyle. To secure a sustainable future, we must change how we live. They also concluded that the prospects would be greatest if decision-makers and all of humanity promptly respond to this warning and declaration of a climate emergency and act to sustain life on planet Earth, our only home.

In almost all nations, we are increasingly witnessing catastrophic changes linked with global warming. Still, we have not become serious, serious enough to address this massive problem. Most of us are making small efforts, but, feeling impotent, we watch helplessly. We are all creating our own destiny. Global warming's impact on biodiversity and climate will alter the course of man's journey. We will soon reach a threshold level. Although human extinction seems a remote possibility at present, other catastrophic consequences may be just as alarming. "Hot Earth" may well be our destiny -- or merely speculation! Some people sincerely believe that the scientific community will surely come up with technological solutions to limit the impact of global warming. Time will tell. In any case, collectively we are consciously designing our own destiny, the destiny in the making.

2.2 Our minds are intimately interconnected. Together they form the collective human consciousness.

In this physical reality, we generally hold a world view of separateness, believing that we are discrete and autonomous entities, totally separate from our fellow beings, because this is what we appear to be perceiving through our senses. However, in ancient times, especially in India, man's views were essentially based upon wholeness. The most significant doctrine expressed in the Vedas and the Upanishads is that Reality is One and Absolute, changeless and eternal, the Brahman. And the ordinary human world of many separate, discrete, and finite things, which our mind perceives through our senses, is merely an illusion. Hence the Vedas speak of a unified field of "pure consciousness" that permeates all of creation. Now modern physicists have established that there is indeed a unified energy field that connects everything, from molecules to plants to animals to planets and galaxies in the universe.

According to physicist/inventor/engineer Nikola Tesla, "If you want to find the secrets of the universe, think in terms of energy, frequency, and vibration." Previously, it was believed that the material universe was the foundation of our physical reality. However, this all changed when scientists began to recognize that energy is the fabric of the universe, and all matter originates from energy. Physical atoms are made up of vortices of energy that are constantly spinning and vibrating. Matter, at its tiniest observable level, is energy. In the scientific world we speak of the unified energy field, and in the spiritual world, we refer to The Universal Consciousness, or Universal Mind. In religion, we call it by various names, including God. Our minds are interconnected through this Universal Mind.

Telepathic experiences and different psychic abilities also give credence to the idea that our minds are connected at a much more intimate level than ever imagined. There are many fascinating incidents of people who have absolutely no communication with each other coming up with almost identical discoveries or solutions to the same problems at the exact same time. Case studies of this phenomenon have been compiled by the scientific community.

There is a perceptible correlation between universal consciousness and the physical world, especially during extraordinary events. Experiments by the Global Consciousness Project (GCP) have shown that human consciousness can make a string of random numbers appear in a slightly less random - or rather, more orderly way - when people hold common intentions to do so, or when there is a special state of coherent group consciousness. In other words, our minds can organize the physical world at a quantum level. In this way, from individual atoms to individual brains to groups of brains emerges global consciousness. *Now, if consciousness is indeed universal and omnipresent, then everything that exists in the universe may ultimately be interconnected and unified through Universal Mind.*

Figure 2.2: Humans are interconnected deeply with each other and together they form universal consciousness or Global Mind.

The GCP is an international, multidisciplinary project involving researchers from several institutions and countries, designed to explore whether the construct of interconnected consciousness can be scientifically measured and validated. The project builds on excellent experiments conducted over the past 35 years at a number of laboratories, demonstrating that human consciousness interacts with random event generators (REGs), apparently "causing" them to produce non-random patterns. The studies conducted by the GCP reveal that major global events that engage our minds and hearts have a measurable effect upon the network's computer, non-random changes that are nearly impossible to have been caused by chance. This means that such incidents impact the global consciousness, which in turn affects REG detectors. In other words, large-scale group consciousness has effects upon the physical world.

Under this project, data is collected and analysed continuously from a global network located in up to 70 host sites around the world at any given time. The purpose is to examine subtle correlations that may reflect the presence and activity of collective consciousness in the world. When millions of us share intentions and emotions, the GCP network data show meaningful departures from expectation. Studies have found that large-scale group consciousness can affect the physical world.

Amit Goswami, a world-renowned theoretical nuclear physicist and a pioneer of the new paradigm of science called "science within consciousness," proposes to place his quantum theory of consciousness within the overall context of monistic idealism. He postulates that consciousness, the ground of all being, is primary. Traditional idealism holds that consciousness is the primary reality and that all objects, whether material or mental, are objects within consciousness. The consciousness of all of us is identical to the consciousness that is the ground of all being. The sense of separation that we feel and observe is an illusion, as has always been claimed by the sages. The separation among us does not exist in reality. However, ignorance of our true nature gives us the illusion of separateness.

This means that what appears to be individual consciousness (mind) is in reality Universal Consciousness/mind. In other words, the consciousness/mind that I think is mine is identical to the consciousness that you think is yours. This does not mean that the contents of my mind are the same as the contents of your mind. These are individual and depend on our brain's structure, individual sensory mechanisms, and the conditioning of mind, as discussed earlier. There exists a nonlocal Universal Consciousness, or Universal Mind, and the effects on this nonlocal mind are clearly evidenced when people are meditating in a group. All material objects are really mental objects. Mind can affect them because there is no difference between mind and matter.

Across the world large numbers of contemporary thinkers, scientists, philosophers, and spiritual gurus are advocating the emergence of a new era of growing collective consciousness. *We are entering a new world of evolutionary transformation as human awareness expands.* It is widely believed that the transformation of our world civilization has been prompted by a rapid increase in technology, advances in quantum science, and expansion of social media through the Internet. Global connectivity is growing at an ever faster pace. We all are getting connected with others irrespective of age, nationality, and religion. Like-minded people can share their concerns, beliefs, and emotions across the globe. Millions of people channel their energies for a common cause through digital media. As our collective awareness starts to flower into spiritual awakening, people around the globe show increasing interest in non-religious practices like mindfulness meditation, TM, yoga and breathing exercises. Eventually in future, sooner than expected, humanity will evolve into a global mind, deeply interconnecting each and every human on the earth.

2.3 What does being "spiritual but not religious" mean? To meet life's challenges, we need to become more spiritual than religious.

Religion goes back to ancient times, when primitive man perceived all objects, including animals and plants, as being imbued with supernatural aspects (animism). Later, the concept of God arose, an all-powerful and omnipotent Supreme Being watching humans from on high. Then as civilizations developed, organised religions were born and started to proliferate. There are now billions of followers of organised religions such as Christianity, Islam, Judaism, Hinduism, and Buddhism. There are also lesser known but equally established religions such as the Baha'I faith, Sikhism, and Zoroastrianism. Gradually, devotional practices, superstitions, and rituals were developed in each religion. The basic characteristics of all religions are similar. There is firm belief in an omnipotent and loving Supreme Being. All religions also have their own set of beliefs, which their followers are required to respect and follow. Religion provides cohesiveness and harmony within their communities.

It is necessary for the unseen, controlling power to give psychological and emotional succour to humans. Hagel's philosophy maintains that humanity invented the idea of God as a consolation and distraction from the sorrow and grief of the world. God is a human creation over which humanity has authority and control. Karl Marx too has left us his frank opinion: "Religion is the opium of the masses." In his mind "God is simply a projection of human concerns. Human beings look for superhuman being in the fantasy reality of heaven, and find nothing there but their own reflection." This is the reason that faith and firm belief in God's existence has not abated despite tremendous progress in science and technology. The majority of the population continues to believe in their religion and/or God's role in their lives.

Christians form the biggest religious group of all, with 31% of the world's population. Next come Muslims (24%), then Hindus (15%) and Buddhists (6.9%). Of the remaining population, though some may not be affiliated with any religious group, they may believe in God's existence. Then others are "spiritual but not religious," meaning that they do not practice any religion, but are likely to believe in a Higher Power, or feel their mystical union with same. It means that worldwide, the majority of the world's population still affiliate with one particular religion, but their absolute numbers are declining. According to India's 2011 census, the number of "people without religion" rose fourfold to about 3 million. Though this number may seem insignificant compared to India's population, the trend is clear. In many developed countries like the USA, religion as a whole is losing ground, rather than increasing.

According to a Gallup survey, 68% of Americans in 1975 had a great deal or quite a lot of confidence in the church or organised religion. Now this percentage has dropped precipitously to 36%. Fewer Americans indicate that they identify with an official religion these days, and fewer say they are members of a church, mosque, or synagogue. All of this seems to dovetail with people now seeing themselves as spiritual but not religious. However, religion continues to expand in economically and socially insecure places, such as many African and Muslim dominated nations. Where conditions are more stable, the number of churchgoers continues to decline.

Figure 2.3: Consistently, more and more people, throughout the world, are moving towards spiritual practices rather than engaging themselves in religious activities.

In India, though recent figures from such surveys are not available, it's certain that more people, especially from the younger generation, while not members of any organised religion, are becoming more in tune with their spirituality. However, absolute numbers of people belonging to any religious group may not be declining. Thanks to meditation and other spiritual practices, more people are joining the ranks of "spiritual but not religious." Interestingly, millennials (individuals born between 1981and 1996) who tend to be passionate about their careers, fitness, and the Climate Crisis, but not interested in religion. For many of them, the gym or a beautiful national park is their temple. While hi-tech pursuits consume many of their waking hours, millennials tend to keep their minds open to the possibility of higher realities.

As previously discussed, the majority of people -- especially in India -- have opted to remain cozily nestled in their comfort zones. They have barely any time for spiritual practices, and are generally ignorant as to what exactly spirituality or spiritual life may be. The difference between being religious and spiritual is unclear to them. Each one of us has our own ideas about spirituality ; there are many myths and misconceptions involving spiritual practices in India. On the other hand, the majority of us find comfort and emotional security in spending whatever time we can take out from our schedule in religious activities. We are actively involved in an organized system of practices, rituals, and prayers to facilitate closeness to God. Our belief system has room for a pantheon of personal gods and goddesses, which are in great supply in the Hindu religion. Therefore, a large population are fine with just being religious, rather than venturing out for spiritual practices.

Recently, an interesting study has found that the majority of older people are inclined to remain religious, rather than switching over to spirituality. They have more faith in religion. The research study, published in the *Journal for the Scientific Study of Religion*, confirmed that in many developed countries where the older population is increasing (as in Japan), the older people tend to be more religious than the younger generations. Following solid religious beliefs, rather than tuning in to their own inner experiences of God, may be more aligned with their comfort zones. Among its conclusions the study reminds us that "as the developed world greys, they will become the majority by 2040."

Let's understand what, in simpler terms, spirituality actually means. The essence of spirituality is to know our true selves and to discover the real meaning and purpose of our life. The self we know, the individual ego, is a limited representation of our identity. Since we are largely ignorant of our true selves, we derive a false sense of identity from what we feel about ourselves, and how others see us. When we discover our deeper sense of Self, we are freed from many of the fears that unnecessarily plague our mind. We can then experience inner peace, an inner security that does not depend upon the behaviour and actions of others or the events taking place around us. Therefore, through spiritual practices like meditation, we increase self-awareness and gain better understanding of ourselves.

Through spiritual practices, our awareness expands, resulting in better mental and emotional control over ourselves. With this we can grow in empathy, extending greater compassion and lovingkindness toward others. In this way, we not only manage our mind in far better ways, but also meet life's challenges in a more effective manner. No one's life is smooth. In fact, life is full of challenges. We are very often subjected to ups and downs and may experience pain and suffering. The real test of life comes when we pass through a troubled phase. Abiding in true spirituality helps put the mind at ease while also giving us courage, strength, and patience to understand and overcome. We develop a greater sense of resilience. This is what we mean when we say, "being spiritual but not religious."

2.4 In modern era of reason and rationality, We still largely believe in God's role in creating our destiny

Before the emergence of the scientific viewpoint on destiny -- that we are all empowered to create our own destiny -- most religions considered God to be the only supernatural power controlling our lives, and thus our destiny. Destiny, which is variously referred to as fate, is a predetermined course of events or predetermined future for the human race as well as individuals. Some religions give comfort to people with the belief that God decides their destiny, and that if something goes terribly wrong, they may justify the event as God's Will. In this age of science and technology, the majority of the population is not completely convinced that we are wholly and solely responsible for creating our own destiny. Ancient beliefs, both religious and spiritual, persist. Many feel that God is the only agent who writes our fate and destiny. Whatever happens in our life is according to His dictate. Others believe that we can tweak that dictate a bit via petitionary prayers and righteous deeds. Even among the highly educated, people don't rule out the role of God in deciding their lives.

Figure 2.4: Majority of the people still believe God's role/hand in creating our destiny

In some denominations of Christianity, the followers consider an all-powerful God to be the only force with complete control over one's fate. God make a plan for every individual. The Bible speaks of a divine plan, or God's plan. Fate is under God's plan. God is holy, wise, and benevolent. Only God is sovereign, and His sovereign control is called divine providence. In other words, everything that happens in the world is made to work out according to God's plan. This plan includes a reward for good behaviour and for those who trust Him. Similarly, in Islam, fate is the decree of Allah. Fatalism is a major premise of Islam, which demands total submission to the sovereignty of Allah. Fatalism is: whatever happens, happens, and we can't do anything about it. However, in Hinduism, instead of God, past deeds and acts play a crucial role in creating our destiny.

The lives and destiny we create is the sum total of the consequences of our deeds. However, there are problems in accepting this theory of karma. The timing and nature of the outcomes of our deeds are unknown to us. When a blind child is born, believers in karma tend to blame it on some evil deed of his parents, or of the baby himself, in past lives. When an innocent is murdered brutally, the suspected cause is again assigned to karma. Of course, no one knows about his or her past life; no concrete evidence exists. In this way, karma can always be the scapegoat. In the Hindu religion, reincarnation justifies our present sufferings and also gives hope for the future as the energy of good thoughts, words, and deeds comes back to us like a boomerang.

The Bhagavad Gita (often referred to as the Gita) is an ancient Indian text that became an important work of Hindu tradition in terms of both literature and philosophy. It is a 700-verse Sanskrit scripture that is part of the Hindu epic *The Mahabharata*. According to the Gita, "*Karmanye vadhikaraste ma phaleshu kadachana*," which means that one should not consider oneself the doer of his actions – God is responsible for everything. When we assume doership for an action, it means that we feel we are doing an action instead of realizing that God is getting everything done and we must simply surrender our actions to God. In other words, we should make efforts and focus on the efforts but not on the outcome.

Ramana Maharshi (1879-1950) was one of the most respected Indian sages and of international repute. He approved a number of paths and spiritual practices but recommended self-enquiry as the principal means to remove ignorance and abide in Self-awareness, together with devotion or surrender to the Self. He accepted the laws of karma but said they are applicable only as long as a person imagines that he is separate from the Self. He says that *"Whether or not one is performing actions, if the delusion of individuality – the ego, 'I am the doer of actions' – is completely annihilated, that is the attainment of actionlessness.*" He proclaims that the loss of doership alone is the right kind of actionlessness, meaning the action done without any desire for the result/outcome.

This concept is often misunderstood : how we can lose the sense of doership. If a person kills another person then he is the killer, and the "doer" of that killing. That being so, he must be punished. How can we say that a murderer is a "non-doer?" Ramana Maharshi explains that we are responsible, in a worldly sense, for the actions we take. Hence, the killer is a doer in the worldly sense. However, in a spiritual sense, the execution and consequences of any action arise as a result of the totality of various related actions by different individuals, which influence the particular action or situation. He is not a single, discrete person taking a particular action. His past conditioning of thoughts and behaviour, childhood experiences, etc., must have directly or indirectly contributed to the action. It means the person is not the "sole doer" of that particular action. In worldly sense, though, he *is* the doer.

Times are changing; faith in God and religion is declining. People are gradually realizing the importance of their potential to script their own journey. Notwithstanding the uncertainty and unexplainable events that happen in everyone's life, more and more people are dissociating their destiny from God's role. Millennials in particular, who are turning away from religion and inclining more toward spirituality, don't see their destiny as being in the hands of a Supreme Being. For them, career and relationships - often illumined by the recognition and celebration of unity -- is their newly discovered God. Millennials are of a generation that is very much about owning and controlling their destiny, and not in the way that previous generations saw it. They prefer spending quality time with their friends and family to Sunday worship and religious pilgrimages. Therefore, over time, as the world changes, so too does one's understanding of the relationship between God and destiny.

2.5 We need God for emotional and psychological support. Religion is still deeply embedded in our collective psyche.

As long as humans are insecure, vulnerable, and living without some kind of faith, they will continue to need God. Not only are we hardwired for

God, but He is very much there in our collective psyche. Ideas about God have successfully survived for hundreds of thousands of years as man evolved from hunter-gatherers to the complex being that he is today. Even scientists who seek and find answers to many questions such as -- What was there before the Big Bang? What is the nature of dark energy and dark matter? What exactly is consciousness, and how did we become conscious? What is beyond the horizon of this universe? -- Often evoke some sort of mysterious entity or pervading consciousness that constitutes and governs all.

Numerous concepts and hypotheses have been postulated by philosophers, religious scholars, and other thought leaders which reinforce our faith in the existence of God. From St. Thomas Aquinas's Five Proofs, to ontological arguments, to the anthropic principle and the theory of intelligent design, we have much to ponder. However, this question will remain unsolved in the absence of any conclusive or empirical proof. In any case, each one of us has their own ideas about God which are unique and personal. Given the unknowable attributes of God, everyone's ideas are highly diverse. In any case, the primary advantage of believing in the existence of God is consolation and the reassurance we continue to derive from the faith. I believe that is why most of us do need God.

For many, there is a personal God, who very minutely oversees their lives. He makes elaborate plans for each life. He writes our destiny before we come into this world. We will get punished or rewarded according to our deeds in this generation or perhaps in our next incarnation. There is a famous and relevant quote by George Carlin, an American author that goes like this: "*Religion has actually convinced people that there's an invisible man – living in the sky – who watches everything you do, every minute of every day. And the invisible man has a special list of ten things he does not want you to do. And if you do any of these ten things, he has a special place, full of fire and smoke and burning and torture and anguish, where he will send you to live and suffer and burn and choke and scream and cry forever and ever till the end of time ..... But he loves you !* "

For some, there is a God who doesn't interfere in the lives of each and every individual. He has broader plans for humanity. Why do we need God in this modern age of science, reason, and rationality? For one thing, just about everyone needs psychological and emotional support.

Life is full of uncertainties, sorrows, and tragedies. No can escape such eventualities. At the most trying times, support from God is sought. We can justify deaths and other loss by believing that this is God's Will, or part of His greater plan, or maybe for a greater good. We get solace from such beliefs, attributing ultimate love and wisdom to God. Experiencing a Heavenly Father helps millions of people to bear and sometimes overcome tragic or simply difficult experiences. Without such support, misfortunes and any personal challenge can be far more painful. Therefore, the eternal being and presence of God is required for humanity to fill the gaps when no other comfort or explanation is available.

During our life's journey, when we are faced with situations that make us feel uncertain, insecure, fearful, and vulnerable, we need God. He is believed to be all-powerful, all-loving, and sensitive to our needs. Many find that God also responds to their prayers and the rituals they perform to seek His blessings. Occasionally, God also bypasses the laws of nature by showing us miracles or supernatural events, some of which become the fodder for myth and folklore. This is what we call a religious or personal God. A very large segment of religious individuals believes in a personal God. However, there is also widespread belief in a God of Science. Here God is seen as the cosmic intelligence behind the order, harmony, and complexity, which is beyond the human's capacity to comprehend. God has created an intelligent, conscious, and self-organising universe. Modern science has, in large part, embraced the God of Science.

Despite (and sometimes *because of)* scientific and technological advances in almost all areas of life, it appears that even the most literate populations have belief in God. Many of us simply feel safer and more secure believing in God's presence rather than denying and rejecting that which might be the Ultimate Reality. There is a popular philosophical argument called Pascal's wager that asserts that it is wise to believe in God, even if God's existence cannot be proved or disproved through reason, and even if it turns out to be false.

This argument was presented by seventeenth-century French philosopher, mathematician, and physicist, Blaise Pascal (1623–1662). According to his thinking, if we wager that God does not exist, and there is indeed no God, then it doesn't matter. There's no point in even making a wager. If, however, there *is* a God and we deny His existence, then we risk God's wrath and may be sent to hell after death. The most felicitous outcome, of course, would be that God does exist and we believed it right along, in which case our reward would be eternal, unlimited happiness. Therefore, it's better to believe in His existence even if there is no God : The unbeliever has nothing to gain and perhaps everything to lose, whereas the believer may have everything to gain and nothing to lose. Many people tend to remain neutral even if they have serious doubt about God's existence.

Figure 2.5: The invisible hand of God that provide us emotional and psychological support on many occasions.

There is another very relevant question that usually arises when we talk about God. It's that if God is so powerful, benevolent, and all-loving, then why does He permit people to commit cruelty and crimes against their fellow beings ? Sometimes the intensity of the cruelly is beyond our imagining, and on those occasions this question invariably comes to the mind of theists. This problem is also called "theodicy." Theodicy is a theological construct that attempts to vindicate God in response to the fundamental problem of evil in all its expressions.

There have been diverse arguments, with different philosophical approaches to this problem. Two dominant responses prevail. First, God allows evil in order to create a greater good. If there were no cruelty and evil, people would not have the necessary contrast against which to appreciate goodness, compassion, and love of others. Second, since God allows us to exercise free will, evil is its natural consequence. As an inevitable result of human freedom, evil motivates humans to grow and evolve ; God therefore allows evil as the price of freedom/free will. However, many don't accept this argument because there are occasions when human atrocities and even devastating acts of nature seemingly cannot be justified as a cost of freedom. At the same time, many feel that this world of good and evil is a perfectly conducive and enabling environment for growth and development. Amidst infinite possibilities for good and evil, humans may evolve toward that for which they were "created" by God.

In any case, people feel safe and secure in believing in God, irrespective of whether God exists or not. It's better not to reject or deny God, especially when people are subject to uncertainties and the inherent vulnerability of life. Any situation can be explained by the existence of God. For emotional and psychological support when in trouble, God helps. There are studies that support the relationship between belief in God or Higher Power and mental health treatment. People who believe in God respond better to treatment for depression than those who do not. Even in loneliness, God can be of great psychological support. Some studies have also established the tonic link between faith or belief in Higher Power and psychological wellbeing. Many of us would do well to turn to God for support and guidance.

ooo

3

The Adaptation of Life – Recognize the Impediments Coming on Our Way to Redesign Our Life Journey

We all encounter innumerable complexities during our life journey. We are deeply interwoven with the social fabric of our society. Not only we are intimately connected with many others but also an integral part of our highly intricate social, political, and economic system. As population grows and humanity evolves, resources are becoming increasingly scare while competition among ourselves to get our due share intensifies. Not many efforts are required if we continue to live in our own comfort zone. If we want to create our own destiny, or achieve something meaningful in life, then rigorous efforts are required. This is especially so if we are not born into a rich family or live in a developed nation: we must struggle extra to achieve success. To lead a life of purpose and design our life's journey, we first need to recognize the impediments that we need to overcome. We need to identify all of them and then make efforts.

The obstacles and challenges that we face may be on a personal or professional front, and may also be from social and environment fronts. The most important are personal challenges, relating to our mental and psychological aspects. If we know how to manage our mind, life can be very smooth. We must never lose sight of the fact that negative, toxic, and distressing thoughts can badly affect our mental health, and, by extension, our physical health. Mind and body are two sides of the same coin. The mind can be our most valuable ally or our worst enemy, depending on how badly or well managed it is. Sensitive and fragile, the mind needs care. If we are flexible, resilient, and mindful, we can face any kind of opposition in life. With a clear, confident, and steady mind-set, we express our thoughts and feelings in the best, most life-giving way.

Social and environmental impediments must also be addressed. Some people go out of their way, to be helpful, while others mainly create obstacles for us. The former delight in sharing opportunities, while the "troublemakers" place hurdles along our path. It is our great challenge and privilege to build relationships with people who are both kind and supportive. Unlike our personal relationships, over which we do have control, unexpected environmental conditions present a different kind of challenge. Yet, a mindful person can always "rise to the occasion." There is of course usually a gap between our decisions and the desired outcome. Often, plans fall through due to unforeseen circumstances. In any case, it helps to have a clear understanding of possible scenarios and likely consequences when we embark upon something. Obstacles and challenges are part and parcel of life's complex -- some would say "messy" – journey. In this chapter many such impediments, ranging from habitual and conditioned behaviour (which includes the human tendency to live in a comfort zone) to primitive and reptilian brain functioning, are discussed. Above all, they may be experienced as motivators to redesign our life's journey.

3.1 We are modern humans with primitive mind.

Humans have evolved from primitive humans, known to have been hunter-gatherers. Like all other animals, plants and other living species on the planet, humans are a product of evolution. All species on Earth have evolved through genetic changes and mutations. Genetic changes of course lead to new and improved traits. Generation after generation, evolving species adapted themselves to their environment and therefore survived. Through the processes of adaptation and natural selection, the "fittest" prevailed, and this has been going since the first single-celled organism came into existence. Likewise, humans have evolved through the lengthy process of change and adaptations from apelike ancestors.

We humans very likely first evolved across the African savannah around 2.5 million years ago. Life at that time was very short and fragile.

Living conditions were extremely dangerous for those primitive humans. They were called hunter-gatherers because they hunted wild animals and gathered wild plants. They lived in small, nomadic bands of a few dozen individuals who scrounged for whatever food they could find. There was scarcity of food, clothing, and shelter. They were constantly under threat from predators, harsh weather conditions, and impending natural disasters. They therefore relied heavily on their instincts, which helped them survive extremely adverse conditions. In this way, *our ancestors spent well over 99% of our species' evolutionary history living as hunter-gatherers.*

Over millions of years, natural selection very beautifully and pragmatically designed the human brain, which evolved gradually to solve the day-to-day problems of our earliest ancestors. Day and night fearful because of their hostile environment, early man was also highly aggressive due to limited resources available for their survival. Violent conflicts among themselves led to anger and aggression. It is believed that because of their extremely vulnerable existence, fear and aggression got imbedded in their collective psyche – and ours.

In particular, those parts of the brain that developed for managing fear and aggression during those brutal times are still prominently present in the primitive part of our own brains. Though the size of the brain has increased throughout the evolutionary process, it still includes those parts that were especially useful during earlier periods. Moved by fear and aggression -- the "fight or flight" instinct -- our ancestors bequeathed these dominant impulses to us. According to evolutionary biologists, the brains of humans living in the modern world have their origin in our Stone Age forebears, the hunter-gatherers. In a very real way, we humans still carry their ancient legacy.

The ubiquitous kind of fear that hunter-gatherers experienced is completely unknown in our contemporary world. But since fear is so deeply embedded in our psyche, our behaviour and actions are often triggered by imaginary fear, working behind the conscious mind. Modern humans may suffer from anxiety, a negative emotional state triggered by the presence of threat that may be real or imaginary. For example, many students who take exams suffer from anxiety because of an anticipated threat of failure. Likewise, many people suffer from social anxiety because of an underlying fear of being socially awkward or 'weak', and consequently, disliked. Although not in a social setting, a young executive who has to make her maiden presentation before other executives may also suffer from social anxiety manifesting as extreme self-consciousness.

Figure 3.1: Despite living in modern age, we also carry primitive brain/mind along with newly developed neo-cortex part of brain.

Millions of people from every demographic across the globes suffer from social anxiety. This mental disorder is characterized by excessive fear, anxiety, and discomfort in social gatherings. While it is normal for people to feel anxious in those situations, people with social anxiety have a profound fear of interaction with others and are worried what others will say or think about them. These anxious thoughts and feelings persist and are chronic in nature. The amygdala, a part of brain that plays a key role in processing emotions, gets activated in those anxious situations.

Human evolution has always been an extremely slow process. Modernity – just a blip on the evolutionary timeline -- has not given our brains a long enough time to adapt to our modern lifestyle. Even relatively simple changes in the human body can take tens of thousands of years. Our minds, therefore, have not sufficiently evolved to solve the problems that are typical of our modern times. That it is still well equipped to meet the challenges of hunter-gatherer ancestors is slight consolation. *Though our brains are far "brainier" and more efficient than the best supercomputer ever made, they're ill-suited for handling the stress, anxiety, loneliness, and depression of modern times.* It's therefore rightly said that we are Stone Age thinkers living in modern times.

Indeed, our brains have not been rebooted or updated for thousands of years, and are therefore incapable of meeting modern-day requirements. Our "computer" now needs a 2020 version of that software that was critical for survival in ancient times. The good news is that there are many proven ways to update those outdated systems. Practices like mindfulness and meditation can definitely make our primitive part of brain more responsive and conscious. The choice lies with us whether we let our primitive mind governs our behaviour, desires and urges or we use rational part of brain i.e. neocortex to control them. We can therefore update our mind by strengthening the newer part of our brain.

3.2 Plato's Allegory of the Cave – We must leave the mind to embrace the true reality of the world.

Reality is merely an illusion, albeit a very persistent one. — Albert Einstein

The reality we perceive is highly subjective, interpreted by everyone in their own unique way. To know the true reality, if indeed there is one, is extremely difficult. We are mostly ignorant and imperfect human beings. We are prisoners of own habitual and conditioned thought and behaviour.. We need to go beyond the realm of the physical world to know the true reality of the world around us. More than 24 centuries back, the philosopher Plato wrote his best-known work, *The Republic*, which contains his famous Allegory of the Cave. This short story illustrates the inability or unwillingness of the human mind to inquire into and discover the true nature of reality.

Plato (429 B.C.–347 B.C.), born in Athens, Greece, is one of the most celebrated and honoured philosophers of the Western world. Many consider Plato, the student of Socrates and teacher of Aristotle, the most important philosopher who ever lived. He is perhaps best known for his Allegory of the Cave. To briefly summarize the allegory, there is a group of prisoners in a cave. Their arms and legs are chained to the wall and their heads are tied so that they cannot look at anything but the stone wall in front of them. Behind them burns a fire, casting shadows on the wall. These prisoners have been here since birth, and have never seen the outside world. In front of the fire is a raised walkway, along which walk people who are outside the cave. They are carrying objects like animals, plants, wood, and stone. The prisoners cannot see anything behind them. They can only look at the wall in front of them.

Figure 3.2: Plato's allegory – to know the true reality of the world, we need to come out from the cave i.e. the mind.

As people walk along the walkway, the prisoners can see shadows on their wall of the objects that those outside are carrying. Since they have never seen these actual objects before, they obviously believe that it is only the shadows of the objects that are "real." Finally, the day comes when *one* of the prisoners breaks his chains and leaves the cave. He is shocked at the world he's now seeing outside the cave, and unable to see it as real. But as he becomes used to his new surroundings, he realizes that his earlier perception of reality was wrong. He then begins to understand the real world, outside the cave. When this prisoner returns to the cave and describes for his cave mates the reality of the outside world, no one believes him. He then urges his cave mates to go out and see the real world. On hearing this obvious falsehood they grow enraged and threaten to kill him if he tries to set them free.

The prisoners who are chained inside the cave can perceive their reality only through their senses. There is no other possible way. So the truth to them is nothing but the shadows on the wall. When one of the prisoners leaves the cave, he starts experiencing the unknown, and sees bright light for the first time. He has no explanation for such light. He then realizes that everything his eyes were fixated on in the dim cave was just a false sense of reality, an illusion, and, having seen the light, questions the reality he was perceiving inside the cave. He therefore begins to feel pity for the ignorance of those still in the cave who cannot even imagine what he saw outside. When he returned to the cave and shared his experiences, they ridiculed him. They couldn't imagine the existence of *anything* outside their cave. Likewise, unless we experience the true reality ourselves, how can we possibly appreciate and understand it?

The allegory points out the ignorance of people who are mentally chained and living inside caves of their own making. They are oblivious of the outer world, the true reality of the world. The cave represents superficial physical reality. The chains of ignorance and apathy prevent the prisoners from leaving the cave. They are in fact trapped in that ignorance, their chains holding them back from truth. For those who see the wall, all of reality is represented by shadows. The shadows symbolize the limitation of our thinking and perceptions. In Plato's opinion, the appearances on the wall are false and not reflecting the true reality. The prisoner who escaped from the cave represents the one who seeks knowledge through intellectual adventuring outside of the cave. It means suggests that to find truth and to gain wisdom, one has to go beyond the senses and physical reality (i.e., the cave).

From Plato's allegory, we can draw a very relevant lesson for our contemporary lives. Like people in the cave, the majority of us are limited to our tunnel vision, pursuing material goods and comforts. For us, this is the real reality. Throughout our life, we believe in and pursue the fleeting shadows of money, status, fame, power, and so on. Since so many of us haven't awakened to the spiritual and true essence of life, we feel no need to exit the cave. Only very few among us dare to gaze into the sunshine of true reality. Since it's extremely difficult for the majority of the population to venture out from their comfort zones, many remain chained for life.

In the allegory, Plato describes the physical world as a "dark place" in which we can perceive objects only through our senses. Therefore the physical world is not a realm from which we can obtain knowledge and wisdom of true reality. We need to go beyond the physical world. This allegory alludes to the world of spiritual reality. Once we know the true reality, ignorance will automatically vanish. To conclude, we must leave the mind (the cave) to embrace the true reality (the sun outside the cave) of the world. Plato's story might be centuries old, but it's totally relevant in today's world. There are areas of our existence we may never fully comprehend.

3.3 We have been designed to suffer, but there are ways to handle it.

Sujjan Shrestha was driving his car to meet a friend in the late evening. His wife was accompanying him. At the outskirts of the city, in a crowded area, he accidentally hit another car in which were four heavily drunk men. Sujjan offered apologies to them for his mistake. However, arguments erupted and suddenly got ugly. One of the men hit Sujjan on the head and fled the scene. Later, when admitted to the hospital, Sujjan was found to have sustained multiple wounds, especially to his left hand. The bottom line is that he had suffered a traumatic experience in front of his wife, one that he had not handled well at all. Somehow, he could not accept the situation. He kept on fighting a legal battle for a long time, unfortunately, without success. In brief, he suffered physical injury that was compounded by mental suffering. Was this suffering avoidable?

The first of the Buddha's Four Noble Truths is the Truth of Suffering (Dukkha): Life is suffering. Aging is suffering; sickness is suffering; death is suffering; sorrow and lamentation, pain, grief, and despair are suffering; association with the unpleasant is suffering; dissociation from the pleasant is suffering; not to get what one wants is suffering—in brief, the five aggregates of attachment are suffering (from Samyutta Nikaya, a Buddhist scripture). When Siddhartha Buddha (563 BC–483 BC), the prince stepped outside of his palace, he famously encountered scenes of four kinds of suffering: poverty, disease, old age, and death. These experiences affected him deeply, impelling him to seek answers to the question, "Why do people suffer?" It was the beginning of his journey to enlightenment.

It is true that Buddhism begins and ends in the study of suffering. Suffering lies at its root, just as it lies at the root of life itself. We are born into a world of pain, and all must experience sadness and loss. Obviously, we experience great joy as well, but suffering seems to be a dominant influence in our lives. *We spend most of our days entangled in a spider's web of desires and aversions.* When we analyse the various forms of suffering and their root causes, we see that they may be reduced to attachments and aversions, based on the illusion of a real and discrete self. Buddhism aims at the demotion of the self, the creation of subtle mindfulness, bliss, great compassion, and moderation and gentleness (*A Buddhist View of Suffering* by Peter Morrell).

Suffering is an outcome of distressing thoughts and emotions associated with physical pain, fear, anger, helplessness, guilt, shame, loneliness, sadness, depression, etc. When we keep on mulling over any distressing, traumatic, or negative experience, we aggravate suffering. As seen in the example above, traumatic experiences usually lead to severe mental suffering. If we are temperamentally sensitive, then even small incidents of emotional distress can lead to prolonged suffering. We generally don't know how to handle negative thoughts, so suffering becomes inevitable. To come out from mental suffering becomes a big challenge. When we fail to confront and manage our thoughts, anxiety and/or depression will persist. More particularly, we tend to suffer over fear from real and imaginary threats, and negative ideas about the future. Disturbing thoughts may focus on violence, sex, and past traumatic events. Psychologists call these types of thoughts intrusive thoughts because they pop into our heads, often without warning, and cause us distress. Even though most of us have these thoughts, some people worry and obsess about thoughts that they would never act on.

Figure 3.3: Mental suffering is widespread among all age groups, but it can surely be avoided.

As we have seen, we often resist change because of the ease and seeming safety of the familiar and predictable. *Locked in our comfort zone, change is perceived as a threat.* This is a common cause of suffering. Imagine someone who has been working in the national capital region (NCR) for the past decade. His children are studying at Delhi University and he is living nearby, most happily. But then he gets a transfer order to one of the remote states. Anticipating that his life will be completely disturbed, his mental suffering begins. Despite his rigorous efforts to stop the transfer, he is forced leave for the new place. Feeling he has been wronged, he continues to suffer. We come across such situations quite often when we are working at a transferable job. It goes almost without saying that changing circumstances do not cause suffering; it's the reactive thoughts and emotions associated with those changes that lead to painful feelings.

If we are open, flexible, and creatively responsive to changes, we can minimise the suffering of our limiting, negative thoughts – or be free of them altogether.

Our minds are generally in a state of subtle, unrecognized dissatisfaction, no matter what we possess for leading a comfortable life. Even if we have excellent relationships, a harmonious working atmosphere, and a warm home environment, our mind may still be open to disturbance at the slightest provocation. Potential for negative reactivity can underlie all the better things in life. Most people are congenitally unable to remain contented for a sustained time. Feelings of vague dissatisfaction will invariably arise. This seems to be an inherent feature of mind. It becomes restless. We are generally looking to "improve" our situations, to accumulate more and more material things, to gain more power and prestige. Such desires can be never-ending. In their pursuit, we create mental distress and unhappiness, resulting in mental suffering.

We suffer most when we take the experiences of life personally, and resist them. However, when we realise that happiness is a choice and that suffering is optional, and can accept circumstances and incidents as they are presented to us, everything changes. Acceptance has a great healing effect. When we lead a mindful life, suffering is mitigated to a great extent. We conclude with a thought from Japanese writer Haruki Murakami, who observes that "Pain is inevitable but suffering is optional." Suffering is a choice when we allow painful thoughts to persist. We become victim to those very thoughts. However, when we learn to manage negative and harmful thoughts, we can easily get rid of them and avoid much suffering. The choice lies squarely with us as to how we interpret any situation, whether we allow it to cause suffering or not. Mental suffering is unavoidable, but the choice of letting any situation cause suffering les with us.

3.4 We are imperfect humans with 'flawed thinking' – cognitive bias

We are imperfect humans. Our thinking is often far from perfect. It is not always based on logic, reason, and rationality. However, we remain ignorant of many things when we act, decide, or make choices. Each one of us is prone to such errors, also known as cognitive bias (cognition means the thinking process). We tend to make illogical or irrational decisions on many occasions. Let's take a look at some common examples of cognitive bias in our everyday life.

- We tend to attribute success to our own superior/better qualities while blaming failure on others or outside factors.
- We tend to believe things because many other people also believe the same. This is also called crowd mentality or herd behaviour.
- We have a tendency to overestimate our own abilities.
- We tend to search for or be on the lookout for information that confirms our beliefs or perceptions .
- We have a tendency to follow or adopt the opinions or behaviours of the majority so as to feel safe and to avoid conflict.

As we can see from the biases listed above, we are inclined to process and interpret information in a biased manner. The result is that we sometimes make poor and irrational decisions. Rarely are we aware of such cognitive bias in our thoughts, words, and deeds. Some of these biases are inculcated at an early age, mostly from our parents. Then gradually we see others and start interpreting information and imitating the responses of our peers.

The question now arises as to why we are prone to such biases. One simple explanation is that the brain continues to process huge amounts of information/data during the day, but we consciously attend to only a small portion of that information. And because the conscious part of our brain is capable of focusing on only one thing at a time, our brain looks for shortcuts to help in making decisions. We are mostly in a hurry to make choices based on our past experiences. Cognitive biases may also be described as the inherent imperfection in thinking that we all make in processing information. These thinking errors prevent us from accurately understanding the reality around us. This is true even if we have gathered all the necessary information or data, but are still sticking to our earlier experiences.

Broadly speaking, there are two types of biases. First, there are information biases, which include the shortcuts to information-processing that produce fast and efficient – though not necessarily accurate

– decisions. We often attempt to simplify information-processing and, as a result, our thinking becomes biased. The second kind of bias involves our ego. Here the decisions are motivated by our emotions, moods, and feelings. Social influences such as peer pressure, or what others will think, become the bases of our errors. Such biases invariably lead to irrational decisions based on distorted perception, inaccurate judgment, and illogical interpretation.

Sometimes small errors in our decision-making can have wide implications in our lives. We never know when a simple error in judgment will have huge ramifications, affecting not only ourselves but also others. Not all biases are bad; however Psychologists have found that many of our biases serve an adaptive purpose so that we can take quick decisive action based on the available information, especially when we are in a hurry or in any dangerous and threatening situation. Sometimes

Figure 3.4: On often practice 'herd mentality', a kind of common cognitive bias, to follow others by adopting certain behaviour mainly on emotional rather than rational basis

From the time we get up in the morning to the time we sleep, we keep on making choices, mostly routine and repetitive ones but many times fresh choices. We are completely unaware of the fact that quite often we make choices wrongly because of cognitive biases. Over the past few decades of research, a good many cognitive biases have been identified. More than one hundred biases are documented now. Some of the commonest biases are negativity bias, confirmation bias, overconfidence effect, outcome bias, choice supportive bias, bandwagon effect, gambler fallacy, self-serving bias, post-purchase rationalization, herd instinct, and hindsight bias. While making decisions, we are very often being influenced by these biases. We may have always considered ourselves as being better than others --- more quick-witted and intelligent, for instance. Many people see themselves as being "above average." Their bias is one of overconfidence.

Most people have a tendency to search for or interpret information in a way that confirms their pre-existing beliefs. This is called confirmation bias. For example, the investor would seek only information that will confirm his existing belief, filtering out most of the rest. Many people assume that self-described "religious" people who frequently visit religious places are morally honest and incapable of sinful acts. Some think that left-handed persons are more emotional and creative than right-handed ones. Likewise, many medical practitioners have confirmation bias in particular aspects of their practice, especially the diagnostic. Due to this bias, we tend to commit errors of judgment or make faulty decisions while making choices or decisions. Such errors can have cascading effects on others.

Another extremely common cognitive bias is negativity bias. No one can escape from it. The media industry, including print and electronic media, suffers from this bias. When we read any newspaper or watch television, we can't help but notice how negative news items are highlighted and repeated over and over again. They know very well that people love watching distressingly negative news, giving far more weight to negative experiences or information than to positive ones. One more example of unconscious influence is bias of the self-serving kind. We have a tendency to attribute success to our own self while blaming failures on others, and outside forces. This is how; our thinking and choice making ability become flawed through cognitive biases.

It's extremely difficult to overcome those biases that are hardwired into our thinking. Since early childhood, many beliefs have been embedded in our mind and become part and parcel of our identity. It was these beliefs that gave rise to our belief system. The most effective way to overcome biases is to be aware and pay attention to our internal environment. Through the practice of mindfulness, we can make our decisions and choices more rational, unaffected by our biases and prejudices. We can observe things nonjudgmentally, with an open mind. Many biases are related to the problem of attention. We don't pay adequate attention while making choices. Therefore, being aware and paying attention in non-judgmental ways addresses the problem of cognitive biases to a great extent.

3.5 The mechanics of decision making –'free will' is largely illusionary in nature

Swaminathan, age 45, was arrested for a violent attack on his colleague at work. On trial in district court, he took the defence that he was not responsible for the attack. He explained that he had a strained relationship with his wife, and that over the past several years, his behaviour had become impulsive. A loose cannon, he would lose his temper at the slightest provocation. He was taking medicine from his psychiatrist and showed his prescription to the judge. On the fateful day of his arrest, his colleagues had provoked him with a nasty comment on his relationship with his wife. So he lost control and attacked the main offender. He argued before the court that he had gone "unconscious" the moment he felt insulted and had no memory of the attack. Did Swaminathan use his free will while attacking his colleague? This was the core question before the judge. Should he be convicted for the crime he committed?

The decisions we make, the way we behave, and the choices we make have profound impact on our future. Though our decisions are influenced by a complex blend of external and internal circumstances, we are still capable of making free, logical, and rational choices based on the available information. However, this is not an easy task. Very often our decisions are impulsive, automatic, and based upon our conditioning. We are imprisoned in our own inner world. When our behaviour is driven by unconscious and conditioned mind, that behaviour and the decisions we make are commensurately unconscious. In that scenario, we have no internal locus of control over life. To create destiny of our own choice, not only do we need to have control over our mind, but also the ability to manage the outer world to whatever extent is possible and prudent. Most of the time, we are not aware of the mental and physical state of a person taking action. We take their action at face value, unaware of anything more.

Figure 3.5: 'Free Will' is illusionary in nature – our decision making process is highly influenced by our life's past experiences, habitual and conditioned thinking and behaviour.

The emergence of thoughts, intentions, and, subsequently, the choices that we make is basically a mysterious process. *Thoughts arise out of the void in an unexplainable manner.* German neurobiologist and geneticist Martin Heisenberg further explained that due to random processes in our brain, much of our thought could be considered truly "self-generated." Suppose we close our mind and start observing it in a very relaxed manner. No thinking. Just let the thoughts flow freely. Within a few moments, we have no idea what thoughts might be coming next. So based on the thoughts that come in that particular moment, we make choices. Suppose a different variety of thoughts comes; we are then likely to make different choices. Seen in this light, the issue of having control over choices become debatable in regard to the destiny we design.

Throughout the day, we keep on making choices -- small choices, such as whether I should take a drink, to bigger choices that directly impact our life. These are conscious choices, but at the same time, at the unconscious level, our mind is making an incalculable number of choices all the time. These very choices have direct and indirect influence over our decision-making and the consequent actions we take. All thoughts, words, and deeds eventually determine our future, the destiny that we may design. The conscious mind is what we know to be at work when we are attentive. We use this mind for making choices and decisions after interpreting and analysing the information available. It makes us aware of what is happening in our outside world.

The conscious mind communicates with the outside world and with the inner self through speech, pictures, writing, physical movement, and thought. It is like the pilot of a plane, giving out orders to the crew that will ensure a safe trip. Generally, the conscious mind concerns things that we are either at that particular moment aware of, or thinking about them. Within the ambit of short-term memory, our conscious mind works. Our conscious mind is described as our objective mind because it deals with the outside world through our senses. Our conscious mind is continually observing and categorizing what is going on around us.

Behind the conscious mind, we have the far more powerful unconscious mind. The visible tip of an iceberg is like the conscious mind, while the hidden part is the vast unconscious. It's the storehouse of all memories and past experiences, including those that are repressed.

It's from these memories and experiences that our beliefs, habits, and behaviours are determined. The unconscious mind is always running its innumerable programmes, like an autopilot. When we are not consciously present, we are in a "default mode" in which the unconscious mind is completely absorbed in internal dialogue. *The mind is occupied by its own thinking process and we are not consciously aware of those moments.*

Over millennia, to ensure the survival of mankind, various specialised processing areas have been developed in the brain. These regions work incessantly behind the scenes of our conscious experiences. We are in fact completely unaware of such unconscious processes, which are responsible for our conscious thoughts and intentions. This is why this powerful hidden part of our mind is as important as the conscious mind. Moreover, our unconscious mind is the seat of our emotions, beliefs, past memories and experiences. If we have a repository of self-limiting beliefs, negative memories and experiences in the unconscious mind, they will be reflected while making decisions on those matters. We therefore need to establish a harmonious relationship between both parts of our mind. Destiny is a result of active participation of the conscious as well as the unconscious mind.

Similarly, American neuroscientist and famous author Sam Harris, in his *Free Will,* arrived at the conclusion that "thoughts simply arise in the brain. What else could they do? The truth about us is even stranger than we may suppose: The illusion of free will is itself an illusion." He further argued that in addition to having no control over the genes we got from our parents, neither did we choose the environment in which we were nurtured. This all contributes to unconscious neurological conditions that are responsible for our thoughts and beliefs. *We feel we are the author of our conscious decisions, but these decisions are greatly influenced by our lifetime experiences, which differ significantly from one individual to another.*

Though most of us feel that we are completely free when we consider options and then make a choice, the reality is that unconscious factors influence the process of decision-making. The assumption that we are the conscious author of our thoughts and actions does not hold well. Our decisions are made on the basis of thoughts generated at that very time. First, we have no control over the thoughts that come into our mind, and second, the thoughts are greatly influenced by many other factors, such as past experience and belief system. Sam Harris has intriguingly concluded that *"We do not have the freedom we think we have. Either our wills are determined by prior causes and we are not responsible for them, or they are the product of chance and we are not responsible for them."*

It's therefore clear that the decision-making process is highly complex because of the involvement of so many processes/factors relating to both realms of our mind. How we make decisions depends on our perception, attitude, behaviour, and preconceived notions. Likewise, we judge people on the basis of our unconscious thoughts, beliefs, and feelings. How we interact with others also depends on our beliefs, behaviour, past experiences, background, etc. We always have a doubt as to whether the decisions and the choices we continue to make are really conscious and fair. In fact, we need to fine-tune and synchronize both conscious and unconscious processes in designing our destiny. If we want to become master of our own destiny, we need mastery over both the conscious and unconscious mind. Otherwise, the free will about which most of us are so confident and dead sure is merely an illusion.

3.6 Is habitual behaviour and mental conditioning the biggest hurdle in our spiritual growth ?

All of us each day perform repetitive tasks. Dozens of times a day, we engage in behaviour that requires little to no focused concentration. Any new activity requires our attention and effort to learn, but then we memorise and become skilled at those tasks. We seem to be conserving our mental and physical energy when we keep on repeating those tasks. We are not required to think about them. Then those tasks become easy, natural, familiar and routine; they are now second nature to us. Similarly, over time, our responses to various situations become automatic. We generally react in the manner that seemed to have served us in the past.

Conditioning starts at a very early age. In our early childhood years, the thoughts, behaviours, and responses we experience get programmed into our subconscious mind. Likewise, when we watch or learn from our parents, other family members and teachers, we start forming our own beliefs about the world. Who/what is right or wrong, we start assimilating in early childhood. Studies show that this is the most crucial time, as foundations are laid during this impressionable period. As we grow, our programmed beliefs become deeply embedded in our thinking patterns. Hence, these beliefs become an integral part of us. We continue to repeat and reinforce those thoughts, behaviours, beliefs and responses. In a very real way, we are strengthening our identity or ego. In the process, we all become habitual and repetitive in our behaviour and thinking.

Figure 3.6: Most of us are prisoner of our own habitual thinking and behaviour – "mind-made prison"

The decisions made by our conditioned mind influence our life in many ways that in turn affect our future and destiny. We perceive and interpret most everything through the lens of conditioning. Imagine a child who has an unconditioned and open mind and sees things as they actually are. As the child grows, the dust starts accumulating on her clear and transparent mind. This is done in all innocence by her parents, siblings, teachers, and friends. Likewise, all of us get conditioned as we grow. Our behaviour, beliefs, and the way we respond to the outer world hardens. Increasingly, beliefs that don't conform to our belief system are rejected out of hand. This is known as confirmation bias, a kind of cognitive bias. Through this bias we keep seeking and seeming to find confirmation for our beliefs. In turn, our mind becomes more and more conditioned in responding to the world we experience.

As we know, the subconscious and unconscious parts of our mind are far more powerful than the conscious mind. When we are engaged in frequently performed activities such as driving, taking a bath, playing our favourite games, and riding a bicycle, our subconscious mind takes over and we need employ almost no concentration or extra effort. We have gained mastery over these skills. On the other hand, the unconscious mind is the repository of our earliest memories, which can't be accessed by our conscious mind. The subconscious mind plays an extremely important role in governing our emotions, behaviour, and actions. Due to its unrecognized influence, we live, more or less, on autopilot. Our conscious mind is like the tip of a massive iceberg, most of which lies beneath the surface, calling the shots.

The conditioned mind is indeed the source of most of our behaviour toward others, and to nearly every situation in life. It determines our perception and interpretation of reality. In a very real way, we spend our days in a "mind-made prison," captives of our small and circumscribed outlook. This is of course a great cause of suffering and the primary obstacle to our growth. We constantly mistake our interpretation of the world, which is almost purely subjective, for the truth. We fail to fully understand or respect the fact that like us, others too have their own set of beliefs, which they take to be true. We keep on labelling things as true or false, and generally do not confront ourselves once the belief is deeply ingrained.

When we are on autopilot mode, we continue to react to various situations in a habitual and conditioned manner. Consequently, we don't always respond appropriately to the requirements of more novel or challenging situations. Many times, our behaviour is impulsive and automatic. These conditioned responses prevent us from living our life mindfully. This in turn is apt to retard our personal growth. Our habitual and highly conditioned responses also become a major impediment to our spiritual growth. We miss many opportunities in our life's journey because we are not open and receptive to them. Of course, mental conditioning is not always harmful. In fact, we can train ourselves or be conditioned to think and act positively. We can learn to respond to the challenges of distressing conditions in a mindful and harmonious way.

Figure 3.6A: For success, we need to jump out from our comfort zone of living.

We should be open, receptive, and mindful in our life, whatever the situation. Appropriate action precludes automaticity and impulsivity. It all depends on the degree of conditioning and one's awareness or unawareness of same. We all know people whose actions and behaviour are so unoriginal and repetitive that we can anticipate what they are going to say, or how they will behave. When we interact with them, they keep on repeating the same thoughts and feelings, even to the point of using the very same words. As we've seen, the answer to this lack of mindfulness is self-awareness. Ideally, we would all aspire to full awareness of our every thought, word, deed, and motivation. Meditation and mindfulness are among the best mental exercises that make us more aware. Once habitual behaviour and hard conditioning are confronted and controlled, we can surely begin to undertake an accelerated spiritual journey.

3.7 We don't change a whole lot in our lifetime. Most of us are content with our "safe" and habitual ways.

"*When we are no longer able to change a situation, we are challenged to change ourselves*" – said Viktor Frankl. In *Man's Search for Meaning he further shared his much celebrated conclusion:* "Everything can be taken from a man but one thing: the last of the human freedoms — to choose one's attitude in any given set of circumstances, to choose one's own way."

But sometimes one's attitude remains fixed, barely changing over time. Unless and until there is some drastic turn of events in one's life -- such as death of a very close one, traumatic experience, deep emotional setback, major illness or financial loss -- there is little discernible change in one's personality. When we meet someone we haven't seen for many years, there are usually changes in her/his physical appearance, but once we start interacting, we find that little has changed. Our basic nature remains more or less the same. We call this core personality. Each one of us possesses a unique personality, having a combination of characteristics or qualities. These qualities make us distinct from others. It is a product of social interaction .

Why then is there so little change? There are surely many plausible explanations, but here are four important possibilities.

1. We are social animals who love to stay in our comfort zones. We all construct our "comforts" and generally choose to live there. Unless we are disturbed by external situations that need to be addressed, consciously or subconsciously, we do not want to step out of our comfort area. Due to the negativity bias, we give more thought to possible negative impacts of change than to positive ones. Within the comfort zone, we may be earning a comfortable living, securely set in a fixed routine and with a number of "close" friends and a lovely family. And that's it; we do not wish to get out of that perfectly fine scenario. Should something disrupt it, we feel extremely uncomfortable and react sharply. This is often how we

miss opportunities that we would otherwise have identified and acted upon, had we accepted the change gracefully.

2. All of us have a robust belief system, created over time. The process begins in early childhood when our parents start teaching us about the world. The process continues to maturity – and often beyond -- as the inculcation of various beliefs about practically everything takes hold. As time passes, we harbor beliefs of all kinds – positive, negative, regressive, and progressive. We have been mentally conditioned, coded line by line much like a computer program. We develop fixed perceptions, and our reactions are determined. Further conditioning comes from outside the home – from our teachers and our circle of peers. Instilled in our most impressionable years, many of our beliefs are rock solid and extremely difficult to change or to simply drop. When anyone tries to challenge or change our beliefs, most of us see it as an attack on our self, and jump to the defense. In so doing, we unknowingly make our beliefs more rigid and thus more difficult to change, or even to accept the need for change.

3. Most people tend to ignore their flaws or the weaknesses that they harbor. Most also appear to have a generally inflated image of themselves that they protect at almost any cost. A surprising number see themselves as being "above average," better than others. Some genuinely believe that others are bad, inadequate, and even inferior to themselves. Of course, we all have a desire to become superior or especially talented in at least certain areas. It's a part of human nature. In order to protect our shining image, we may try to blame others or the environment if something goes wrong, rather than blaming ourselves. When we commit any mistake or error, we often try to rationalize what we did. We want to keep our self-image intact by blaming external factors rather than looking inside and finding the fault there. In such an un-insightful person, little change occurs.

4. No matter how much we wish to change our habits and eliminate certain patterns, it's never an easy task. We need the determination of tremendous willpower to harness our mind. Our habitual behavior is hard-wired in our brain. Whenever we experience

something for the first time, new neural connections are formed. Later, when we repeat the action again and again, those neural connections get hard-wired into the brain. Just as we perfect the same technique or skill gradually, as we keep on practicing the same, so too does repetition of undesired actions lead to enduring impressions – "ruts" in the mental circuitry that are difficult to ignore. No doubt, any habitual behavior can be altered, but huge effort in terms of time and energy is usually required.

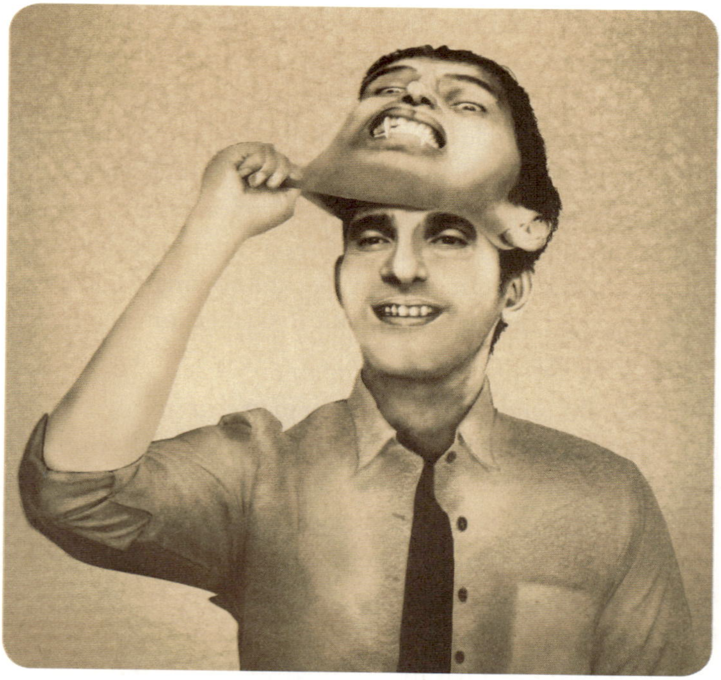

Figure 3.7: Invariably, our core personality and basic nature doesn't change throughout the life. Mostly, there are superficial/outwardly changes in our personality

Those are the reasons that we generally don't change – at least, not significantly. To do so, great energy and effort are required, bringing discomfort that we generally try to avoid (unless the situation is critical). Enter willpower! Complementing and strengthening our determination to change, mindful living becomes essential to willpower. And as we grow in self-awareness, we are better able to identify and address our weaknesses.

OOO

4

Life Journey and Emerging Challenges of the Modern Age

We are living in an era of breath-taking technological innovation. Digital advances affect our lives in almost every area, from the way we think to how we work and interact with others. Digital technology is now deeply embedded in our lives. Children belonging to "Generation Z" will never be able to imagine the life their grandparents lived. For starters, there were no computers or mobile phones. Instead, communication was by landlines (home phones), letter-writing, and telegrams. Money was transferred and payments made mainly via personal checks and money orders. Within the span of one generation (30 years), all aspects of our lives have been radically transformed.

Every day we see the many beneficial effects of digital technologies on our lives, primarily the almost immediate access to and creation of information. Whereas once we waited almost a week, breathlessly anticipating a letter (from, say, our beloved, or a college admissions officer), we may now "hear back" instantly. However, there has been a darker side as well. Through smartphones, networked technologies, and social media, our lives are in some ways also diminished. Our attention span, in general, has been reduced, which is leading to a decline in our ability to focus on any one thing. We are gradually and insidiously disconnecting from others, though we may have thousands of "friends" on social media. People are becoming more self-centred, lonely, and isolated from one another; the incidence of mental disorders like anxiety and depression continues to rise. Individual privacy and online security, fake news, and "deep fake" videos on social media pose big challenges before the government and law enforcement agencies.

Such problems can only serve to aggravate and exacerbate other problems with which the world is currently grappling. Even before this high-tech revolution, we have been living a predominately materialistic life. The developed world has become a wealthier place where the majority struggle to achieve their version of success in order to become "happy." The problem, however, lies in that very pursuit and the assumption that with wealth will come happiness. Ironically, we are becoming more and more unhappy and discontented as we become richer. In our workplaces and in relationships, mental stress is rising. The stress at work and at home is leading to many lifestyle diseases. The stress hormone cortisol is causing illnesses like diabetes, obesity, and high blood pressure. Millions of people worldwide die every year because of stress- related diseases.

Another major problem peculiar to our modern age is loneliness, which is taking an epidemic toll in many nations across the world. As people become more and more disconnected from one another, owing in part to social media, the problem is growing even among the younger generation. Rather than being happily busy, engaging with others face to face, people feel disconnected and unhappier. And because more and more people are now living in nuclear instead of joint families, they are often isolated in older age. Loneliness becomes a new norm, especially in urban areas. A global issue, it has attracted the attention of various governments and institutions, such as the World Health Organisation. In this chapter, many challenges that most of us are facing due to our fast-paced, highly stressed and materialistic life are briefly discussed. The world can't afford to ignore these issues.

4.1 In a far wealthier world, humans are becoming unhappier and more discontented.

Is material success the highest goal in life? Far too many of us are preoccupied with the material world, striving to possess more and more material goods, eager for ever more comforts in life. The measure of one's success becomes not happiness but wealth, status, and power. Many place greater value on those attainments than on their intrinsic spiritual nature. Though most people will say that their first priority in life is to be happy and enjoy life, their real motives may focus on possessing material things. Ironically, chasing material success in pursuit of greater happiness may bring more discontentment in life. In fact, research (and simple observation) reveals that we are becoming less happy than we were 25 to 30 years back. Some studies suggest that hunter-gatherers were probably happier than modern humans. These early humans were living on a day-to-day basis, chasing after food and other goods to stay alive.

The reason so many of us are running after material things is twofold. First, we are living in a culture of rampant consumerism. Since early childhood, we are strongly conditioned to desire goods that are appreciated by society. Thanks to electronic media and enticing advertisements and endorsements by film stars, sports personalities, and other eminent persons, many have a strong desire to possess impressive goods and enjoy the admiration and attention of others. When we sport an attractive suit or wear an expensive jewellery item, or drive a late-model car, we get plenty of "likes" (as expressed on social media) or, better yet, the in-person approval of others. Our brain's neural network conveys signals for "reward" as the neurotransmitter dopamine sends its happy signals to the brain. This biochemical gives us a pleasurable feeling. The more dopamine is released, the stronger our desire to seek even more "likes" or rewards.

Through all of this craving and striving, happiness generally eludes us. The missing realization is that happiness seldom comes from the outside world, especially not from material goods. To a certain extent, money is required to meet our basic needs, the fulfilment of which is, of course, necessary for our happiness and well-being. Once these needs are met, money makes us marginally happy. After this, further accumulation of wealth and possessions will not bring joy. And yet, despite disappointment, we keep on striving for more and more of those things that are supposed to make us happy. Regardless of circumstances, the mind's intrinsic nature is to be restless and discontented -- unless we learn to manage it. This is a skill that most of us have yet to master. Lacking it, we may get trapped in the drive for wealth.

As we keep on chasing and accumulating wealth and goods, we find ourselves increasingly disconnected from the inner Self. Emphasis is purely on the outside world. We forget that happiness and peace lie within ourselves – that, in Jesus' words, "The kingdom of heaven is within." We don't pay attention to the inner governance of our mind. Since we are largely ignorant of the mind's inner workings, we mostly fail to keep it under check. Completely identified with our mind, we are largely dominated by it. Unless we know how to manage our mind, its proclivities, such as negativity bias, wandering, natural restlessness, and dissatisfaction, make our life difficult. Vulnerable in our unawareness, mental illnesses and disorders like depression and anxiety may follow.

Over time, human development has been lopsided. Growth has not been balanced. Progress in science and technology is not seeing a corresponding rise in spiritual development. Technological advances have obviously made life far more comfortable, secure, and easy-going. However, because ways of thinking have remained more or less static, man's suffering has not abated. In fact, in today's materialistic society, we feel more alienated and separate than ever, not only from our fellow beings but also from our inner Self.

Figure 4.1: We are living in a highly materialistic world – driven by material goods and comforts but still becoming unhappier.

All around us we see discontentment, intolerance, anger, and aggression. In many parts of the world, these qualities are in fact increasing. The gap between 'us' and 'them' is widening as conflicts intensify. Since we are not paying adequate attention to our inner Selves, the incidence of mental disorders is also on the rise. The World Health Organization estimates that worldwide, more than 300 million people of all age groups are currently suffering from depression, an increase of more than 18% from 2005. Incidentally, people in India constitute the world's most depressed population. That is also true of social anxiety and other mental disorders.

Undoubtedly, the world is witnessing multiple revolutions in the areas of science and technology. While 36 percent of the world's population (1.86 billion) live in extreme poverty, tremendous wealth is being generated in much of the world. For those fortunate people, life is becoming increasingly comfortable and even luxurious. The scope of pleasure-driven entertainment is increasing. People are becoming increasingly busy and stressed. A large segment of the population is growing more concerned about their physical health and appearance. Almost everyone is connecting socially with friends and acquaintances. At the same time, people are in reality feeling disconnected from one another and their own self. These are the typical signs of a highly materialistic world. There is hardly any genuine emphasis on our own spiritual nature. We have almost no place for soul, spirit, and inner governance. Close attention must be paid to spiritual development. Otherwise, the disconnection -- our sense of alienation and aloneness -- will only deepen.

4.2 Mental stress at workplace and in relationships is becoming deadlier for our mental and physical health

All around us are the signs of a society under stress. Mental stress is becoming endemic in the modern world. Many of life's situations may trigger a stress response in the body, problems such as inharmonious working conditions, overload of work, financial difficulties, and relationship problems within one's family or with a boss or colleagues. The majority of us do suffer from mental stress; however, its severity varies from individual to individual. Stress causes a wide range of physical changes in the body. It generally increases heart rate and may accelerate or depress breathing. Stress itself is not an illness, but if left unchecked, it can contribute to major health problems, such as high blood pressure, heart disease, obesity, and diabetes. Chronic stress not only weakens the immune system but also increases the risk of developing depression and anxiety.

Mental stress is exacerbated when we do not monitor and manage our mind in an efficient and open way. We generally don't know how to prioritise work and time efficiently. Managing intimate relationships and relations with co-workers can be especially stressful. Many stir up tension and harassment for others. Under stressful conditions, the mind becomes agitated and thoughts may become obsessive triggering a cascade of hormones, including stress hormone -- i.e., cortisol. It's secreted by the adrenal gland situated above the kidneys. Increased levels of cortisol in the blood contribute to serious health problems, such as heart disease, high blood pressure, diabetes, obesity, and other illnesses, as well as mental disorders like depression and anxiety. Millions of people in India die each year from these diseases and all because we don't know how to cope with chronic mental stress.

Stress can come from just about anywhere. However, there are two main sources of mental stress; one is from family relationships and the other is from our workplace. A toxic relationship with one's marriage partner or in-laws is also very common, as are financial difficulties, health-related issues, and childrearing problems. Sometimes even a trivial matter can take an ugly turn between the partners. Relationships are often very complicated, and if both partners don't handle their issues with empathy and care, mental stress is inevitable. *Relationships may also be tense in one's social circle and in the romantic arena.*

Mental stress is especially prevalent in the workplace. In today's hyper-competitive world, the working class is the worst affected, especially in India. Most are working in a highly aggressive environment, with pressure to be more productive, efficient, and profit-generating. Long working hours, tight deadlines, and overambitious targets cause an overload of work, leading to mental stress. Unfortunately, senior executives and leaders are far more stressed, and create stress for others. Working conditions are therefore unpleasant and unconducive in most of the private- and public-sector enterprises in India. Though the trend is changing, it's still not encouraging.

The recently released findings of the 2018 Well-Being Survey, conducted by Cigna TTK Health Insurance, show that stress levels are higher in India compared with other developed and emerging countries, including the United States, the UK, China, and Brazil. Nearly 9 in 10 Indians suffer from stress. According to the survey, India has topped work- and finance-related stress levels once more. It further revealed that 95 per cent of Indian millennials between the ages of 18-34 are stressed, and that one in eight Indians has serious trouble in dealing with stress. And while almost 75 percent of those surveyed said they would rather not discuss their stress, many did express their desire for a better wellness programme on the part of their employer. More recently, in January 2019, the Economic Times, citing a survey from HR tech start-up Hush, reported that one out of every five employees of India Inc.is suffering from workplace depression.

Figure 4.2: In India, most of our workplaces have become highly stressed, leading to many diseases caused by cortisol, the stress hormone.

According to *Harvard Business Review*, a mounting pile of scientific research shows mindfulness helps relieve stress and anxiety, improves concentration and memory, inspires creativity and strategic thinking, and fosters a more collaborative environment. This can be especially helpful in high-stress situations in which the chief executives are expected to be the ultimate decision-makers. Its popularity is growing very fast among CEOs to build leadership skills and enhance overall productivity. *Mindfulness practice helps in attaining a high degree of mental clarity, focused attention, and ability to see things in greater perspective.*

There are many ways to cultivate mindfulness at work, from walking at lunchtime to taking purposeful pauses while eating. One of the most reliable ways is simple meditation. Mindfulness meditation is becoming increasingly popular in several Fortune 500 companies, including General Mills, Goldman Sachs, Facebook, Ford, Google, Apple, Aetna, and Nike. *Forbes* reported that 22% of Fortune 500 companies had mindfulness programs in 2016, and this figure was expected to double in 2017. In the USA, mindfulness has already become a billion-dollar industry, with universities, colleges, hospitals, and other institutions offering mindfulness programmes and short-term courses that benefit their employees in a big way.

Even in India, private companies have started introducing programmes on meditation. Separate rooms are being earmarked for relaxation and meditation on each floor. Whenever employees feel the need, they can spend 20-30 minutes there during working hours. Gradually, it's becoming popular. Mindfulness India, a summit for cultivating excellence in leadership, is being organised in Mumbai for the end of 2019. In a large number of government schools in Delhi, children too are being taught how to be mindful. Hospitals have started using it for pain management. However, *in India, the meditation industry is at nascent stage.* Hopefully, the way it's getting popular in corporate and government institutions, more and more people are adopting mindfulness based meditation techniques to cope up with the growing stress at workplace. With the improvement of interpersonal relationships by listening and addressing the problems of co-workers and colleagues, conflicts and resultant mental stress can effectively be reduced to a great extent and this can be done through meditation practice.

4.3 As the technological revolution advances, loneliness is taking the shape of an epidemic.

Manmohan Sinha, age 59, has been staying in Chennai for the past four years. He is presently working as a consultant to a multinational company. He stays in a posh locality alone as his wife died of breast cancer several months ago. His only daughter is working in Seattle, USA, as a software engineer. She is married to a computer engineer. Since she spent a long time with her father due to her mother's long illness, she is not able to join him for the coming festival season. This saddens him, especially considering that Deepawali (Diwali), the most important Hindu festival, is fast approaching. Day and night he thinks about his loneliness. No close family member will be joining him for the joyous festival of lights. As he belongs to Meerut, a populous city of Northern India, he has not many friends or social contacts due to the language barrier. He has been feeling socially isolated, though he has many friends on social media. He does not feel connected to his acquaintances. No one will be around to share his feelings and the joyousness of the festival. Three days prior to Deepawali and at his most anxious and lonely point, Manmohan suffered a panic attack.

Like Manmohan, millions of people feel isolated and alone. These people perceive the world differently. They feel lonely in a wide range of social circumstances. Lonely people may have a large number of friends, but often these friendships are superficial and lacking in meaningful intimacy and trust. They never feel close to them, or they may not even like to speak to their so-called friends. The epidemic of loneliness is a product of modern ways of thinking about the self and society. As we all know, there has been a sharp fall in family togetherness, with children rarely spending much time with their parents, much less engaging in face-to-face interaction. Much of this loss may be attributed to the increased popularity of social media, such as Facebook, WhatsApp, Instagram, and other remote means of communication. While appearing to be tightly connected on social media, many people actually feel disconnected from others. For them, TV and their dog or cats are the main sources of company and entertainment. When the pet dies, the problem of loneliness is further aggravated.

Under the circumstances, loneliness is becoming a widespread phenomenon across the world, especially in developed nations. A study by *The Economist*, published in September 2018, using a sample survey, found that 22% of adults in the USA, 23% in Britain, and about 9% in Japan always or often feel lonely or lacking in companionship ; they also feel “left out” or “isolated.” In January 2018, former Prime Minister Theresa May even appointed a Minister for Loneliness. This shows how serious the problem of loneliness is becoming in the UK, with approximately nine million people reporting that they often feel lonely. Unfortunately, recent figures in respect to India are not available. The last survey of the National Sample Survey Office conducted in 2004 reported that about 4.91 million people in India were living alone. Another finding released in April 2017 revealed that 12% of Indian youth reported feeling depressed often, and 8% said they felt lonely quite frequently. The incidences of loneliness have definitely increased sharply in recent years due to rapid changes in modern society.

Figure 4.3: In a highly crowded and connected world, people are increasingly becoming lonely.

Not even the younger generation -- including school age and college students -- have escaped from this fast-spreading sickness. While elderly age parents are left alone in their home, the children who were brought up under loving care are becoming lonely as not enough attention is now being paid to them. Digital media is distracting them from their studies. When they feel alone, they tend to use mobiles more often and so end up spending more time on digital platforms. Though they are always surrounded by numerous colleagues, they feel isolated from them. They are becoming lonelier even than the older generation. Loneliness in that generation is often associated with compulsive technology use, smoking, and excessive use of alcohol and drugs. For them, family functions, weddings, vacations, and impromptu gatherings may even increase their feeling of being left out, or their dissatisfaction with life.

Loneliness is emerging as a public-health problem. Accompanying the empty feeling of loneliness are acute sadness and depression, along with irritability and self-centredness. Odd as it may seem, the lonely often do not feel like talking to anybody. People experiencing loneliness are more likely to suffer from sleep problems. Preoccupied by continuous negativity loops, they seldom enjoy sound, restorative sleep. According to one study, loneliness may raise the risk of heart attack by more than 40. Another study conducted in 2010 by Brigham Young University found that loneliness shortens a person's lifespan by 15 years, about the same impacts as being obese or smoking 15 cigarettes a day. One 2015 analysis, which pooled data from 70 studies following 3.4 million people over seven years, found that lonely individuals had a 26% higher risk of dying. This figure rose to 32% if they lived alone. They are even more likely to suffer from cognitive decline in old age.

No sector of the society is spared from this sickness. More and more people of all ages are feeling socially isolated. Other than business and social gatherings, people generally don't meet others in person. They somehow believe that they are short of time. Whatever free time is available tends to be squandered on a digital screen. Obviously, to escape from loneliness, we need to nurture meaningful and quality relationships. Better to have a few true friends with whom we meet regularly and share our feelings than to have legions of friends on social media. It is urgently necessary that we spend more time in those places where we can meet others, like parks, gyms, sports complexes, community centres, houses of worship, and libraries. We must also put in time to practice meditation to bring about mindful living. What we need is a strong desire to be an aware, beneficent presence in the world --- and willpower.

4.4 With greater use of technology, attention is increasingly becoming a scare resource

We are entering into an "attention economy." Attention in humans is fast becoming a rare commodity. And everyone seems to be competing to attract the attention of others. As information/digital content has grown increasingly abundant and available on various platforms, attention has become a limiting factor in this age of information and technology. Just about everyone is spending hours and hours "together" on digital platforms like smartphones and computers. Yet they remain unsatisfied; they want to take in more and more interesting and entertaining material. People are getting addicted. Our mental capacity or bandwidth is limited. So, sharp attention is needed to filter the most important information from an ever-growing pool of information surrounding the human on digital media.

Figure 4.4: Increasing use of digital technology especially mobile addiction is leading to attention deficit.

In this Information Age, entertainment, social media, and marketing are constantly vying for our attention. Our minds are therefore diverted from the activities that most need our attention. Though generally conscious of those distractions, the problem is that they are very tempting and often addictive. Checking emails, "likes" on Facebook and Twitter, playing games, and watching videos are all tempting enough to command our attention in an uninterrupted way. FOMO (fear of missing out) effect is affecting our youths, who constantly scan their mobiles for fresh posts. While fun and informative, these trends are making it more difficult for us to focus on the overall purpose we intend to pursue.

The worst impact of digital addiction – especially to cell phones and gadgets – is on our younger generation. Studies are confirming that students, whether in high schools, colleges, or universities, are being adversely affected. Most of the students, whether in developed or developing countries, are strikingly similar in how they use media – and how addicted they are to it. The mobile addiction of children could threaten the very fabric of society. According to a UK study by sociologist Paul Kendall, "Many teenagers are desperate about being always available and are extremely uneasy if unable to contact their friends countless times each day. According to a survey, millennials check their phones even more often: 150 times per day, on average. If the trend continues young people will soon be incapable of forming and maintaining relationships without the help of a mobile." Under the circumstances, how can these students be able to focus on their goals and aspirations?

Digital addiction is having wide impact on youngsters' studies, health, career, and relationships. For instance, students need to pay full attention to their studies. It's now become more difficult for students to pay sustained attention in the classroom. Focus is lacking. To engage students during study hours in and outside of class has long been a challenge for teachers across the world. That so many students are mentally and physically occupied with social media obviously takes a toll on their studies, which in turn impacts their career. And as attention to studies decreases, work pressure from parents and teachers increases, and this leads to chronic stress.

According to a recently published Microsoft Attention Spans Research Report, *this digital lifestyle has made it difficult for not just students but all of us to stay focused, with the average human attention span shortening over a decade from*

12 seconds to eight seconds. Whether it's in the workplace, home, school, or educational institutions, there is an increasing use of gadgets. The Report further says that in the digital age, it seems the ability to maintain focus is now a "superpower." This weaker attention span could be an effect of the brain having to so rapidly adapt and change in the presence of technology. "We are moving from a world where computing power was scarce to a place where it now is limitless, and the true scarce commodity is increasingly human attention." (Satya Nadella, CEO Microsoft)

Daniel Goleman, author of a New York Times best-selling book, *Emotional Intelligence,* has recently written another book, *Focus: The Hidden Driver of Excellence,* in which he very elaborately explains why it's becoming so difficult for us to focus. He explains that attention is the thing that makes life worth living, and helps you develop more of it in every area of life: work, relationships, and your own attitude towards life and the planet. As cognitive overload weakens self-control, our ability to focus on and to design our destiny also suffers. So then, how do we address the issue of mind-wandering, distractions, and the attention deficit that we all experience in normal life? The solution lies in mindful living. When we have a high degree of self-awareness and having ability to focus, be attentive and present on the moments, we are, in other words, mindful. How we can cultivate the habit of becoming mindful is discussed in another chapter.

4.5 We need to use digital media judiciously; its obsessive or excessive use can lead to health issues .

The way we think, behave, and spend our time is becoming completely transformed. We're in an age of many revolutions. Within the information and technology (IT) domain, we are witnessing disruptive technologies impacting our lives in major ways. The most notable effect of digital technology is from social media. The way people communicate and socialize is being transformed. Nearly half of the world's population is connected through social media, such as Facebook, Twitter, WhatsApp and Instagram. About a dozen social networking sites are popular in India. Of India's 1.3 billion population, it is estimated that 241 million are active Facebook users. These numbers are, off course, escalating at a rapid pace.

There have been areas where social media has made a huge positive impact on our lives. We can instantly connect with ease to anybody all over the world. In addition to the joys of socializing and instant communication, social media has increased creativity, spreading awareness and learning opportunities. Many reports feeling more self-confident and empowered. The impact is tremendous and difficult to quantify. However, on the other hand, there can be negative effects, such as social isolation, digital addiction, attention deficit, loss of privacy, and health problems.

Alarming numbers of users, especially among the younger generation, are getting addicted to social media. When we use it, there is a direct neurological effect on our mind. Some even say that social media is like the world's largest slot machine. Whenever we are "on it," we get rewarded, so there is a pleasurable component to it. Since there is the anticipation of content that is rewarding or pleasurable or in some way desirable when we use the Internet, there is an accompanying elevation in dopamine, a neurotransmitter associated with the reward system in the brain. So we get tempted to refer to it excessively. There are virtually unlimited opportunities for pleasurable content from social media, as well as from Internet gaming, videos, movies, email, etc. A large percentage of us, young and old, find ourselves continually checking our cell phones whenever we get notifications, or whenever the desire for something rewarding or soothing arises. This habit may become compulsive or obsessive without our even knowing it.

As we get addicted to our phones and computers for social media and Internet stimulation, it starts effecting our mind and body in many ways. First and foremost, our attention span decreases due to constant distraction and the nature of quick sound bites. We don't want to miss anything important on social media. There is a fear of missing out (FOMO). We are less able to focus on anything for a sustained period. In fact, collective attention span is gradually declining. A study recently published by researchers at the Technical University of Denmark finds that global attention span is narrowing. We have developed an appetite to take in more and more things in a short period of time. The average person's attention span has dropped from 12 seconds in the year 2000 to fewer than eight seconds today. Too many distractions and attractions on digital media are causing us to be less focused on other priorities.

Figure 4.5: Mobile addiction is leading to not only inability to focus and be attentive but also many physical and mental problems.

In this age of information and technology, social media and the Internet seem to be seeking our attention all the time. We are becoming far busier. All around us, we can see the widespread sickness of "busyness." Everyone is absorbed in their mobiles, whether it's on the train, the bus, in public spaces or offices. Any available spare time is now consumed by social media. Not only are we becoming more distracted, less attentive, and less sharply focused, but there is also an adverse impact on our health and well-being. When our distracted mind wanders in various directions, it becomes bewildered and unhappy. So as we get addicted to mobile or other digital screens, happiness flees. Excessive use of social media can also impact our productivity and creativity. It disrupts our normal sleep rhythms. Many studies have shown a direct correlation between excessive use of mobiles and poor sleep quality, leading to mental health problems. Research studies are also showing greater incidences of depression and anxiety, especially among the younger generation.

We are becoming lonely people, seemingly connected on social media but not so much face to face. In this hyper-connected world, disconnection from others has become the norm. Though we may be surrounded by numerous colleagues in colleges, universities, and workplaces, we suffer from loneliness. Not only senior citizens, but even students and younger people have started feeling lonely, sad, and depressed due to the isolation brought about by social media. "Internet addiction disorder," as it is now called, may bring about serious mental problems such as depression and anxiety.

One prophylactic step we might take is to turn off notifications on our mobiles. When there is a sound of any kind, we get distracted, and it takes time to come back to the activity we were doing. Without turning off this recurrent sound, it's very difficult to focus or be attentive to a task for any length of time. Second, it would help if we could use the Screen Time app to keep track of time spent on social media. Becoming aware of the time we spend staring at a digital screen is a critical first step. Lastly but most important is the practice of mindfulness meditation, which brings us more and more into the present moment. Otherwise we don't notice --- let alone enjoy – our precious present moments. With meditation practice, we become more focused, attentive, and aware enough to keep time on social media in check.

OOO

5

Understanding the Inner Life: Learn to Recognize the Inner Workings of Mind

Since the dawn of civilization, man has been struggling to unravel the mysteries of the brain and mind, and their relationship to the body. Brain-mind-body has long been among the central issues in the study of philosophy and an extremely challenging problem, both philosophically and scientifically. Is the mind located in the brain, or is it beyond the structural and functional boundaries of brain? Where, exactly, does the mind reside? This is a contentious question that brain scientists have been trying to answer for centuries. The most straightforward scientific evidence of a strong relationship between the physical brain and the mind is the impact that physical alterations have on the functioning of the mind. On this basis, there is a broad understanding among the medical community that our brain, the visible structure, is located inside our head, while our mind is part of the invisible, transcendent world of thought, feeling, attitude, belief, imagination, etc. To understand mind, it's essential to have deeper knowledge of the brain.

The brain is the most complex organ in the human body. It generates all our thoughts, actions, memories, feelings, and experiences of the world. It's yet to be fully understood by the medical community. While neuroscientists are attempting to map all the neurons of different regions in the brain, they still have a long way to go. The human brain is the most complicated and creative information-processing system in the world. The processing of information starts with inputs from our sensory organs, which transform physical stimuli such as sound, light, and heat into electrochemical signals.

To understand human behaviour and how the thought process impacts our life, it is necessary to recognize the organs that are involved in the discriminatory processes that play a vital role in designing our destiny. It is the nervous system -- neurons, the brain and the spinal cord -- that constitutes the intelligent system responsible for smart functioning of the body. Connected to the brain through the nerves, sensors provide two-way communication that implements information exchange and the control and command to produce action. The spinal cord in the simplest terms is the highway for all the traffic of information exchange and the only connection between the brain and the other organs.

Finally, the most basic unit of this intelligent system is the neuron. Neurons consist of a cell body containing the nucleus, and special extensions called axons and dendrites. Neurons have the amazing ability to gather and transmit electrochemical signals. Each neuron may be connected to up to 10,000 other neurons, passing signals to one another via as many as 1,000 trillion synaptic connections. When a neuron receives a message from another neuron, it sends an electrical signal down the length of its axon. At the end of the axon, the electrical signal is converted into a chemical signal, and the axon releases chemical messengers called neurotransmitters. The neurons in our brains communicate in a variety of ways. Signals pass between them by the release and capture of neurotransmitter and neuromodulator chemicals such as serotonin, dopamine, and endorphins.

In *Incognito: The Secret Lives of the Brain*, American neuroscientist David Eagleman very beautifully explains the intricate structure of the brain. *Your brain is built of cells called neurons and glia—hundreds of billions of them. Each one of these cells is as complicated as a city. And each one contains the entire human genome and traffics billions of molecules in intricate economies. Each cell sends electrical pulses to other cells, up to hundreds of times per second. If you represented each of these trillions and trillions of pulses in your brain by a single photon of light, the combined output would be blinding. The cells are connected to one another in a network of such staggering complexity that it bankrupts human language and necessitates new strains of mathematics. A typical neuron makes about ten thousand connections to neighbouring neurons. Given the billions of neurons, this means there are as many connections in a single cubic centimetre of brain tissue as there are stars in the Milky Way Galaxy.*

It is widely believed that a fully developed typical normal brain contains roughly 100 billion neurons. All these units together form the brain. Weighing in at three approximately pounds, the brain is an intricate and amazingly complex jelly-like organ which is extremely rich in proteins and fats.

In this chapter, an attempt has been made to understand the process and mechanism through which our mind operates. Though prima facie, we feel the process is extremely intricate and perplexing but our mind acts rationally. Like physical laws, there are mental laws that overall govern its functioning. Our emotions and actions are the end products of our thinking process. Most of the time, we do not observe our mind because we are totally identified with the thinking process. As the mind arises from the brain, it is quite natural that its functioning would be equally complicated. Moreover, no one else can know what's going on in our mind. The knowledge and understanding of our mind is purely subjective. Often our self-awareness is inadequate, so we do not know if what's happening inside our skull is objectively right. We will explore main characteristics of our mind and its inner workings.

OH MY MIND

You are a stream flowing with incessant thoughts
And possess a vast reservoir of memories of all shades and times

You amaze me the way you auto generate thoughts in a fraction of moment
And the potentiality to wander in all possible directions in a spur of moment

You don't let me live and enjoy the moments at hand,
You wander from my past experiences to future's anxieties

You are like a monkey, jumping from one thought to another,
You keep on tasting and throwing half-eaten thoughts into the air

Oh ironically, you love to relish negative, repetitive and habitual thoughts
You love vulnerability and insecurity despite embodied in my stable entity

You become a drunken and agitated monkey when negativity arises,
You try to suppress and kill those thoughts but mostly fail to succeed

You create the self-image and selfish feeling of 'I', an identity of me
You encourage my ego to inflate, disillusioning me into a being free

You are the root of almost all of my miseries, sufferings and pain in life
You erect barriers with others and isolate me from the cosmic oneness

You continue to be a prisoner of my past and lost moments,
You carry a baggage load of emotional thoughts and memories,

You are appeased by me by fulfilling your demands, as and when raised
You, however, keep on raising your materialistic needs and desires

No enemy can be worse than you if you are wild, agitated and uncontrolled
No friend can be better than you if you are well trained and disciplined

Over the millennia, mankind has rapidly progressed into a civilized society
But, oh my mind, you chose to remain primitive in evolving humanity

I know, oh my mind, if I am able to control you and your flickering behaviour
I can turn around my affairs towards my goals leading to my 'purpose' of life

I know by doing this, I have an unbounded power to exercise my 'free will'
So as to be the designer and master of my own destiny and the future

5.1 Mind is a theatre and our thoughts are like a movie

Undoubtedly, mind is the most complex and mysterious thing in the universe. It's the product of interaction among trillions of neurons (extremely tiny brain cells) in the brain. Brain scientists are still struggling to answer where mind is located, inside the brain or outside of it? Is mind more than the brain, or is brain the real player, and mind merely an illusion? From antiquity, when man began to think deeply about life's mysteries, mind has held centre stage. Earliest recorded views about mind and its relationship with soul and divine forces were put forward by the Buddha, Plato, Aristotle, Adi Shankara, and many other ancient Indian, Greek, and later Islamic scholars and philosophers.

So then, again --- whence come thoughts? What we know is that thoughts are the product of unconscious neurological processes in different parts of the brain. The human brain is comprised of about 100 billion neurons, interconnected by trillions of synaptic connections, each transmitting signals. On average, each synaptic connection between neurons transmits about one signal per second. Some specialized connections send hundreds of signals per second. According to researchers, in some extremely complex process, trillions of connections and billions of simultaneous transmissions coalesce inside our brain to form a thought. One study has found that human beings have an average of nearly 60,000 thoughts every day. Most of these thoughts that pass through the mind are unstructured, random, and largely incoherent.

David Hume (1711-1776), a Scottish philosopher, historian, and important figure in the history of Western philosophy, has explained mind very appropriately in the following words:

'Mind is a bundle or collection of different perceptions which succeed one another with an inconceivable rapidity and are in a perpetual flux and movement. The mind is a kind of theatre where several perceptions successively make their appearance, pass, repass, glide away, and mingle in an infinite variety of postures and situations. There is properly no simplicity in it at one time, nor identity in different times ." Hume suggests that our mind is just a bundle of perceptions, like links in a chain. We capture, ever so fleetingly, only our perceptions of the scenes in the physical world around us.

Figure 5.1: Mind is a theater and we ourselves become part of the great story line.

We then construct highly subjective mental models of the outer reality we perceive through our senses. These internal representations are based on s experiences, perceptions, and interpretations of the world. This is why each of us perceives outer reality in his or her own unique way. Billions of people on this planet carry their own internal models of the external world inside their minds. No two individuals therefore think in exactly the same manner. Mental models serve to represent real as well as imaginary situations. Whenever we imagine something, we construct an internal model based on our previous experiences. Let's say we're going to a new mall to do some shopping. Never having seen it before, en route in the car we find ourselves constructing an imaginative model of that mall in our mind.

Imagine we are watching a movie in a theatre. We are completely engrossed in the storyline. As the story proceeds, we feel happy, joyful, sorrowful – amused -- a wide range of emotions. The movie to us becomes a real-life happening. Though the events in the movie are not happening to us, we empathetically feel that we ourselves are playing one or more of the roles. We forget that we are merely watching. Similarly, our thoughts are like a movie, running in our mind. Completely identifying with its thoughts and feelings, we feel that this drama is real, and part of "I." We lose our ability to watch our thoughts as a simple observer. Rather than witnessing our thoughts, we become an integral part of the thoughts themselves. We are not mindful. We must learn the art of mindfulness in order to observe our own thoughts. If we are able to do this, we can sit in the driver's seat and direct our own course.

5.2 Beyond our conscious mind, we have a far more powerful subconscious and unconscious mind

Sujan is driving his car along the highway at about 100 miles per hour. He is listening to music and thinking about the meeting he will be attending in the evening with his client. Suddenly, his mobile starts ringing. Though there is a strict law banning mobile chats on the highways, he ignores it and answers the phone. Despite heavy traffic on the road, he is driving his car with ease. After attending to the call, he increases his speed and, within seconds, he sees a villager crossing that road right in front of him. He freezes. However, his body kicks into automatic mode, and within a fraction of a second, his swift movements enable him to swerve around the man. Certainly it's not his conscious mind making decisions within that fraction of a second. His mind had been busy, thinking about his client. Likewise, all of us successfully carry out multiple tasks all the time without being fully aware of them. We recognize that behind our conscious mind, some other part of mind, which is far more powerful, never sleeps.

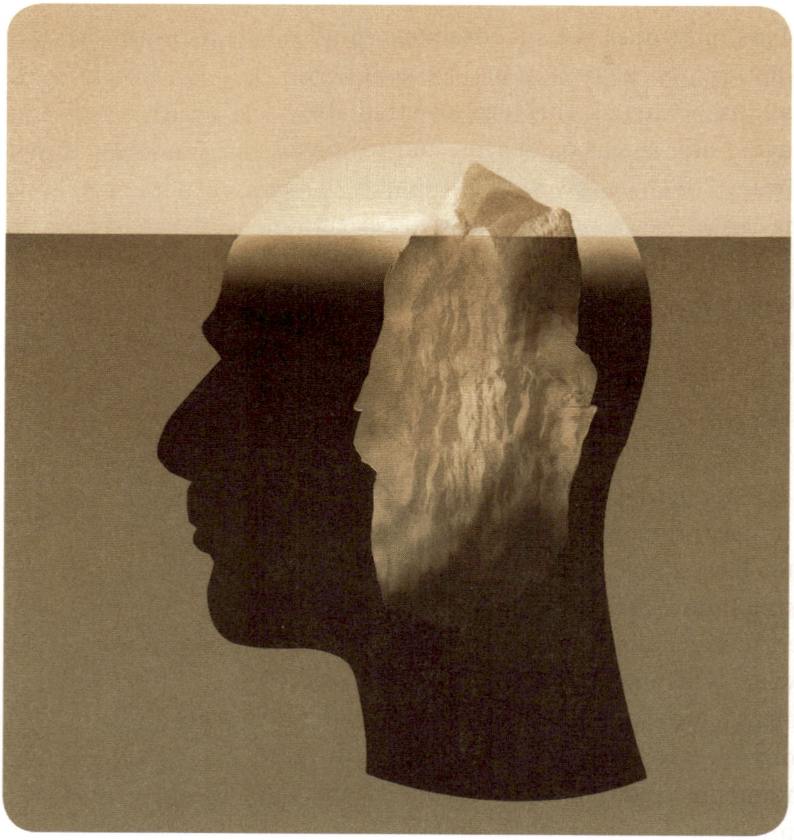

***Figure 5.2:* We have extremely powerful subconscious and unconscious mind working incessantly below our conscious mind.**

All routine and repetitive activities such as driving, walking, eating, bathing, drinking, and playing are performed perfectly by our subconscious mind. It works continuously and tirelessly "behind the scenes" to meet our requirements without ever letting us know. When we undertake such repetitive tasks, it is primarily the subconscious mind that guides us from moment to moment, and even at critical junctures. It is now common knowledge that the subconscious mind is far bigger and faster than the conscious mind. The subconscious mind is what lies just beneath the conscious mind. *Many complex tasks are performed in perfect harmony and accuracy through the subconscious mind.* Even if we are at rest or not doing anything during our waking hours, our brain keeps on working. According to American cell biologist Dr Bruce Lipton, the subconscious operates 500,000 times faster than the conscious mind.

Not only does the subconscious mind direct routine activities; it also anticipates the next moves we are likely to make. Unknown to our conscious awareness, this level of mind always thinks two steps ahead. To avoid any threat or danger, and to maximize potential rewards, it is always "on." In this way, thousands of activities and functions are being carried out round the clock in perfect synchronization with every aspect of the body. And all the while, we are completely unaware of its functioning. As Sujan was talking on the phone, his subconscious mind was coordinating various body parts for driving smoothly on the road. He was totally unaware. Our subconscious mind is vast, deep, and largely inaccessible to conscious thought. It maintains vigilant awareness of our surroundings.

It is popularly believed that the conscious mind forms less than 10% of the human mind, while the rest is either the subconscious or unconscious mind. The conscious mind is what we consider to be at work during our waking hours. We use this mind for making choices and decisions after interpreting and analysing the information available. It makes us aware of what is happening in the outside world. It functions on the basis of information that it gleans through our senses. The conscious mind communicates with the outside world. It is like the captain of a ship, standing on the deck and giving out commands to the crew that in turn ensure smooth sailing of the ship.

In addition to the subconscious, we also have a deeper part of mind called the unconscious mind. It is the storehouse of all the memories and past experiences, including those that have been repressed and those that have simply been consciously forgotten and are no longer important to us. The unconscious mind constantly communicates with the conscious mind, and is what provides us with the meaning to all our interactions with the world, as filtered through beliefs and habits. Most of the time when we make choices or conscious decisions, groundwork has been done by the unconscious mind. It is the source of all the programs that our subconscious uses to carry out routine and repetitive activities on automatic mode.

Most of our mental processes occur automatically, and without the involvement of our conscious mind. This prevents the mind from being overloaded with simple tasks. *When it comes to decisions, we tend to assume they are made by our conscious mind, but to a greater extent, they are made by the unconscious mind.* All the groundwork necessary for decision-making is laid behind the scenes by the unconscious mind. Of course, when we commit any mistake, we obviously take responsibility for it, even though the actual decision was born in the unconscious. It is also true that our unconscious mind, over which we have hardly any control, plays a crucial role in making choices at critical moments, many of them unfortunate. Unconscious "kneejerk" responses to difficult situations can spark impulsive and "mindless" behaviour.

Many times we later justify our decisions and come up with explanations for our motives and actions. We convince ourselves that we were logically and rationally justified in taking a harmful action. This is the defence mechanism known as rationalisation. It is a wholly unconscious process by which the mistakes we committed are logically justified and explained away in a rational or logical manner. The fact is that decisions underlying the behaviour were not made by our conscious mind. This is our artful way of "making excuses" for our irrational or selfish choices. Hence, even after committing an obviously wrongful act, we strongly support and defend it. It is a common phenomenon that we encounter often in life. Hence, it would seem that our life is predominantly governed by our unconscious drives, urges, habitual patterns of behaviour, and especially our belief system.

5.3 The limitation of our inner mind to perceive the objective reality of the world around us

As you read this page, you of course feel that you are stationary. Chances are, it has slipped your mind that the earth is spinning eastward on its axis, making one daily rotation at a speed of 1,040 miles per hour. As the earth orbits the sun, you are being carried along at 70,000 miles per hour. As the sun orbits the Milky Way galaxy, you are moving at 500,000 miles per hour. Consider further that the earth is situated 27,000 light-years from the centre of the Milky Way galaxy. Our galaxy is among the estimated 100 to 200 billion galaxies in the (known) universe. Do you know that one light-year is six trillion miles? Now you know you are largely incapable of visualizing what's happening in the world/universe which is beyond your eyes.

The fact is that we imperfect humans have limited ability to know the objective reality of this world. With limited knowledge and scanty information, we create reality in our mind. There is no reality beyond our mind. Is the reality that we construct in our mind an objective, true picture of the reality that appears to exist around us? Let's examine it. The brain, through our five senses, receives and then processes huge amounts of data from its surroundings, and forms a mental image. *Since incoming data is so overwhelming, it's not possible to process all the raw data. This is why those images that we form may be neither complete nor accurate.* They are simply interpretations, and not the true reality.

The mind however has a unique ability to construct its own reality out of limited information. In fact, our brains have been designed by evolutionary processes to make the best sense of data we receive from the outer world. According to one study, our brain processes around 400 billion bits of information every second, while our awareness takes in only around 2,000 bits of information. This means that conscious awareness is negligible compared to what the brain actually processes. Now here the problem starts. Each one of us interprets this limited information in our own unique way. Different people will analyse, evaluate, and perceive input data in different ways. No two individuals will interpret information in the same way. Let's see how this happens.

Everyone's mind has its own selective filters through which we perceive the world in our own unique way. This so-called filter is built into our minds, allowing us only a partial view, depending upon what we are most drawn to seeing. The selectivity of mind is determined by what one most wants and/or needs to become aware of. Researchers have established that since the mind can receive and interpret only a fraction of the input data/information from its surroundings, it uses that limited information as coordinates by which it constructs a mental model. The brain uses this raw data to create a model of the world, and this is the mental world in which we all live. *As we all construct the inner mental image or model on the basis of limited raw data, passing through the selective filter, the reality becomes highly subjective and unique.* Therefore, thanks to that selective filter, each one of us lives in a world that is quite different from that of others.

The information that we are receiving or gathering from outside sources is very often unreliable. Every day we experience it ourselves.

The news that we receive from print media or watch on television or smartphones is generally not reliable or authenticated. We hardly make any attempt to verify the news, yet many of us are cocksure of that information. Now in the digital world, this problem is becoming very serious due to fake news. We continue to receive and then forward videos whose authenticity is questionable.

When we watch any movie, we all interpret the story in our own unique way. We go to the theatre to see a film rated four stars, then find it to be totally hopeless and a waste of time. Our mind perceives the story based on our past experiences, beliefs, and, more importantly, our expectations. The subjectivity that reigns in the movie theatre goes on all the time in the outside world. From the vast input from the world around us, only a small fraction of it is consciously processed by our minds. Then, from our selective filter of past experiences, beliefs, mental conditioning, ideologies, and other fixed/rigid ideas, we construct reality in our own unique ways. None of us will construct the same reality, even when we are experiencing exactly the same situation.

It is like constructing reality from the tip of an iceberg, while ignoring all that lies beyond our field of vision. This means that we live in a largely imaginary and illusory world, far from truthful representation of the world around us. Now from here, another problem emerges: we mostly don't realize that others will be interpreting the same information in different ways. Others may have an altogether different view of reality than that which we are experiencing. So we don't understand their point of view – sometimes not at all. We think we are right, but the truth is, others are also right because they have their own interpretation of reality based on the same basic information. The result is misunderstanding, conflicts, and disputes, as others' points of view completely elude us. Though it's extremely difficult to perceive objective reality all the time, but we can surely minimize the gap between what others perceive and how we interpret reality by greater awareness and ability to think in other's perspective and point of view as well.

5.4 Heaven and hell - the outer reality: A true reflection of our inner state of mind

"We are what we think. All that we are arises from our thoughts. With our thoughts we make the world." Thus spoke the Lord Buddha around

2,500 years ago. In a very real sense, we are an active participant in the creation of reality around us. If our mind is filled with negativity, angry and fearful thoughts and feelings, we attract similar conditions from the outside reality. Likewise, if we are joyful and full of positivity, the world will look pleasant and cheerful. The outer world is nothing but a reflection, a mirror image of our inner state of mind. The universal law, "As within, so without," puts it more succinctly. That is why our spiritual teachers say that the key to eliminating something from our external world is to eliminate it from our internal world of thought and feeling.

Figure 5.4: Outer world is merely a reflection of our inner mind. While a joyful mind perceive outer world as pleasant and sad, depressed mind will see the world as hostile.

It is well said that there is no reality outside of the mind. Everything we perceive in the world has its roots in our inner world of thoughts, feelings, and beliefs. Tranquillity and serenity of mind will make the world wonderful, with friendliness all around. Similarly, if our mind is in turmoil, then we are certain to see a tumultuous outer world. Buddhist Zen masters say that the reality in the mind is displayed in our outer world. We try to fight the external reality without realising that we first need to address our own thoughts, inner feelings, and the conflicts arising within the mind. Fighting the external world is like breaking the mirror; it serves no purpose and only reflects more negativity. The reason is simple and straightforward: The outer world is a true copy of our inner world.

We all perceive this world in our own way, depending on our state of mind. That is why our mind sees only a partial reality, determined by what we are most interested in, or want to experience. The world around us has no dearth of good people and pleasant things full of beauty, joy, and happiness, but they are perceptible only if we are good at heart, and share love, affection, and compassion with others. Otherwise, plenty of negativity – that appears to be in the outside world – does not allow our mind to be at peace. Therefore, when we look at hostility and negativity around us and allow that to influence our thinking and behaviour, we are unintentionally expanding the scope of negativity. It is hence necessary to first sort out our inner feelings and thought processes before blaming the outer world.

There is a constant loop of energy connecting us and the world around us. It is extremely important that we become aware of what we are sharing with the world because whatever we are giving to the outside reality is coming back to us in one form or another. If we share negativity with the outer world, we must expect more energy of a similar nature to be coming back to us. In other words, all that negativity that we think is coming at us from the outside environment is actually the same energy that we have earlier shared with the world. The reverse is equally true. That is why people who engage in philanthropic activities are found to be happier and more contented than those who do not; they are getting far more in return from the outer world.

Ancient spiritual texts teach us that if we want to see changes in our life and the surrounding world, then we must start from inside. Once again, this means that if we change and reform ourselves internally, these changes will naturally be reflected back to us. Though it is difficult to think how such a shift would be possible, many of us have succeeded in demonstrating this principle. Life can be far more peaceful and enjoyable by adopting this simple mantra: *If we want happiness in our life and the surrounding world, we must inculcate happy and pleasant feelings inside.* If we love others, we will see that love in our reality mirror, which is our perceived external world. Rather than changing the forces operating in the outside world, we must follow this simple mantra.

It's abundantly clear that what we are experiencing inside is reflected in the outer reality. If we are creating heavenly feelings inside ourselves by way of positivity and happiness, we are living in a heaven. The reverse is equally true. If we are trapped in a loop of hellish thoughts and feelings, we are living in hell. Both heaven and hell are human constructs. We create the reality through our thoughts and intentions. The choice is ours: heaven or hell. Our ancient scriptures convincingly explain that we will go to heaven if we do good deeds and make good karma. Otherwise, our front-row seat is reserved in hell. This belief in the Law of Karma continues to be widely accepted to this day.

5.5 Thoughts think themselves: we are completely unaware of the process by which thoughts are generated in our mind

As we've seen, streams of thoughts flow through our mind continuously. The only exception is during the deepest, dreamless stage of sleep, characterized by delta brainwaves. Unless we are consciously attentive to the present moment, our mind goes into default mode. In other words, our mind starts wandering in different directions. Thoughts are mostly random, unstructured, and largely incoherent. When we are thinking about something other than what's currently happening, we are more or less unaware of our surroundings. The mind is also unaware of time – we "lose track" of it. We are also unaware of the ongoing sensations of the body. Although completely identified with our mind, we are generally unaware of the movement of thoughts. We just take it for granted that our mind has its own separate identity, like any other organ of the body.

We hardly notice the time, even when we are sitting idly, doing nothing. Although we do have the ability to watch our thoughts, we seldom exercise that ability. When we are sad or worrying about something, we do notice our feelings of sadness and say, "Oh, I am sick of negative thoughts." This, however, happens rarely. Most of the time we are.so engrossed in our thoughts that we are oblivious of the very act of thinking, and the thoughts that are moving seemingly on their own – without intentionality – in and out of consciousness.

Where do all these thoughts come from? This is a perplexing question that neuroscientists have long struggled to answer. They do know that thoughts are electrochemical responses, which arise from neurons in our brain. Some specialized synaptic connections send up to 1,000 signals per second. Through some complex unconscious neurological processes, thoughts arise in our brain. In some mysterious way, trillions of connections and billions of simultaneous transmissions coalesce inside our brain to form a thought. With new brain-imaging techniques, researchers are making inroads in their understanding of how thoughts arise in the brain. Despite thinking all the time, most people do not seem especially curious as to how and from where these thoughts simply appear in their mind.

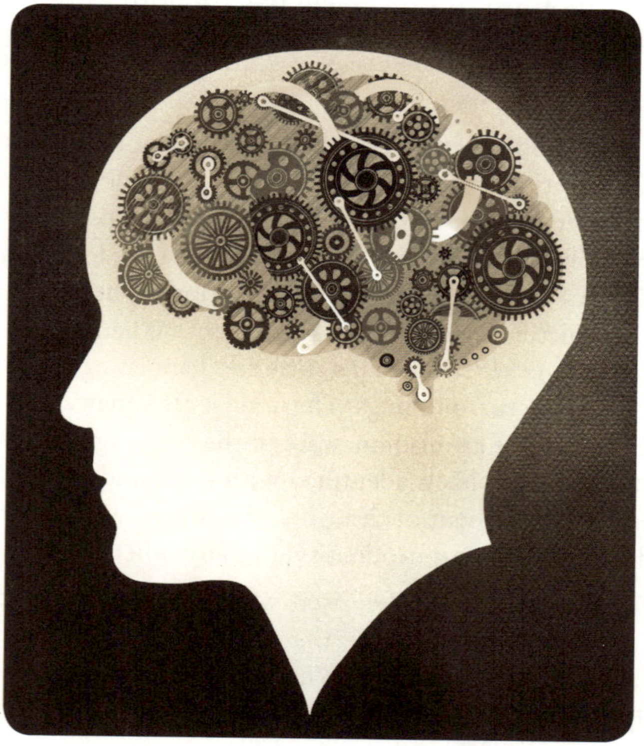

Figure 5.5: Mind is thought generating machine – we are unaware of how thoughts arise in consciousness.

Samuel Harris, a popular American author, cognitive neuroscientist and philosopher, firmly claims that we are not the author of our thoughts because we don't control them. They just mysteriously show up, uninvited. Not only do we not control when a thought comes upon us, but also, "The thought thinks itself." However, we have been conditioned to believe that we are the voice behind our thoughts. In his book, *Waking Up: A Guide to Spirituality Without Religion*, Harris writes that "*Thinking is the substance of every social relationship and cultural institution we have. It is also the foundation of science. But our habitual identification with the flow of thought—that is, our failure to recognize thoughts* as thoughts, *as transient appearances in consciousness—is a primary source of human suffering and confusion."*

Robert Wright, author of *The Evolution of God* and *Why Buddhism Is True: The Science and Philosophy of Meditation and Enlightenment,* has also written on this subject. He explains, "*You might have thought all your life that you're thinking thoughts – the thing you think of as 'you' is thinking thoughts. It's closer to being the case that the thoughts try to capture you, the thing you think of as 'you.' Right. They come from somewhere in your body, somewhere in your brain. It's just that the thoughts are arising and there's a strong habit of mind to be identified with them* ." He further says in *Why Buddhism* Is *True: "While observing the mind during meditation, it could seem like 'thoughts think themselves' – because the modules do their work outside of consciousness.*" He describes mind having modular structure, with different modules competing for one's attention as mind wanders from one module to another. In this way, thoughts are generated on their own. Somehow and somewhere, the thoughts arise and we are completely unaware of this process.

Brain scientists have not been able to track how a single thought is generated in our brain. No one knows what prompts neurons, the tiniest brain cells, to fire signals to adjoining neurons to make their synaptic connections.. Throughout our lives, billions of indefatigable neurons keep firing and wiring in a synchronised manner. What kind of thoughts will arise a few moments from now is anyone's guess. All thought that can potentially visit our mind may drop in at any moment. All thought therefore is in potentiality and then "collapsed" into reality. On the basis of random thoughts, we quite often make choices. After making the choice, we assume that we ourselves have authored the choice. Did we make the choice? It's the prime philosophical question posed when we deliberate "free will." Off course, the time will soon come when neurologists will unravel the mysterious process concerning thoughts.

5.6 Mind's wandering - wandering mind is an unhappy mind

Observe your mind carefully for just two minutes. You will notice that despite trying to stay in the present, your mind keeps wandering off to thoughts and physical impressions. Mind's wandering increases when we perform boring tasks. When we attend any lecture or meeting and the topic is either not relevant or not to our interest, our wayward mind will not be attentive to subject at hand. We will invariably get lost in our own thought processes. We are either planning or anticipating the future, worrying about something, or reliving the past. There is no shortage of upcoming tasks and duties to think about. Even if we don't have anything pressing to consider, we will slip into daydreams. We are lost in fantasies. If we arrive at the venue in a disturbed state, our mind will be preoccupied with related thoughts. In fact, on those occasions it's all the more difficult to stay present. Mind's wandering is a very natural phenomenon. It's the very nature of our mind.

Unless it is focused, attentive, or engrossed in some activity, the mind is moving randomly and incessantly. When it wanders, we don't remain on any one activity or task for very long, particularly when we are not engaged in any interesting or attention-demanding task. The mind wanders mostly when we are busy performing routine, monotonous, or repetitive tasks. When we drive, eat, walk in the morning, read a book or perhaps get trapped in conversation with a bore, the mind wanders broadly afield. (If that bore is boring enough, the mind may even "blank out," occupying neither past, present, nor future!) *Mind-wandering allows one part of the brain to focus on the task at hand, while another part keeps a more interesting idea or goal in mind.* We can also see mind wandering in "multitasking." We shift our attention from one task to another task. The mind is actually focusing on open goals or unfulfilled intentions, which are generally many at any given point in time.

In a way, it's our default mode of mind. A wandering mind is in its natural state. Researchers have recorded people's brain activity and observed mind-wandering. When test subjects reported that their mind was wandering, their brains showed activity in several cortical regions that are the same ones that are active when our brains are "at rest." These areas are always operating in the background. So mind-wandering is a natural feature of how our brains work. Normally, 50% of the time our mind is not focused or attentive; in fact. it's on wandering mode. When we are bored or doing routine or any other uninteresting work, mind's wandering is as high as 70%. However, when we are engaged in mind-absorbing or concentration-demanding tasks, this percentage is low, as low as 10%.

Figure 5.6: Mind wandering – our mind is, nearly half of the time, wandering in different directions. Our attention is not at the task at hand.

Harvard researchers Matthew Killingsworth and Daniel Gilbert found some very interesting facts about mind-wandering in their 2010 study. They collected real-time data from volunteers on an iPhone app developed by Killingsworth called "Track Your Happiness." Participants were asked to record their feelings when the app contacted them at random intervals. One question was, "Are you thinking about something other than what you're currently doing?" (Either yes or no – If no, people were asked to indicate if they were thinking of something pleasant, unpleasant, or neutral.) They gathered and compiled over 6,50,000 real-time reports from a diverse group of more than 15,000 people. The subjects belonged to a wide range of categories on the basis of income, education level, and marital status. There were 86 occupational categories. They analysed data on 22 different activities such as eating, working, playing, and watching TV. Their findings were:

First, approximately 47% of the time, people's minds are wandering, which means thinking about something other than what they are doing at that time. Second, people are substantially less happy when their minds wander compared to when their minds are on the task at hand. When the mind wanders, people often think of unpleasant things, which make them enormously less happy. Also when people have neutral thoughts, they are considerably less happy than when their mind is on what they are doing. Even when people have pleasant thoughts, they are still slightly less happy than when their mind is not wandering.

These are very interesting findings about the relationship between the mind's wandering and unhappiness or happiness. The conclusion of their study is that the wandering mind is an "unhappy mind." This may be why when we exercise or engage in dancing or playing games that require a high degree of concentration, we feel happy. That a focused mind is indeed a happy mind is the finding of many other studies conducted later. In fact, being present is the road to happiness. No doubt money is important for happiness, but beyond a certain point money doesn't help in realizing happiness. However, to have inculcated the habit of being focused and present on any task or activity that we do at any moment makes us happier.

Many spiritual and religious traditions teach us that happiness is found by living in the present moment. These traditions also maintain that a wandering mind is an unhappy mind. Mind-wandering has also been associated with vehicular accidents. Unrelated, fragmented thoughts are common in people in a low or depressed mood. Mind-wandering is especially common when a person is drunk or drugged. *Studies have established that we tend to engage in more future than past-related thoughts during mind-wandering.* When thoughts are unrelated to the task at hand, the mind then processes both task-relevant and unrelated sensory information in a less detailed manner. It is said that while daydreams offer a welcome mental escape from uninteresting tasks, they also have a positive, simultaneous effect on task performance.

In our contemporary world, we are very frequently distracted by social media such as WhatsApp, Facebook, Twitter, and email. We tend to use dozens of apps actively throughout the day. We are tempted to visit sites relating to media and entertainment. In doing so, frequency of distraction is increasing. Attention span is decreasing too. It's becoming increasingly difficult to focus on any specific task. The result is before us. We are becoming more unhappy. Though apps like Screen Time can help in reducing time spent on social media, we must become more self-aware so that whenever we are distracted or attention is diverted, we become conscious and return our attention to the task at hand. Awareness of getting distracted is the first step to limit mind's wandering. Despite our best efforts we can't reduce the extent of wandering beyond a certain point. However, on the practical side, there is no harm in allowing our mind to wander or distract as long as our performance is not adversely affected or joy and happiness is not compromised.

5.7 Negativity Bias – we all have a natural inclination for negativity in life.

"Bad news is a good news!" Isn't that true of most media, especially in India? When we switch on any TV channel or scan any national or regional newspaper, we find predominantly negative news. Do we have a natural inclination toward negative news? This question comes up quite often. Ask any media person about it and he or she will tell you the reason. People love sensationalistic news; that's why newscasters air more news of a negative nature. The space generally allocated to negative news is more than that given to neutral and positive stories. The main reason behind the media's focus on negative news is not that there are more unpleasant and negative stories for them to report, but rather that mental bias toward negativity. We are more inclined to pay attention to bad news than good news. We remember and recall negative news more clearly and quickly compared to positive news.

In other areas too -- not just the media – we tend to pay more attention to negative news or events than to positive ones. We often experience this bias in our relationships. After even one single negative incident with our spouse, we need more positive experiences for neutralizing the negative one. It's far more difficult to forget anything unpleasant that happens to us personally, sometimes taking days to overcome the fallout on our relationships. On the other hand, we tend to forget positive incidents more quickly.

The negativity inclination is seen in every sphere of life, from the individual and family level right up to the national level. We are especially sensitive to negative thoughts and emotions because our capacity to weigh negative inputs is comparatively very high, whereas positive ones are less compelling. To know the reason, we need to see this inherent aspect of mind as serving critical evolutionary and developmental functions. Because of our past, living the life of hunter-gatherers for millions of years, this negative bias got deeply embedded in our mind. During those times we lived in constant fear of wild animals and other predators. Living conditions were dangerous and frightening. So we became highly sensitive to any threat – whether real or imagined -- due to prevailing living conditions. That's how the negative bias got hardwired into our brain. *We became very sensitive and adept at identifying threats and then remembering negative experiences so that we could better handle such situations when they happened again.*

Figure 5.7: Negative emotions are dominating (heavier) – we are more sensitive towards unpleasant news, experiences and relationships in life.

After only 70-80 generations of civilized conditions – compared to about 90,000 generations as hunter-gathers -- our minds have still not fully adapted to this modern era. In a way, we are still as sensitive to threats and as prone to fear as we were in ancient times. We are modern humans with a semi-primitive mind. Our older part of brain, which evolved during the Age of Mammals, still remains active. It coexists with the newly evolved part of the brain -- i.e., the neocortex. Fear is, by and large, an outdated requirement for our existence. We fear far more by way of the imagination than actual impending harm. Our older (reptilian) brain is still conditioned to react automatically in threatening situations. Because of this reactivity, we humans have more of an inclination toward negativity than positivity.

When negative thoughts arise, they obviously attract more thoughts of a similar nature. And as we unconsciously attend to those thoughts, we end up strengthening them. We increase their intensity with our emotions. As we all know, negative thoughts act as a magnet to attract negativity in our life. So we trap ourselves in a vicious cycle. We all harbor enormous goodness inside of us. However, because of in-built sensitivity to negativity, this goodness is often overshadowed by negative experiences/memories, which we do not easily forget. This inherent tendency of humans, a legacy continuing from the period of hunter-gatherers, has been researched widely by neuroscientists in the recent past. Neuropsychologist Rick Hanson refers to this as "the brain's negativity bias."

Because of this inherent tendency toward negativity, the mind is kept busy thinking about negative events/moments, not only of our own experience but also those of others. *Under stress, the harder we try to distract ourselves from negative thoughts, or to suppress or repress them, the more frequently and persistently they resurface.* Considered one of the most problematic features of mind, this disturbing tendency can play a big role in almost all the lifestyle diseases, including heart ailments, diabetes, and cancer. At the deepest level of connectivity, body and mind respond to negative thoughts with life-sapping insecurity and anxiety, born of fear.

The only way to free our lives of negativity is to start starving negative thoughts by paying less and less attention to them. It's an undisputed fact that no thought can survive for long if we do not give it our attention. The frequency and intensity of negative thinking gradually diminishes, as thoughts become "weak" and disappear from our awareness. Watching and observing thoughts in a nonjudgmental way can bring about a big change in the way we normally respond to negative situations. The more we pay attention to what makes us happy and feeling good, the greater would be our capacity to manage what makes us feel bad in the first place. We should look for positive experiences whenever and wherever possible. We must frequently recall our past experiences which reinforce pleasant feelings. To the extent possible, we should avoid watching negative news. We should share good experiences among ourselves. We need to highlight the good work done by others. There is no dearth of good things happening in the world. What's required is to pay more attention to those experiences and events, rather than falling into the trap of negativity.

5.8 The more we suppress negative and unwanted thoughts, the more forcefully they resurface and the longer they persist.

> *Sujata, a young executive in charge of a marketing division, had been working in a multinational company stationed in Gurgaon for past three years. Her performance had been consistently good. However, due to a sudden change in the policy of competitors, sales started going down. To review the position, one day the regional head from Mumbai, a short-tempered and impulsive gentleman, came by to speak with all executives in the marketing division. Barely listening to the local executives, who were attempting to explain the problems they were facing, he started shouting at Sujata. Having never faced such a situation, Sujata was humiliated before her colleagues. Somehow the meeting finally ended, and the bullied woman went home, emotionally shattered. Unable to control her thoughts about the meeting, she tried to divert her attention to other pleasant activities, like watching TV and listening to music, but failed miserably. The more she tried to suppress angry and distressed thought about her boss, the more forcefully those thoughts came back for another round. She'd fallen into a vicious cycle of toxic thoughts. She continues to have no idea how to come out from that situation.*

Such mental habits are not uncommon. Most of us fall into them at some point in our lives. We are in fact *bombarded* by unruly distressed thoughts. We try to divert our attention to other things. We talk to friends, watch movies, go to games, and engage in various other entertainments, but gain only temporary relief. Those disturbing thoughts just don't want to quit! In fact, the more we suppress them, the more forcefully they continue to come to mind. The mind loses control. We become increasingly agitated and disturbed. Our mind becomes disobedient, clicks off, and is no longer "listening" to us. *One of the worst characteristic features of negative thoughts is their 'stickiness'. They get stick inside the mind and not easily leave our head.* It's not an easy task to remove 'stickiness' from negative thoughts.

This is a psychological phenomenon known as "ironic process" or the "white bear problem," wherein deliberate attempts to suppress certain thoughts make them more likely to resurface. For instance, when someone is trying hard not to think of a white bear, the same bear is likely to appear more in our mind. Many people get trapped in constantly anxious thoughts; they fail to recognise that their symptoms of anxiety are produced by their thoughts themselves. They keep trying to stop these thoughts through different methods, but generally fail. Without acknowledging the real problem, they cannot suppress or ignore their troubling thoughts. They may also try to bring logical thinking to the fore, expecting to neutralise such thoughts, or attempt to balance them with positive thoughts, but none of these methods generally work.

Figure 5.8: Ironic process – more we suppress distressing and negative thoughts, more strongly they resurface and persist.

This tendency of mind was studied elaborately in experimental psychology, originally and most notably by social psychologist Daniel Wegner. Ironic mental processes have been shown in a variety of situations, where they are usually created or worsened by stress. It is always counterproductive when we try to suppress or avoid anxiety-producing or depressing thoughts. Persistent negative thoughts, including those pertaining to past trauma or acute suffering, can lead to depression or other psychological disorders. Daniel Wegner asked test subjects to verbalize their stream of consciousness for five minutes, while trying not to think of a white bear. If a white bear came to mind, he told them, they should ring a bell. Despite the clear instructions to avoid it, the participants thought of a white bear more than once per minute, on average.

Wegner also attempted to explain why it is so hard to avoid unwanted thoughts. He found evidence that when we try not to think of something, one part of our mind does avoid the forbidden thought, but another part "checks in" every so often to ensure that the thought is not coming up -- therefore, ironically, bringing that thought to mind. The result is often a vicious cycle of negativity. *Studies have shown that suppression of negative thoughts makes the situation worse.* Thoughts rebound, regardless of one's attempts to divert attention from those disturbing thoughts.

The ironic rebound effect explains many recurring problems in modern society. Individuals who strive to inhibit or suppress their emotions when upset, for instance, are especially inclined to experience depression as well as anxiety disorders. These unpleasant emotions tend to recur, compromising well-being. Many of us experience a similar situation when we try to fall sleep with a disturbed mind. Trying hard to avoid our disturbing thoughts, we attempt to distract ourselves with other thoughts. We are then trapped in the "paradox of insomnia." No amount of self-inflicted pressure will shut off the troubled mind!

What does one do under such circumstances? Here is the practical solution. Unless we release the accumulated energy of those negative thoughts, their recurrence and intensity will not decline. Generally, people get impatient too soon after failed attempts to suppress their thoughts. One easy and effortless method to encourage relaxed awareness is to just sit back and fully allow whatever arises in the mind. Watch and observe how thoughts and feelings come and go. Once we do this, our awareness increases. As we stay in this state of relaxed awareness, we feel the intensity of those disturbing and distressing thoughts reducing.

We need to be patient and non-judgmental while observing our thoughts. With a sense of equanimity, simply allow the thoughts that are disturbing us to arise and be seen. Though difficult to practice, we should certainly do this if we want to overcome recurring regrets, resentments, and fears. We should never try to suppress distressing thoughts; rather we should confront and neutralize those thought at the very first place. We must never allow them to stay and stick in our mind for a long period. Longer they stay, more difficult it becomes for us to get rid of them. This is possible only when we either don't pay attention to them or to neutralize those negative thoughts with positivity. But never try to suppress them.

5.9 We easily surrender before our distressed mind We mostly become helpless in managing our mind in troubled times

Mehram Singh is a middle-level executive working in a private-sector company for the past decade. His initial few years were excellent for the company but then, due to stiff competition in the ITES sector, profitability started dwindling. Consequently, mental stress started building among his fellow executives as they were required to contact their clientele and bring in more business for the company. Mehram now sits in the waiting room, anticipating the results of testing by his personal physician. His sugar levels have risen alarmingly and he is now officially diabetic. Within the past month, secondary symptoms have started to surface. His marital relationship has also deteriorated because he has been irritable, and not able to spend much time with his family. Stressed almost to the max, Mehram is not able to manage his mind, which unhelpfully accuses him of being a "failure."

If we closely observe our mind for a few moments, we see a nonstop stream of thoughts. From one set of thoughts to another, the mind is always engaged in permutations of these largely recycled thoughts. Most of the time, the mind is restless. Like a monkey, it jumps and swings from one branch of thought to another, alternately nibbling on and throwing out ''half eaten" titbits. Buddhists call it the "monkey mind" to describe its unsettled, restless, or confused nature. Unless we calm this monkey, it never rests, and keeps darting in all directions. When it's not darting and dashing, it's dreamily wandering, blurring the attention we need to effectively work and joyfully play.

Like Mehram Singh, there are millions of people suffering from stress-related diseases as well as mental illnesses. Mental stress is the result of our inability to manage our mind. When people don't manage their mind well (for a variety of reasons), they suffer mentally. When conditions become chronic, the sufferer may fall into mental illness. Despite advances in medical science, mental illness has become an intractable epidemic.

Figure 5.9: We become helpless in managing our thoughts and emotions especially during troubled times.

As previously stressed, what we see in the outer world is a faithful reflection of our own inner state of mind. Our fears, anxieties, and other negativities are fully reflected in the outer world. Likewise, our joy, faith, gratitude, generosity, and sense of beauty are also projected outward. When we fail to control our mind, negativity builds and then, under pressure, bursts into the reality of the world around us. The result is, unless we counter this negativity with positivity, the distressing situation inside our mind starts to escalate. Our mind is inherently very sensitive and vulnerable. Unless we handle it with utmost care, it can't be managed. Even if we start taking medication on doctor's orders, we can at best get temporary relief by way of suppression of symptoms. In most cases, there seems no other way than to go to the doctor because we find ourselves helpless in managing our thoughts.

For all its exquisite complexity, the brain lacks the ability to perceive the objective reality of the world around us. Each one of us interprets the same information, situations, and circumstances in different ways because of vast variation in our genetic constitution, upbringing, past experiences, belief system, and so on. Additionally, there are other inherent limitations of our mind which further distort the perception and interpretation of reality. Humans are highly emotional. Emotions like love, fear, anger, hate, sadness, joy, and happiness influence our behavior and decision-making. Each one of us reacts differently under similar circumstances. Most of the time, emotions affect our behavior and decisions more than logic and reasoning.

Just how this incessant stream of thoughts makes its way into our mind we have no idea. According to one study, an estimated 2500 to 3300 thoughts pass through our mind every hour.. Most of these thoughts are routine and habitual. However, when we are disturbed for any reason, the aforementioned monkey mind becomes highly agitated. It's extremely difficult for us to calm this riled up monkey. And the more we try to suppress it, the more irrational or even violent it becomes. Further, our mind has that previously discussed negativity bias -- the inherent inclination toward negative things. It very promptly and eagerly picks up unpleasant news, messages, and emotions from others.

In summary, due to a combination of many factors, our mind is highly sensitive and vulnerable to any stimuli from both the outer and inner world. We all interpret information in as many ways as there are individuals. Cognitive biases through which we process incoming information are very strong. Our mind seems wired to wander. Unless and until we are focused on a particular activity, it moves as it will. Mental wandering can take up as much as 70% of our time. Evidently, it seldom finds what it's looking for because the more it wanders, the more unhappy it is. Unless we make a deliberate attempt to calm and relax the mind, it will be restless and distressed. That's its default mode. It's not an easy task. It requires persistent efforts to calm this wanderer.

6

Chasing Success, Happiness, and Pleasure in the Modern Age

There are two widely held misconceptions about success, happiness, and pleasure. First is the idea that happiness comes with success, that those who are successful in life are happier compared to those who are not.. Second, some assume that there is little to no difference between happiness and pleasure, that happiness is nothing more than sensual and pleasurable feelings. For instance, many see exotic resorts, night clubs, expensive liquor, and gourmet meals as potential happiness-makers. However, the fundamental reality behind the relationship between success, happiness, and pleasure is different from what is generally believed. Due to these mistaken beliefs and perceptions, people have misplaced priorities in their lives.

One of the main drivers behind these misconceptions is our highly materialistic world, where wealth, status, power, and material goods are central to modern culture. When we pursue mainly success, generally overlooking those things that give us genuine happiness, we naturally end up becoming more unhappy. Various studies have shown that, compared to our ancestors, we have become in general more unhappy. The reason is simple and straight: hunter-gatherers were living on a day-to-day basis. Their main imperative for survival was to forage for wild plants, seeds, fruits, and berries, and to hunt animals. It's believed that there was no competition among them as available resources for consumption were plentiful. The lifestyle of hunter-gatherers required little planning for the future. Aside from the threat of wild animals and extreme weather events, there was little reason to worry or occasion for stress in their living style. Therefore, they were likely to have been happier than modern humans.

Regardless of whether we are successful in our life or not, our primary aim would ideally be happiness and enjoyment of life to the fullest. However, our actions are mostly directed at becoming successful. There is often a contradiction in what we aim for and what we do in life. What is required is a fine balance and complementarity between success and happiness. This is achievable. We need to prioritise our personal and professional life. We must have a good idea of from where we can derive happiness, a sense of overall contentment, and satisfaction. Similarly, we should enjoy life through pleasurable pleasers of the five senses, but again in a balanced way. It goes almost without saying (almost!) that we shouldn't pursue pleasure at the expense of happiness in the long run. Most of us are aware that instant gratification is, by its very nature, short-lived. To experience more happy moments in life, we need to passionately pursue some hobby or interest, especially those activities in which we lose the sense of time. These issues have been briefly deliberated in this chapter.

6.1 Chasing success, pleasure, and happiness in a modern world driven by materialism

Narayan Swami is a top executive for one of the largest fertilizer manufacturing companies in India. Because of sharp cuts in subsidies on controlled fertilizers by the central government, profit margins have been significantly reduced over the past two years. Imports have also risen, seriously affecting the profitability of his company. In any case, Swami has been extremely successful in his career. After graduating from IIT Bombay, in Mumbai, within ten years he had reached the pinnacle of success in the fertilizer industry. He has a spacious bungalow in the state capital. He enjoys a chauffeur-driven Mercedes and high perks for different facilities.. This success, however, has come at a high cost. He is working with chronic stress and has recently been diagnosed with diabetes. Hs weight has increased, also due to stress. Nowadays, he is not able to sleep for more than four hours at a stretch. For the past two years he was unable to take vacations, due to high pressure on the job. Highly successful in his professional life, he is miserable in his personal life.

All around us, we see extremely "successful" people leading highly stressful and unhappy lives. They have all the money and comforts but little to no time to enjoy. The pursuit of money and/or success, and what it means to happiness, is a much- discussed topic. With success comes wealth, material goods, and comforts, status in society and more powers to enjoy. Most of us strive to be successful in life, in whatever way we may define "success." Since early childhood, many were told (implicitly or explicitly) by their parents that it is success that really matters in life. They were led to believe that without success, life is purposeless, and that with it comes everything that is said to be good and meaningful for a long, rewarding life.

Many people, whether consciously or unconsciously, tend to confuse success with happiness. They generally believe that it is success that leads to happiness and not the other way around. As they see it, to be happy, we must first achieve success, and success, they believe, must involve struggle. Another unexpected bump in the road is that, generally speaking, the more success we achieve, the greater is the desire for more of it. Throughout the almost inevitable struggle, it helps to remember that happiness does not come from the outside world. In regard to our work, happiness comes from the sense of satisfaction and contentment from our own achievement after we've given it our all. Still greater happiness comes when we extend gratitude to others, and share with them our love and compassion. The joy of deep connection with a few close friends and family members trumps anything that money can buy!

As we have seen from the case above, success generally comes at a cost. It often leads to stress and unhappiness because of the demanding nature of successful positions. As we move up in the hierarchy, responsibilities and work pressure generally increase. We then either want to rise further on the ladder of success or we strive to maintain our present position ; in both cases, the struggle creates stressful situations. Expectation also rises as we succeed. Human nature is like that. We normally don't feel contented with our success. Mostly, there exists a gap between the level of expectation and the reality we experience. Only occasionally do we hear about successful people giving much of their wealth to charity, or surrendering their authority and notoriety to live in relative obscurity. Off course, there are many rich people who do defy categorization.

There's no denying that money plays an extremely important role in our society. A mad race to generate wealth is evident in India, where I live, as well as in many other countries. It's a harsh reality. Money is undoubtedly very important for us in at least clearing the way to happiness, but, as most of us have noticed, that's true only up to a certain point. Beyond that point of "enough," money can easily become counterproductive.

Figure 6.1: To climb upward for more wealth and higher social status, at whatever cost, is a key determinant of success in modern life.

A life of physical ease, with plenty of money and comforts all around us, can indeed be pleasurable. However, like a great meal or a "roll in the hay," bodily joys are, by their very nature, fleeting. Temptations abound in this pleasure-driven world. "Quick fixes" such as tobacco, alcohol, sugar, social media, drugs, and the Internet, where we can uninterruptedly watch anything, are readily available. However, pleasure never offers *true* satisfaction or lasting happiness, and in fact can make us more miserable than ever.. This happens when, in order to maintain the pleasurable feelings, we increase the frequency, quantity, or intensity of things that give us pleasure. This phenomenon is known as the "hedonic treadmill" (to be discussed later). In its extreme, it becomes outright addiction. Few can resist it because the cause lies in our brain – especially in its secretion of dopamine.

These are just some of the ways that millions of people fall into the vicious cycle of chronic stress, unhappiness, mental illness, and, ultimately, addiction. Unaware of the inner qualities that generate true happiness and well-being, they often become disillusioned with the life they lead. Life's priorities get skewed and derailed. Absent peace and joy, they pursue pleasure, thinking erroneously that it is, or will grow into, happiness. People from all walks of life can, owing to confusion between pleasure and happiness and ignorance of the inner Self, fall into this trap. Fortunately, the answer to all this pain and confusion is found in self-awareness and mindful living .

6.2 Pursuing pleasure can be a trap; we in fact end up becoming more unhappy and dissatisfied.

One of the greatest gifts that humans have received through the evolutionary process is the ability to enjoy their life in a variety of ways, and live to the fullest. Life can be filled with a range of pleasurable and joyous experiences. Inner happiness may last for months and even years. It is through these positive emotions that the meaning of life becomes clear. Humans would not have survived without the inner sunshine of joy, pleasure, love, and happiness. They give us a reason to live, even in extremely adverse and painful situations. Short pleasure events are among the essential ingredients of leading a happy and joyful life. Pleasure is nothing more than a short-lived feeling of intensity, superficially mimicking happiness. We may feel wonderful and elated when we experience it, unable to distinguish whether these emotions are a result of pleasure or the outcome of happiness.

Of all the positive aspects of life, pleasure falls into its own category, one of physical sensations. Following its momentary bursts of wonderful feelings, it has the potential to create extreme unhappiness and even addiction if temptation is not resisted. By contrast, who has ever heard of intense joy or happiness ever leading to anything harmful for body or mind? Things that give us pleasure like milk and cookies, tasty and spicy food with wine, expensive whisky, watching movies or any of the performing arts, visiting nightclubs, or travelling to exotic destinations give us joyful and happy moments and add flavour to our life. Moreover, we are living in a world where tremendous opportunities and easy accessibility to such pleasures are pretty much laid at our feet. On the other hand, a search for happiness is far more subtle. Temptations associated with finding happiness are far less than those than those that may accompany seeking pleasure. Therefore, the easiest and laziest choice for those who can afford it is to pursue pleasure.

Figure 6.2: The more we enjoy pleasure, the more we seek it. The earlier we interrupt the cycle, the easier it is for us.

When pleasurable things are easily available in a material-driven world, it becomes all the more tempting to enjoy them often. When we are stressed, unhappy, and in a depressed or distressed mood, we feel a need for immediate relief, to relax and be happy through pleasurable feelings. Studies have now established that the release of dopamine is occasioned not only by pleasure, but also by the mere anticipation of pleasure. In fact, the anticipation of pleasure inspires dopamine release even more than the actual experience of pleasure. Like a salivating dog looking at his food bowl, we find ourselves experiencing pleasurable feelings long before the actual experience of pleasure. We generally get excited even as we're undertaking activities that will lead to the expected pleasure. Dopamine causes us to desire, seek out and pursue pleasure. Dopamine makes us feel great. It hence plays a very big role in our pleasure-seeking behaviour.

Now we know why our actions and behaviour are generally motivated by the pursuit of pleasure and avoidance of pain. However, there is a catch. According to one researcher, our "liking system" makes us feel satisfied, and we pause our seeking. But there is another system, a "wanting' system," which is stronger than the liking system. We therefore tend to seek more, even when we are satiated. Now we fall into a dopamine loop. The more we enjoy pleasure, the more we seek it. Unless we break or interrupt this loop, pleasure-seeking can only increase. Dissatisfied, we step onto the hedonic treadmill. Even after we achieve just about everything – such as living in a luxurious mansion, having an expensive car, huge wealth, and working in a high-status post, we may still feel the need for *more.* The hedonic treadmill is a major problem in our life. The only way to step off the treadmill (see it as a hamster wheel, if you're a pet lover) is to be aware of the difference between pleasure and happiness, how neurotransmitters in our brain incline our behaviour toward pleasure, and to recognize the mechanics behind that treadmill. The earlier we interrupt the cycle, the easier it is for us. Mindfulness meditation also helps in increasing awareness and mindful living.

6.3 Three main pillars of happiness; ultimately it's simple happiness that gives meaning to our life

Undoubtedly, a good part of the world is steadily becoming wealthier and more prosperous; most developed nations are growing economically, registering a positive change in their gross domestic product (GDP). The world is, overall, becoming a better place as we are now richer, healthier, more literate, and enjoying greater comforts compared to two decades earlier. Various indicators not only on the economic front but also on the Human Development Index are showing significant improvement over the years in most parts of the world. We are also witnessing multiple revolutions in science and technology. As we enter this "Fourth Industrial Revolution," we are seeing ground-breaking discoveries that are changing our lives in multiple ways. And yet, unhappiness is a serious twenty-first-century issue. People are now realizing that their ultimate aim is not just surviving but thriving. To do so, they must deal with the gravity and imminent peril of climate change, increasing inequality, and the spiritual crises that humanity is currently facing.

Fortunately, there is growing awareness of the importance of happiness in our life. It's becoming a high priority for government as well as the corporate sector to take specific measures to promote workforce happiness. There are courses on happiness in universities and colleges, and classes in schools ; separate ministries have been established in the government, and research into various aspects of happiness is underway. Various government and other institutions, acting on the assumption that human well-being is the most important indicator of success, have taken to monitoring it, especially when any new programme or initiative is implemented.

Figure 6.3: There is a strong and direct relationship between happiness and close friends/family members.

Some may wonder whether we're actually becoming happier or it's just the hype associated with increased awareness of happiness. In many ways, some nations, like India, are becoming less happy, while other countries give every sign of becoming happier. For instance, India ranks 140th (out of 156 countries) on a list of the happiest countries, according to World Happiness Index 2019. India was ranked 118th in 2016. Are we becoming unhappier? If we observe the statistics relating to the number of people suffering from mental illnesses, chronic stress, and lifestyle diseases, as well as people getting involved in acts of aggression and intolerance all over the world, then we become sceptical. What *is* happiness, and what are the factors that contribute to happiness? How to court it?

Happiness is a feeling of contentment. It comes when feel satisfied, safe, grateful, and eager to experience more of life. Happiness is of two kinds. First, we may feel conditionally happy on a day-to-day basis, and secondly, there is a long-term contentment that runs deeper. We feel good, elevated, joyful, and generous when we are happy. No doubt, all of the ingredients that lead to happiness lie within our mind.

I cannot overstate the importance of distinguishing the difference between pleasure and happiness. This doesn't mean that we should be leery of pleasurable things ; we simply need to enjoy pleasures in a mindful, balanced way. We must never let hedonism dominate our actions and behaviour in any way. To create a welcoming environment conducive to happiness, three things are being recommended here. These are the three pillars on which a strong foundation for happiness can be built. First, we must see to it that we have a healthy mind and body. Second, we should hold high priorities and ideals alongside reasonable expectations; and lastly, it is our privilege and greatest joy to nurture and maintain true relationships with friends and family members. These pillars, once erected, can protect us from situations that compromise our stability and happiness. These pillars are briefly explained below.

Learn to live peacefully: Can we even conceive of enjoying our life without a healthy mind and body? As we know, the two are intimately connected. The way we think and the thoughts we entertain and process throughout the day affect the physical body in many ways – some would say, in *every* way. Almost all of those suffering from mental disorders and more than 90% of people with other diseases must first look within themselves, as these illnesses are usually the by-products of their modern lifestyle. Many fail to understand and appreciate how the mind works and how to manage it well. It's ultimately our inner world that must be set right if we want to lead a happy life. We must learn to live peacefully within our own skin. We should handle both mind and body with great care and sensitivity. In this modern world, the majority don't exercise, or don't exercise enough. And rarely do most of us devote any time to mental exercises, such as meditation. If we want to lead a happy, contented, and productive life, we must take care of mind. If we succeed, our body is very likely to be in good shape.

Reasonable expectations with right priorities: As we are economically and socially progressing, our expectation levels, in general, are also rising. Rather than being happy with our higher standards of living, however, many of us are growing wildly ambitious, or even greedy, as our desires increase. Our expectation level very often decides our happiness. If our expectations exceed what life is currently delivering, the result will be unhappiness, intractable dissatisfaction until our expectations are met. Since expectations are based upon priorities, the blind pursuit of wealth, fame, and pleasure is sure to make us (ultimately) miserable. Indeed, we must have right ideals and priorities in pursuing our goals, both short-term and long-term. If our priorities are not set straight, and we keep on pursuing our every little fancy, our stress levels will soar. One must learn to see things in the broadest-possible perspective. In fact, one of the biggest causes of stress and unhappiness is that we fail to take in the Big Picture. There is of course nothing wrong with spending money on things that make us happy ; that is, after all, the aim of earning money. We can certainly make our life more enjoyable, easier, and happier with money. Therefore, to lead a happy and contented life, we must keep our expectations in a reasonable range, directed by right priorities.

Nurture and maintain meaningful relationships: True happiness comes with human relationships, especially when we are really connected with a few (or several) close friends and family members. In fact, they often prove to be the ones who truly help us in overcoming any stress, adversity, or even tragedy. Likewise, it is they who can truly rejoice in our good fortune and happiness! True wealth comes from such relationships. A long-term, loving and trusting partnership also makes people's lives really worth living. Many studies have confirmed a direct relationship between social connections and happiness. People become happier – and live significantly longer -- when they are close to their true, long time (and/or new) friends. The greater the social interaction, the more rewarding and meaningful life one lives. It also has a direct impact on our mental and physical health. People who spend more time with their friends feel happier than those who spend less time with friends. However, it's always preferable to have a few true friends than friends in large numbers (business associates, acquaintances, golf buddies).

Decades of research studies have shown that social relations predict mental well-being over time, and that people who actively endeavour to cultivate and vitalize their connections with others often report becoming happier. Similarly, the longest-running study conducted in the Harvard Study of Adult Development has confirmed the same results. The Study has found a strong association between happiness and close relationships, such as family, friends, and social circles. "Personal connection creates mental and emotional stimulation, which are automatic mood boosters, while isolation is a mood buster," says the project's director, Dr Robert Waldinger. Likewise, many other studies confirm a direct relationship between social connectivity and happiness.

6.4 Each one of us experiences happiness in his or her own personal way. Among many other things, happiness requires a delicate balance of certain biochemicals in the brain.

Happiness is a very fine mix of well-being, positivity, and overall satisfaction with life. It's far more than the absence of unhappiness. It's neither easy to define what it is nor prescribe how to achieve it. Happiness is in fact the outcome of many internal factors, including the delicate balance of neurochemicals that are secreted in our brain. It is also a product of our thoughts, and the feelings they generate. If thoughts are toxic, fearful, angry, or even vaguely negative, we can't feel happy. Mental peace is prerequisite to experiencing pleasant feelings.

We must also understand that feelings of happiness arise spontaneously, and no matter how hard we may try, we just can't chase happiness. If we try to capture the Blue Bird of Happiness, or are obsessed with finding his whereabouts, we may even become more unhappy. We should not, therefore, put pressure on ourselves to feel happy. Moreover, we must also accept that never in our life can we expect to be perfectly happy for sustained periods. We have not been designed to be happy all the time. Life will not make us perfectly happy. We need to work consistently to realize happiness.

So then, how do we achieve happiness? Is it achievable or do we just stumble upon it? What's the secret behind a happy life ? It's generally believed, and truly so, that the genes we have inherited from our parents do play a role in determining our happiness level. We have seen many people throughout history (and perhaps in our own lives) remain happy and balanced, even in adversity. They will surely experience hours or days of unhappiness, but they will invariably bounce back to their baseline level of happiness. For others, it may take much longer to regain their original level.

One study has found that 50% of our happiness is biologically determined -- i.e., through genes. Then 40% of happiness is controlled by our thoughts, behaviour, and the actions we take. Our choices are entirely in our own hands. The remaining 10% is determined by life's circumstances. If we react automatically to all difficult situations, how can we remain happy? Appropriate, mindful response to life's circumstances, driven by clear, insightful thoughts, can, to a great extent, make our life happy.

Alert people tend to notice that regardless of what they may experience, they generally return to their usual level of happiness. Each one of us occupies a particular place on a scale of, let's say, 1 to 10 (1 being most unhappy and 10 the happiest). We more or less hover around that emotional baseline, which remains relatively stable through all our days. This is known as the hedonic treadmill gradient. The hedonic treadmill is a common phenomenon in which people repeatedly return to their baseline level of happiness, regardless of what happens to them. Since so much of our happiness is determined by our thoughts and actions, which tend to be habitual and unchallenged, our happiness level remains generally static, with only slight fluctuations. .

An extremely critical factor in determining happiness is our biochemical system. All emotions and sensations have a profound effect on our biochemistry. It's a two-way communication of feelings affecting the secretion of chemicals in the brain, and vice versa. Any imbalance is likely to lead to many kinds of mental illnesses, such as depression and anxiety. Happiness is also the outcome of four basic chemicals – namely, serotonin, dopamine, oxytocin, and endorphins. These chemicals are known as neurotransmitters, chemical messengers that transmit signals between neurons (nerve cells).Around 100 billion in number, neurons are the building blocks of our nervous system.

Figure 6.4: Happiness is an outcome of right mix of biochemical in our brain - any imbalance in their secretion can lead to mental illnesses.

The sensations and feelings that underlie happiness are a result of the intricate interplay between these neurotransmitters. Some call it "chemical happiness," as it's a by-product of bio-molecules. There are innumerable factors that influence their secretion and delicate balance. If there is any disruption, consequences can be disastrous for our mental health and well-being. The first such biochemical is serotonin, which is also known as the 'happy chemical." It brings a feeling of well-being, peace, and relaxation. When there is deficiency in its secretion, it may lead to depression and anxiety. It also regulates our sleep, mood, and positive emotions. It's further released when we act in a way that benefits others, such as giving to charity, expressing gratitude, or helping a friend.

The second neurotransmitter that is crucial for our happiness and pleasure is dopamine. This is also known as the "reward molecule." Dopamine is responsible for pleasure-seeking and all manner of reward-driven behaviour. Whenever we achieve something, or are rewarded in any way, we get a kick of dopamine. This chemical can even give us the feeling of euphoria, greater energy, and elevation of mood and overall power. It's also linked to addiction to many pleasurable habits, such as alcohol, drugs, and tobacco.

The third category of neurotransmitter is called 'endorphins'. These biochemicals, also known for their painkilling properties, are secreted when we do exercises such as running and swimming.. When we laugh, eat chocolate and raw green pepper, or take wine, the same chemicals are produced. These are like an "internally produced morphine," natural painkillers for the body. They give us a feeling of euphoria and well-being, thereby generating happiness in us.

The last basic neurotransmitter essential for happiness is oxytocin, the "bonding molecule." It's a biochemical directly linked to human bonding and increasing trust and loyalty. It's sometimes referred to as the cuddle hormone or the love hormone. Oxytocin-induced happiness may be experienced when we give and receive love and affection. We come close to another person. According to a study, when we are attracted to someone, our brain releases dopamine, serotonin levels increase, and oxytocin is produced. This causes us to feel a surge of positive emotion, i.e. happiness.

While other hormones and neurotransmitters have roles to play in creating feelings of happiness, these are the four main ones. There is also an overlapping of their influences on many aspects of our thought and behaviour. Their deficiency and imbalance can result in mental illnesses of varying severity. Depression is the most common mental illness, accompanied by deficiency in serotonin. Whether deficiency of these biochemicals causes mental illness or is a result of mental illness is not yet known.

Happiness is a highly complex state. Life's purpose and passion come on the wings of happiness. For the past two decades, this subject has taken global centre stage. And rightly so. Happiness is far more vital to holistic human health than growth in any other area.

6.5 Flow with time! Through focused and 'absorbing' activities, we can create plenty of happy moments in our life

One of the inherent tendencies of mind is that it never stays in one state for more than a few moments. Try to concentrate on any one thought and see how the mind slips within seconds. It keeps on moving all the time in different directions unless we are attending to any activity or object. Perhaps this was essential from the evolutionary point of view. For survival, our ancestors had to almost constantly think about all possible situations and seldom be at ease. This particular feature of mind is not required in the usual present-day scenario. In fact, worriedness and guardedness are obviously counterproductive when we are focusing on one task but the mind is wandering off to another concern. On average, half the time our mind is wandering. For example, a college student is attending a class but her mind is at her home, working out details for an upcoming party. Restless and anxious, she is missing the entire lecture.

There is seemingly no harm in doing one thing while thinking about other things. However, many studies have established that a wandering mind is an unhappy mind. When we are not focused and attentive, we are not happy. Studies have, on the other hand, also shown that a focused mind is a happy mind. Each one of us must have noticed that when we are absorbed in an activity of our interest, not only do we feel good, but also time moves fast. We may even lose track of time. We don't know when an hour has passed. Everyone must have noticed that when we are focused and attending to one particular endeavour, our mind doesn't wander. Mind's wandering can be as low as 10% on occasions such as when we make love or are engrossed in an interesting conversation. We can't be unhappy while doing what we love. The greater the interest or passion, the happier we are while performing that activity. That's why we often advise others to follow their hearts. In the unforgettable words of mythologist and author Joseph Campbell, "Follow your bliss."

When we are listening to our favourite music, painting on canvas, practicing dance with our instructor, playing games of our choice, running on a treadmill, or being engrossed in conversation with a friend on any hotly debated topic, time seems to fly. People can forget that they are hungry or even tired when they are absorbed in interesting activities. Mihaly Csikszentmihalyi, a Hungarian-American psychologist and one of the co-founders of positive psychology, coined the term "flow state" (commonly known as being in the zone) to describe the focus, absorption, and enjoyment of full immersion in any activity. According to him, "Flow is a state in which people are so involved in an activity that nothing else seems to matter; the experience is so enjoyable that people will continue to do it even at a great cost, for the sheer sake of doing it."

***Figure 6.5:** When we are fully involved and absorbed in our passion, we experience happy and blissful moments.*

If we want to increase happiness, well-being, and creativity, then we would do well to court periods of flow. Happiness, as we all know, doesn't come from externals ; it is in fact an internally derived state of being. Csikszentmihalyi's popular book, *Flow: The Psychology of Optimal Experience* is based on the assumption that happiness levels can be raised by introducing opportunities for flow in our life's experiences. Csikszentmihalyi found that people were their most creative, productive, and happy when they are in a state of flow. He interviewed athletes, musicians, and artists because he wanted to know when they experienced this state of consciousness. He coined the term flow state because many of the people he interviewed described their optimal state of performance as the sense of their work simply flowing out of them, effortlessly.

When we experience flow state, our activity and our awareness are merged, and we are completely absorbed in the task. Our mind is laser-focused on what we are doing. The default mode network (DMN), which is a cluster of many brain regions, is always active when our mind wanders. Whenever we perform an uninteresting task or are just thinking randomly, DMN is overactive. It is busy daydreaming, eager or anxious about the future, or ruminating about past events. On the other hand, when we are completely absorbed or lost in any activity, the thinking mind (or, as it is unflatteringly called, the "monkey mind") is not at work. "I" is lost completely. Ego is on hold. Self-consciousness is lost, and the surrounding world fades away.

In a way, we have disappeared from the world for some time. One can spend hours like this, unaware of how the time has passed. Most people can recall such experiences in their life. Flow is a universal experience. Many activities are intrinsically rewarding, especially when the experiencer is fully in the zone, flowing. Each one of us needs to accentuate or cultivate some interests or passions through which we may experience flow. In addition to awakening our inner creativity and improving our performance, flow states can also show us true happiness.

7

Learn to Live - we are potentially capable of scripting our own destiny

Sanjay, a young man working as a bank clerk, used to take a local train for work at 9 a.m. sharp every morning. One fine morning he missed his train by two minutes. While waiting for the next train a young girl arrived, heading for the same destination. After boarding the train, both incidentally both sat on the same seat. They introduced themselves and started chatting. As luck would have it, their friendship grew, and after a few months they got married. The girl's uncle was working as a top executive in a corporate office of the same bank, and some posts had become vacant abroad. Sanjay then applied for those posts and his wife's uncle helped him to get posted in Europe. Thereafter, they started living happily in The Hague, Netherlands.

Let us see one more example.

After completing her graduation, Swati, whose ambition was to become a police officer, started preparing for civil services exams. On her first attempt, her high grade on that exam got her into the Indian Police Service. Swati was expected to join the police academy in a few months' time. The day finally arrived and she boarded the train for the Service. However, the train met with a serious accident and her coach was derailed. The girl somehow escaped death but lost both her legs. Now she can't join the Service. She later took up voluntary work in a charitable organisation.

In both cases, Sanjay and Swati's normal life got radically changed. Were these outcomes destined by some guiding force? In the first case, the young man was destined to work in Europe, which is why he accidentally met with the woman in the metro train. In the normal course of life, he might have spent all his days working in the same branch of that bank. In the young woman's case, it was not in her destiny to become a police officer despite gaining admission to the premier Service. Since her events were all predetermined by the God, her destiny was evidently to work voluntarily for a charitable organisation. In both cases, there was an invisible, unexplainable guiding force working in their lives. The development of events was beyond their control. The events were predetermined. This is what we call destiny .

Figure 7.1: We, the sole architect of life, create our own unique pathways by way of our thoughts, actions and choices we make from time to time.

Destiny is the event that will necessarily happen in the future. The idea is that we can't avoid destiny. This concept assumes that we humans have no control over the events that take place in our life. Destiny means the future is completely determined by the present (and therefore by the past). Hence, the events are completely determined by pre-existing causes. Everything that happens to us is not under our control and we are merely puppets in the hands of some Unknowable Power, or, if you will, God. Destiny presumes that everything we do is already decided.

Fate is is another word used to refer to a predetermined course of events. Though "fate" and "destiny" are often used interchangeably, fate defines events as unavoidable or inevitable. We have no role to play in their occurrence. For instance, we had no voice in choosing our parents, place of birth, characteristic features, and so on. Mostly, we use this word to describe events that appear to be divinely driven. The belief that events are fixed by fate and we can't change them is called fatalism. The word destiny is more often employed to refer to predetermined events leading to some destination.

The notions of fate and destiny suggest a situation in which we have no freedom. There is no free will. Someone (or something) else is deciding the course of events. As in the first example, some external force appears to have decided for Sanjay's marriage to that particular woman, so that he can work in Europe. In the case of fate, there is a preordained course of action that no personal efforts can change. However, in the concept of destiny, we are seen as participants in the events, but the outcome is fixed. Destiny can also indicate that there is a given direction, and hence a possible purpose of our life.

There is one popular line of thinking that some divine force is working behind us, orchestrating a predetermined course of events. The polar opposite to this dreary fatalism is the equally compelling point of view that we are the architects of our own destiny. We are wholly and solely responsible for our actions. No one else is deciding on our behalf. However, there is always a high degree of uncertainty, especially in predicting the outcome of our actions and decisions, and no one can deny that there are unexplainable events that continue to take place in our life. There may be some meaningful but elusive patterns in these seemingly from-out-of-the-blue events. This somehow gives us the impression (or hope) that some unknown guiding power is working for us. Therefore, both positions – that all is in our hands, or out of our hands -- can be reasonably argued. Even now in the contemporary world, most people still look to destiny when they fail to justify or explain an event that takes place with them or around them. Seemingly senseless or tragic events are said to be part of "God's plan."

Despite the scientific and technological revolution taking place around the globe, a large section of population believe that there is an Unknown entity or God that governs our life and that this entity creates destiny for us. Nothing happens in our life without the dictate of God. Though the percentage of such people is gradually declining, their numbers are still large. According to a Gallup Poll, most Americans believe that God has the major (or only) role in creating human beings, whether in their present form or as part of an evolutionary process over millions of years. In this group of believers, 38% of USA adults accept the theory of creationism. It is a religious belief that humans were created not through the process of evolution but solely by divine invention. The universe and all forms of life were and continue to be created by God. Fewer than one in five hold the secular view of evolution, meaning that a divine being had no role in creation/evolution of humans in their present form. More recently, as science joins seamlessly with religion, many people see no argument between Divine Creation and the natural processes of evolution.

The debate over destiny - especially about how much control we can exercise over the events that take place in our lives -- rages on. Our Stone Age ancestors, constantly under siege from predators, diseases, and a hostile environment, probably believed in the role of destiny and fate for the important events that took place in their life. In those times, food was obtained by collecting wild plants and pursuing wild animals. They were living on a day-to-day basis, and anything could happen to them at any moment. For millions of years, humans were at the mercy of nature and therefore developed strong beliefs in supernatural entities, - gods, goddesses, and a single God. It was therefore very natural that essentially helpless humans would believe in supernatural power having complete control over their lives.

Destiny is, undoubtedly, shaped by our choices, the decisions we make, and actions we take throughout our lives. So the main question is whether we can create our own destiny or everything is pre-planned. The answer lies in the extent to which we exercise control or free will over our decisions and actions. If we have no control over our actions, then obviously our destiny is a reality. Whatever is to happen will happen as destined. If we feel and also exercise complete control over our choice, decisions, and actions we make or take, then we are the architect of our destiny. We can design destiny according to our wishes.

If we ask anyone whether they believe they have complete control over the events that take place in life, the answer would mostly be yes. However, some people would use excuses like destiny, fate, or bad luck when something goes wrong in their life. They seldom dare to own responsibility for any wrongdoing. A person with an internal locus of control believes that he or she can influence events and their outcomes, while someone with an external locus of control blames outside forces for everything. This concept was brought to light in the 1950s by Julian Rotter and since then has become an aspect of personality studies.

People who have an internal locus of control believe that they have better control over their lives ; those with an external locus feel their life is controlled by outside factors which they cannot influence, and that chance or fate controls their lives. While a person having an internal locus of control attributes success to his or her own efforts and abilities, a person with an external locus of control attributes his or her success mainly to luck or fate.

To understand the concept of determinism and destiny better, it's necessary to know the role of free will in our life. Free will is the ability to choose between different possible courses of action. It is the freedom to choose. If we exercise free will while taking any action, we are responsible for its outcome. In that case, the decision is self-determined. No outside force, including divine entity, is responsible for that action. The devil did not "make me do it."

We generally think we all exercise 'free will' while making choices and decisions ; however, quite often this is not true. If we make conscious choices, then our decisions are not determined. We are responsible for our behaviour, including our every thought, word, and deed. However, our actions and decisions are quite often impulsive and based on unconscious thought processes that reference our past experiences, beliefs, conditioning, and behaviour. In these cases, we don't have complete control over the events. The greater the control we exercise, *commensurate with our degree of self-awareness*, the more certain we can be about outcomes.

In most areas, we can have better control over our life. Our chosen course of action obviously has profound impact on our own and others' lives. William Shakespeare very rightly said that "It is not in the stars to hold our destiny, but in ourselves." We are in full control of what we choose to express. Spiritual leaders, thinkers, and philosophers have long emphasized the role we have in shaping our destiny. We create the reality we hold and wholly believe. Lord Buddha said, "We are what we think. We are the product of our thought." Destiny is not based on chance. It is a matter of choice.

Since ancient times, many spiritual traditions have been stressing that we are the sole architect of our own life. More specifically, our thoughts are the creative force constructing the reality that we perceive and experience. We navigate our lives based on what we believe about our world, ourselves, our capabilities, and our limits. Ancient wisdom, especially from the East, became the foundation of the New Thought movement, which began in the early nineteenth century, and later the New Age movement of recent times. One of its most important beliefs is that the human mind has vast powers, capable of overriding or shaping physical reality. We create our own reality.

In creating our own destiny, however, we very often lack the requisite conviction to build inner strength that will move us in that direction. While we may agree theoretically that we can build our own destiny, many are fearful and not confident enough to move forward. We remain in the seemingly secure comfort zone. Inner resistance to cross self-built boundaries is greater than our desire to achieve what we want. Inertia is stronger than the zeal to create our destiny. This is because we've developed a fixed set of strong beliefs and attitudes, held in place by a rigid mind-set. We are not flexible and responsive to fresh ideas and beliefs. We keep on thinking through our own deeply conditioned mental programming, based on our earlier life experiences. Unless we challenge those static and regressive beliefs, it's difficult to grow mentally and spiritually. If we truly want to script our life's journey, we must revisit and challenge all our beliefs and habitual behaviours. If we succeed in clearing away these hindrances, our journey to exactly where we wish to be becomes far easier.

7.1 We need to live meaningfully – otherwise, life is not worth living

Here is a real-life story of one Anand Kumar, a mathematics teacher in Patna, Bihar. His father, a clerk in the postal department, couldn't afford private schooling for his children, so Anand had attended a Hindi medium government school. Wishing to help children in the position that he once was, Anand started an educational program called Super 30 in Patna, under the banner of Ramanujan School of Mathematics. It was co-founded by an IPS (Indian Public Services) officer, Abhayanand, in 2002. The program selects 30 talented candidates each year from economically underprivileged sections of Indian society (who are unable to afford coaching classes) and trains them for the Joint Entrance Examination for IITs, globally recognised as India's best engineering institutions.

Anand Kumar's mother, Jayanti Devi, volunteered to cook for the students while Anand, Abhayanand, and other teachers tutored them. The students were also provided with study materials and one year of free room and board. In 2010, Time magazine included Super 30 in its list of "The Best of Asia 2010." In 2017, all the candidates again cracked the IIT-JEE Advanced 2017. In 2018, Kumar and his team reported that 26 Super 30 students achieved success in IIT-JEE : 422 out of 480 students had made it to the IITs, and the Discovery Channel showcased his work in a documentary. These exceptional candidates are working at high-profile jobs across the globe.

Is Anand Kumar not leading his life with meaningful purpose? How many of us succeed in achieving this goal of living creative and beneficent lives? While we may be awfully busy in pursuing "more," at some point each of us is compelled to ponder some of life's bigger questions. And one of the most challenging of those questions is: *What is the purpose of my life?* The follow-up to that question is: *Am I pursuing meaningful goals?* We all do have a purpose or purposes,, even if those purposes seem insignificant to others. The security guard, sitting the livelong day outside of a big warehouse with no work at hand, is as purpose-driven as anybody else is. Maybe his daughter wants to become a police officer and he's working overtime to fulfil her dream. On the other hand, the richest industrialist in the country may also be a great altruist, working tirelessly for the poor and underprivileged. We can see that the word "meaningful" is highly subjective.

When we say *meaningful purpose*, it broadly means doing something for the greater good in one's life, something more than leading a routine and self-centred life. When we start looking beyond "I," "me" and "my," and bring others into the fold of "us," then we can say we are doing something meaningful for society. Those who pursue mainly wealth and (their idea of) success live a purposeful life but not necessarily a meaningful one. Viktor Frankl (1905–1997), an Austrian neurologist and psychiatrist and a Holocaust survivor of World War II, wrote an extraordinary must-read book titled *Man's Search for Meaning*. Frankl's account of his experiences in Nazi concentration camps inspired millions of people to identify their own purpose in life. By identifying a positive purpose under back- and spirit-breaking conditions, and then holding on to that purpose while imagining its desired outcome, Frankl was able to live with both meaning and purpose through the horrors of the Holocaust.

Frankl says we are always freer to live a meaningful life than we recognise, and that life's meaning lies in finding a purpose and taking responsibility for ourselves and others. He enjoins us to not see our suffering as useless. Informed by purpose, suffering may be seen as a challenge. Therefore, even in extremely adverse conditions, we can find a purpose that inspires enough strength to endure and eventually overcome pain and suffering. Our attitude toward adversities is always subject to change. In every circumstance, we can find a solid purpose to live and create meaning in life. The meaning in life will not just come automatically. We need to discover it.

During earlier times, when the majority of people believed in God, their predominant purpose was to live a "good" life. Their purpose was to do good works so that after death, they would be welcomed into heaven. Minus the good deeds and obedience to the mandates of their faith, they would be consigned to eternal torment in hell. In Hinduism, the doctrine of karma was the greatest motivator for leading a meaningful life. Karma has to do with the thoughts, words, and deeds that we send out into this world and their good or bad results in this and future lives. It means that all actions good or bad have similar consequences for the individual who acts. If something really bad happens to anyone, it may be due to the bad karma of his present or past life. It's this general moral law which governs not only the life and destiny of all individuals, but even the order and arrangement of the physical world. This theory was a powerful incentive to lead a life of meaning and harmlessness (*ahimsa)*.

In Christianity, people who have been good and obedient to Church law, may expect to enter into the Kingdom of Heaven -- the blissful abode after death. This ambition, along with pleasing their personal Lord and Saviour, provided Christians a strong meaning and purpose. People aspired to enter the Kingdom either after death or, in some cases, during life itself. This idea remained entrenched in the Western world for over a thousand years. For Christians, the purpose of their earthly existence has always been to live in accord with 'the will' of God. However, things started to change as the scientific revolution got underway. Man's faith in a personal Father God started to decline in the face of reason and rationality. A sense of meaninglessness and pessimism began to stir among the masses. And as a material-driven culture set in, passion for wealth and material goods began to take hold and, in the process, connection to ourselves and to nature lose hold. The emphasis had shifted from a meaningful life to a "successful" one.

Far too many people live for the sake of simply existing. Life goes on automatically. They lead a routine, repetitive, and familiar life, "making all their nowhere plans for nobody" (in the words of a Beatles song), with hardly any change for years. As they take stock at the end of their lives, what can they say they've really contributed to the world? They have been busy as can be, while achieving hardly anything worthwhile. We have not come into this world to "waste time", much less to "sit it out." Life is as meaningful as we make it ; we must not lose track of what really matters in the grind of everyday life. We need to be focused and set our priorities right. We need to see things in as large a perspective as we can. The essence of meaning lies in connecting and contributing to something bigger than ourselves, something that will further the greater good of our fellow man. We are here for some larger purpose than existence and ego gratification, one that we have to pursue and discover. That's how we can live life to the fullest.

7.2 Meaningful Coincidences – Some incidents have a bigger purpose in life

Sujata was looking for one particular book, a rare one, of ancient history written by some author. He spoke to many colleagues but no one knew about that book. One day to buy some stationary she visited one local book shop. As she entered the shop she got a pleasant surprise to see that book on the shelf. In yet another case, Vimlesh, age 30 got divorced a week earlier and feeling relieved to get rid of strained relationship of 10 years with his wife. He planned to visit his USA to meet his uncle. When he boarded into US bound flight from Delhi International airport, he was surprised to see his old college mate on the next seat. After exchange of pleasantries, they entered into long intimate conversation. His college mate is also a divorcee. After a month, both got married and started living happily thereafter. These two incidents though seem accidental but are meaningful.

Our life is full of coincidences and many of them prove to be very meaningful and important in determining our destiny. Like, someone is thinking about his very old friend that he hadn't met him for several years. Then incidentally he met the same friend on the next day itself. Similarly, we may see a person at work that we think we might like to know, only to find that that that very individual sitting across at a restaurant later that day. Coincidences are, at many times, meant for some purpose which may lead to new opportunity and those very opportunity then changes one's path. Is this a luck or chance or should we say it a meaning coincidence?

At some level, we may sense that such events were destined in some way that they were supposed to happen in that period of life. Those incidences happen to give us new opportunities that can potentially change our life. Carl Jung (1875-1961), a famous Swiss psychologist/ physicist was the first modern thinker to define this mysterious phenomenon. He called it synchronicity, the perception of meaningful coincidences. Jung maintained that synchronicity was a causal principle in the universe, a law that is operated to move human beings towards greater growth in consciousness.

His concept of synchronicity came through many surprising coincidences his patients shared with him during his practice time, especially as he began to realize that the occurrences went beyond what could be attributed to mere chances. He further explained that 'meaningful coincidences are unthinkable as pure chance--the more they multiply and the greater and more exact the correspondence is. They can no longer be regarded as pure chance, but, for the lack of a causal explanation, have to be thought of as meaningful arrangements'.

Since then this subject has been widely deliberated and researched even by modern physicists especially in the field of quantum physics.

The meaningful coincidences happen in everyone's life but very few of us are able to appreciate those events because of the reason that superficially those events look random and merely the chances. *If those events are looked closely, we find them significant in shaping our destiny.* Often we attribute such events to a divine power or God. It's quite natural as in normal circumstances; the possibility of happening that event must have been very remote. That's why we say, 'Oh this couldn't have taken place without the intervention of God'. They lead us to newer opportunities, which, in turn, can change the direction of our life. They help us in growing to a higher ladder of life.

Many a times, coincidences can make us realize that those are the significant events though look accidental. Like meeting someone unexpectedly and then that meeting proved to be a turning point in our professional life. However, some other coincidences can be very subtle and fleeting, and thus easily be dismissed as a mere chance. But later at some stage, we find those events very significant and meaningful. As we pay more attention to those events which we were, till that time, treating them merely the chances in fact were purposeful. *As we become more self-aware and attentive towards our experiences, we find more such meaningful events in our life.* These are the improbable events that give us some meaningful message or new opportunity that redefine our destiny. When we look at the past then we may realize their significance in shaping our destiny.

7.3 The foundation for our growth and development is laid largely during our early childhood.

We tend to underestimate the role of our genetic blueprint and the tremendous influence of early-childhood experiences in shaping our life and determining our destiny. We are not simply the product of independent thoughts and actions, but also of our parents, who played a significant role in making us who we presently are. If we are successful and living our life to the fullest, then obviously a hefty share of credit goes to them. If someone is impulsive, aggressive in temperament, or violent in behaviour, parental input also needs to be considered. Though they may have had little to no role in our development at a later stage of life, their genes and the way they treated and cared for us before we reached maturity did play a great role.

Most of us come into this world with a perfect set of genes. We have our parental genetics to thank for our physical attributes, talents, and many personality characteristics. The genetic material in every cell carries the unique blueprint for everything, from our height and complexion to our risks of serious illnesses like cancer. No two humans are genetically identical, but we are all 99.9 percent the same. The genes we are born with remain constant, but their expression does change with age. How they work is a highly complex study. Experiences leave a chemical 'signature' on the genes that determine whether and how the genes are expressed.

Figure 7.3: Very often children who suffer traumatic and abusive behaviour during early childhood become violent and criminals at later stages of life

The debate over the role of genetic blueprint vs. environmental factors that impact us is one of the oldest philosophical issues within psychology. In the past, the widespread view was that genetic endowment plays the greater role in determining our life. Later medical science suggested that nurture (i.e., the environment in which we grow (both in utero and after birth), is far more important. However, today, most experts recognize that both nature and nurture play a significant and complementary role in determining our lives.

Neurological research shows that the early childhood years play a key role in children's brain development. By the age of five, 90% of the brain's capacity has already developed. A child's brain is more receptive to learning during the first five years of his life than at any other point in time. The brain is most plastic and flexible in these initial years. As new neural pathways are established and strengthened by learning experiences, the foundation is laid for the child's further development. If this foundation is weak and vulnerable, it becomes very difficult (though not impossible) to reinforce it in subsequent years. This is the critical time on which the child's future largely depends.

In early childhood especially, the parents leave a deep imprint on the child's mind, some of which may overshadow aspects of genetic constitution. The interaction of genes and experience determines childhood mental health. In turn, the physical, emotional, and social development of young children shapes the adult they will become. The emotional well-being of young children is directly tied to the functioning of their parents and the families in which they live. When these relationships are mentally and/or physically abusive or stressed, children are at high risk of developing mental health problems. Numerous studies have shown that traumatic experiences during childhood and adolescence often lead to violent and criminal behaviour. Young children who experience recurrent abuse or neglect, domestic violence, or an addicted parent are particularly vulnerable.

An adverse childhood has undeniable effects on a child mental and physical health. The cost of damaged children and young adults to their families and society is huge. In families that experience recurrent marital discord between the parents, children suffer immensely. Many are subjected to other chronic stress conditions as well within their families, with similarly negative impact. Many diseases such as diabetes, cancer, heart and lung ailments can consequentially develop at later stages of life. In many ways, our children are extensions of ourselves. Their destiny is our destiny. Therefore, our lives can never flourish if something goes wrong with the care and nurturing that we provide to our children.

7.4 Plasticity of Brain – we can mould and redesign our brain at any age during our lifetime

Professor Ramakrishnan, age 75, retired at the age of 65 from the Indian Institute of Technology, Madras, after an active life of teaching and research. He never had interest in music, but about a year ago, he wanted to learn to play the piano. He discussed his newly found interest with his wife. She expressed her surprise and remarked, "At this age, you want to learn piano! How is it possible?" After a few days, he bought a piano and engaged a teacher for lessons. To everyone's surprise, he learned to play remarkably well in just 10 days, and within three months had become a virtuoso. Somehow or other, he had learned an altogether new skill at the age of 75, with practice. Like the Professor, senior citizens in large numbers learn new skills, develop new hobbies, start pursuing new interests, and gain admission to learning institutions to pursue their interests. Inspiringly enough, we all have an inherent capacity to undertake any new task or learn new things in life at any age, thanks to neuroplasticity, the plastic nature of our brain.

Whenever we think, act, or react, various brain areas get excited and "charged up," due to neural firing. Each and every thought we experience changes the structure and function of our brain at the micro level by altering the neural connections. Even imagination can produce structural changes in neural pathways. It has been found that simply imagining doing a physical exercise increases muscle strength, because the neurons responsible for the activation of movement are used and get strengthened.

There has recently been a radical change in our understanding of the human brain, especially the way our brain is reshaped in light of continuing experiences. Now researchers say that the brain has potential for change and development throughout one's lifetime. It is believed that all experiences make new neural connections which change the structure in various parts of our brain. The brain is highly dynamic and changing all the time. In fact, throughout one's lifetime, not only are new brain cells/neurons continually being born (neurogenesis), but also changes taking place in brain structure (neuroplasticity). While neurogenesis refers to the birth of new brain cells, neuroplasticity stands for the brain's ability to mould and change (plastic nature) because of our experiences. Recent findings suggest that neurogenesis occurs not only during embryonic development, and also until the day we die.

Although we come into this world with a genetically predetermined body, we have enormous potential to structurally and functionally change our brain. This is a paradigm-shattering discovery made by neuroscientists in recent times. For centuries, neuroscientists were of the opinion that our brain is immutable, unchangeable, and static, and that therefore whatever genes we inherit from our parents would to a large extent control our destiny. Now the fact is, we are all amazingly empowered to change ourselves. Mind has unlimited potential to upgrade itself to learn and create new skills, behaviour patterns, belief systems, etc. We actually have the capacity to remould and rebuild certain regions of our brain. Neurologists call this "brain plasticity" or "neuroplasticity," which refers to changes in the brain via modification in neural pathways and synapses.

As we learn to adapt to changes in our life, our brain also changes, both structurally as well as functionally. With each new thought, we begin to create a new neural pathway along which information travels through the neurons (nerve cells) of the brain. With every repetition of a thought or emotion, we reinforce that pathway. These small changes, that are repeated frequently, lead to changes in how our brain works. Neuroplasticity is like a "muscle- building exercise" of the brain. By this process, we gain experience and develop mastery of that particular activity or skill. When we don't repeat certain activity we lose those pathways. That is the physical basis of how we develop and improve our skill, expertise, capability, efficiency, and competence. Over time, it becomes automatic, a part of us.

All around us are living examples demonstrating the power of neuroplasticity. People at the age of 90-plus are running marathons, learning new skills, and performing difficult exercises. Age is no bar for any activity or skill which is performed by youngsters. Buddha, around 2600 years ago, rightly preached that "we are shaped by our thoughts; we become what we think ." Now it has been proved by neuroscientists that we do indeed have the ability to become what we think or intend. We have the ultimate tool to fulfil our dreams and, in turn, our destiny. In earlier times most people assumed that they were too old to learn a new skill or venture into a new area. Not so now : within each one of us is the innate potential to design and shape our destiny.

This remodelling of brain structure and function through neuroplasticity continues throughout life. Our behaviour and thought patterns evolve (or may, devolve) with the passage of time. We also adapt to new experiences, learn new information, and create new memories. Our mind has infinite capacity to learn and bring about permanent changes in our brain all through our lives. As a result, we are constantly being shaped by our experiences.

Figure 7.4: At any stage of life, we can learn anything new, thanks to the inherent power of brain's plasticity

We can therefore be encouraged by the fact that at any age of life, we are capable of learning, practicing, and improving any skills. Brain plasticity does not significantly decrease with age. Earlier, scientists were of the opinion that as we age, our ability to form new neural pathways decreases and therefore brain plasticity decreases. Research in recent years has established that as we age, the rate of change in the brain, or neuroplasticity, does decline but does not stop. We further know that new neurons can appear in certain parts of the brain until the day we die. However, as we age, our brain size decreases, particularly in forebrain (frontal cortex). In any case, through the power of neuroplasticity, we can start transforming our life at any stage of time by venturing into any new areas of learning. Through physically rewiring our brain, we can change our lives.

7.5 Thanks to "switch-on" and "switch-off" genes, harmful genes can lie dormant throughout our life.

The genetic blueprint of the new-born sets the stage on which the new being will interact with the outer world. Every cell carries the blueprint for everything, from height and complexion to the risks of critical illnesses like cancer. It is a great wonderment that while no two humans are genetically identical, every human's DNA is 99.9 percent the same. The remaining .1 percent of our genetic makeup makes every individual unique.

Each one of us is brought up in a particular and unique way. We had no role in choosing our genetic makeup. A combination of genes or even a single gene surely influence many biochemical processes. However, the environment in which we are nurtured determines the expression of those genes in many ways through a complex process. Experiences leave a chemical "signature" on the genes which determine whether and how the genes are expressed.

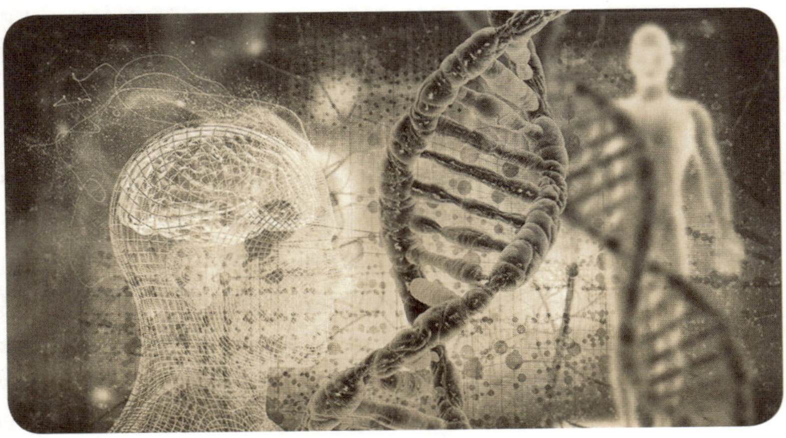

Figure 7.5: Harmful genes can lie dormant throughout our lifetime; otherwise they can be triggered at any age due to environmental factors

People often argue about whether our genes also influence our destiny. There's no question that the hereditary material we receive from our parents influences our life. Earlier, the consensus was that the genes have a far greater role in shaping our life than our experiences – that to a great extent they determine our destiny. However, with the advance of medical science, these views have changed. Our genes are not our destiny. We have a great deal of power over our own genetic behaviour. The science of epigenetics has changed the way we used to think about the role of genes in our life. Epigenetics is the study of the biological mechanism that switches genes "on" and "off." These mechanisms act by changing the structure of DNA, deoxyribonucleic acid, the molecule that contains our genetic code. It's the interaction between our environment and the genes that determines whether we remain healthy or develop diseases.

We may carry the genes of certain chronic diseases, but it's the environmental factors that switch on those particular illness-producing genes. Our bodies may harbour harmful genes for serious illnesses like cancer, but they may lie dormant throughout our lifetime. Such genes can be triggered anytime, depending upon specific environmental factors. Unless we make conscious and healthy choices, there is a high probability of activating those harmful genes. Numerous studies have confirmed that the environment in which we are nurtured is primarily responsible for chronic diseases. The environment includes our food and drink, the air we breathe, the thoughts we entertain, and the quality of our social relationships. The environment is the primary driver of our health and longevity, and not the genetic blueprint.

It's therefore the mix of genetic as well as environmental influence that shapes our life. There is a very important study carried out by California Life Company, which is known as Calico and also the longevity lab. Calico has been carrying out research on aging with the hope of finding breakthroughs for delaying or defeating death one day. This company, in collaboration with other institutions, collected and analysed a database of millions of families around the world. The results were then published in the journal *Genetics*. The study has concluded that our DNA, the genetic material, has far less influence on how long we live than previously thought. Previous estimates for how much genes explain variations in lifespan had ranged from around 15 to 30%. Now the study concludes that this percentage is merely 7. It means humans have more control over how long they live than their genes do. If someone dies early, it is generally due to one's lifestyle and the environment in which the person has grown.

There is now broad consensus among researchers that it's ultimately the nurturing that matters the most in our life rather than the genetic blueprint that we inherit from our parents. However, nature and nurture are deeply and intimately interwoven with one another. Genes have an influence on the environments we experience. We have certain genes that largely determine how intelligent, empathetic, or antisocial we are. In fact, DNA differences account for about 50 percent of the differences between us, in our personality, mental health and illness, and cognitive abilities and disabilities. Quality of parenting, education, social contacts, and life events and experiences account for the remaining differences. Our environment and experiences can directly change the level at which certain genes are expressed, which in turn alters both our brain as well as the physical body. Now there is broad agreement in the question of nature and nurture, and nurture is the winner.

7.6 We are what we believe – Our Belief System

Life is all about believing in ourselves and the world around us. What we believe and tell ourselves from moment to moment determines the journey we undertake during our lifetime. The beliefs we carry along with us shape the contours of our life. These beliefs create our future, the destiny we design. These are both the catalysts and inhibitors of our growth. So deeply are embedded our beliefs that we hardly care or dare to challenge them. For the most part, we live with them throughout our lives. The quality of our beliefs exerts significant impact on our day-to-day life. What we do and what happens to us are reflections of our core beliefs. Emotionally bound by our belief system, if someone confronts us with opposing beliefs, we become offended, and are often "hurt."

We all have a whole system of beliefs that usually continues to grow and petrify along our life's journey. We keep on accumulating beliefs as we age, thinking and acting on the basis of those beliefs. They are the foundation of our identity, the "I" powerfully influencing our personality, physical health, and overall quality of life. In a way, they act either as catalysts or inhibitors, depending on the belief system. Our successes and failures, mental and physical health, joy and happiness, pain and suffering, are born of our core beliefs. If we want to change our life, we first need to change our beliefs.

Life is not easy in any situation. It's critically important to believe in yourself. Opportunities are available in almost all situations. Beauty lies in the belief about oneself, in one's strength and ability to handle whatever comes our way. Our well-wishers, friends, and colleagues can help in making opportunities available to us, but belief in ourselves is required to make good of those opportunities. *Beliefs in ourselves are, in fact, the precursor to success.* Success starts with the belief that we are the creator of our own destiny through our actions. If we change our thoughts, we can change our reality. It all begins and ends with our beliefs. The main difference between successful and ordinary people is their belief system.

Unfortunately, during our life journey, many negative and regressive beliefs become part and parcel of our belief system. For example, *"The world around me is hostile and unfriendly*"; *most people, except family and close friends, will never help me*"; "*I am a worthless individual who can't succeed in life*"; *"no one likes or loves me."* Many such notions, especially during early age, may get into our belief system. Such core negative beliefs become part of our personality and are expressed in our thinking, behaviour, and decision-making, colouring the quality of our lives.

The strongest evidence that beliefs can influence our physical body comes from the placebo and nocebo effects in the medical world. We can change the biology of our body simply by holding to what we believe to be true. The placebo effect is among the most mystifying phenomena in medicine. The medical community and individuals too, have seen innumerable instances of patients being given just sugar pills or some other placebo, who were fully cured or whose symptoms were relieved as if they were taking medicine. When we expect a pill to make us better, it generally does. *Doctors have even gone to the extreme of conducting fake surgeries and found that their patients got well, or were relieved.*

How a doctor treats his or her patient, and the overall context in which medicine is given, can greatly influence the outcome of medication. The greater the confidence in one's doctor for the treatment of illness, the greater likelihood would be for a speedy recovery. Undoubtedly, our mind can usually be a very powerful healing tool. When our brain convinces our physical body that the treatment is the real thing and not a fake one, the placebo effect works its magic. Numerous studies have been conducted to learn the exact dynamics working behind the placebo effect.

According to an article, "The power of the placebo effect, 'Treating yourself with your mind is possible, but there is more to it than positive thinking', published in Harvard Men's Health Watch of Harvard Medical School, *"How placebos work is still not quite understood, but it involves a complex neurobiological reaction that includes everything from increases in feel-good neurotransmitters, like endorphins and dopamine, to greater activity in certain brain regions linked to moods, emotional reactions, and self-awareness."*

Figure 7.6: Through positive beliefs about one's potential, anyone can achieve near impossible tasks. Seriously disabled girl is climbing a steep mountain.

Modern science has now, beyond any doubt, established that mind and body are "two sides of the same coin," and the way we think and feel has a tremendous impact on our health and well-being. For instance, when the mind is engaged in negative thoughts and emotions, there is noticeable impact on healing; even medicines and other interventions do not work on those occasions. This is called the "nocebo effect." The same mind-body power that can heal us can also harm us. The mere suggestion that a patient may experience negative symptoms in response to a medication, or even a sugar pill, may be a self-fulfilling prophecy. For example, if a doctor tells a patient who is being treated merely with sugar pills that he might experience nausea, there are fair chances that he would feel nauseous. If it is suggested that the person might get a headache, then most likely that person will. There are even instances of patients dying due to negative beliefs, coupled with the extreme fear occasioned by misdiagnoses.

Now the question arises as to how our beliefs influence our life to such a great extent. One very obvious way is through our behaviour. When we have positive beliefs about ourselves and the world around us, our behaviour is confident, pleasant, and impressive. This self-motivating and confident behaviour can obviously lead to positive outcomes. The reverse is of course true for negative and self-limiting beliefs. Such people exhibit self-defeating behaviour, which leads to poor or negative results. In this way, beliefs, as expressed through our behaviour, can exert a great influence on outcomes, especially when people are trying to identify and take advantage pf opportunities. Through their own positive-belief-based behaviour, people can even influence other people's behaviour. As they pleasantly and easily interact, positive thinkers can impress others with their own positivity, which easily "rubs off" on their associates.

Destiny and our belief system have an intimate and deep relationship. To design our destiny constructively, our beliefs must be positive and rational. These beliefs help us to move in the direction of fulfilling our goals. On the other hand, if we carry with us a load of negative, self-defeating and regressive beliefs, the realization of intended goals becomes extremely difficult. Unless one consciously and persistently decides to replace such beliefs with a positive and progressive system of belief, it's almost impossible to extricate oneself from that negative loop. *The choice of belief system upon which we build our future is solely ours. Destiny needs to be designed or earned.* Despite the presence of opportunities that can change the course of our life, we often fail to notice or seize them. That the same opportunities are utilized differently by different people is due to their respective belief systems.

We must therefore look into our operating system, the belief system, and identify the beliefs we've been carrying since our early days. Are those beliefs positive and growth-oriented? Revisit them, if required. Then move ahead. Beliefs have the power to create anything positive in our lives. Our beliefs in fact decide the contour of our life's journey. It's well said by Denis Waitley, an American motivational speaker, '*if you believe you can, you probably can. If you believe you won't, you most assuredly won't. Belief is the ignition switch that gets you off the launching pad*'.

7.7 Though the Law of Attraction is powerful and potent, But we find it very difficult to attract what we desire in life?

What we focus on, we attract. This statement very succinctly summarizes the Law of Attraction. Though there is no direct scientific evidence or study that confirms the working of this law, there have been, and continue to be, references to it in spiritual texts, sacred manuscripts, and ancient wisdom. Most compelling evidence of its power comes in the form of personal experiences, accompanied by the knowledge of quantum mechanics that corroborates the unexplainable power behind the Law of Attraction. Strong support for this law came from the New Age Movement, which started the '70s and '80s, though there were plenty of forerunners to it in the nineteenth century. In fact, the Law of Attraction is the main tenet of this movement. In a sense, it's a metaphysical-religious movement in which people believe that our thoughts, intentions, and beliefs, if properly held, can bring about transformational changes in our lives.

The scientific basis behind the law is that all matter is nothing but energy. The world which appears rock solid to us is, in fact, energy. Everything in the physical world is interconnected, at the deepest level, by invisible energy fields. Similarly, our thoughts are vibrations of energy that is transmitted by our mind. All thoughts, words, and emotions have unique frequency. According to the Law of Attraction, whatever energy we transmit, the same kind/frequency of energy will come back to us. If we give positive energy to the world, the same kind of energy is what we receive. The same is true of negative energy, based on the natural principle of "like attracts like." If our thoughts and intentions are more focused and consistent, they have far greater energy and accordingly manifest the reality they project. Therefore, our intentions and focused thought patterns can create the reality that's desired and attracted by us.

In other words, whatever comes into our life has been attracted by our dominant thoughts and intentions. If we are living in the pathetic conditions that some describe as "a living hell," it is because of the quality and intensity of our thoughts, past and present. If we keep on thinking and reinforcing our negative thoughts, regardless of how conscious they may be, that same reality is manifesting in many ways in our life. On the positive side, suppose I am consistently imagining that I have my own lovely house and am happily staying there with my family, then circumstances will unfold in such a manner that allow me to have a house. In other words, we quite literally have the ability to shape events, circumstances, and relationships in our life, based on how we choose to think, imagine, and believe. We create the reality we wish by becoming co-creators of that reality. We are not helpless bystanders, but active participants in creating the reality we desire.

The Law of Attraction works perfectly, and for that our body, mind, and spirit are aligned and in harmony with the universe. Ideally, we should achieve the goal that we set for ourselves in life. For that, every single day we must visualise what we want to achieve. We should use affirmations and visualizations for achieving our goal. Many successful manifestors develop a blueprint, a plan with details as to how they are going to get from where they are now to where we want to be. The universe will do the work, but we ourselves also need to do what's required.

We also need to keep in mind that while practicing to attract what we want to achieve, we should use only positive language. We should not think or speak about what we do not want in life. When we give emotional thought or expression to what is not desired, we generally strengthen its presence in our lives and attract more of the same. We must keep this simple mantra in mind. We should all think big, and dream of only good things in life. There is no dearth of opportunities in our life's journey. All that is required is focused and consistent attention, with our mind set steadily on what we desire.

If Law of Attraction is so powerful that merely through our focused thoughts and intentions we can manifest major changes in life, then why don't people experience better outcomes in their life ? There are four main reasons. First, people don't believe so strongly that merely through their thoughts they can manifest changes in their life. Since this looks so simple and effective, it's very natural that doubt will arise over the utility of the law. Second, when we think something very positive -- say, receiving an out-of-turn promotion or a luxury car for the family -- simultaneously serious doubts arise. *Oh, this will not be possible because of reasons x, y, and z.* What then happens is that doubts become more powerful and focused than thoughts of the desired goal. We keep on blaming others or doubting ourselves or criticizing "the system," as we are conditioned to think in that way.

More importantly, the third reason why conscious use of the Law of Attraction may not seem to work is most people's inability to focus or concentrate consistently on something. The mental focus – most potent when it is like a laser – is lacking under normal circumstances. Divided attention commonly occurs in everyday life when we are performing multiple tasks at a time. Nearly half the time, our mind is wandering in other directions rather than focusing on the task at hand. Sometimes, mind - wandering is as high as 70% when we are engaged in boring work. This tendency of mind makes it very difficult to focus and attend wholly to the present moment. It is rare for someone to be engaged in just one task for a long time. We lack focused attention because our average attention span is only 6-10 seconds per minute. That is why it's so difficult to concentrate on anything, regardless of how attractive it may be to us. This is the main reason why we are not able to see positive results from utilizing the Law of Attraction in our life.

Lastly, it's also true that though our conscious mind may be concentrating on the goal we intend to achieve, our subconscious and unconscious mind may be tuned to an entirely different channel – one of pessimism, for example, or unworthiness. Suppose I want to get an out-of-turn promotion but my belief is that I am not capable of handling the job I desire. Since my belief is deeply embedded in my unconscious mind, it's very difficult to be aware of that belief. It's an established fact that our subconscious and unconscious minds are more powerfully influential than the conscious mind. Repressed and suppressed beliefs and feelings of limitation can make it nearly impossible to attract what we desire in life through the Law of Attraction. For this reason, the law which would act powerfully – "miraculously" -- under the perfect conditions of a clear mind and an unguarded heart may be blocked from proving itself in our life.

ooo

8

Life and inseparability of Self, Mind and Body – learn to manage psychosomatic entity

Where is "I" in my body? Isn't it a funny question? Since we are so sure about the answer, we seldom think about this aspect of Self. However, this is a highly debatable question in philosophy as well as in neuroscience. Let's first examine our physical body. Over a lifetime, all of us change significantly. As an adult of 68kg, I have about 34 trillion (34,000,000,000) cells. In every minute, 300,000,000 (30 crore) cells die and are replaced by new cells. In about 7 to 10 years, most of the cells are replaced. Baring a few cells in the brain and some other parts of the body, all other cells are replaced. I have a new physical body.

Given that my body has changed completely, how is it that my Self, my identity, remains intact? Is it because of the fact that my name, my family, and my background stay the same throughout life? Or is it that my body changes so slowly that I and others usually don't notice the changes? Suppose there is a bus and that has a name. It's standing in one fixed place in a city. Every year, someone replaces one part with another identical part. After 20 years, when all of its parts have been replaced, people still call the bus by the same name. Unlike this bus, however, "I" is a lot more than a body. It is an amalgam of physical body, mind, emotions, experiences, etc., and all of these constituents of "I" are changing constantly. It means there is no permanent Self in me. In that sense, the Self is not real. That's why the question about Self becomes very relevant and perplexing too.

In Buddhism, the term anattā (Pali) or anātman (Sanskrit) refers to the doctrine of "non-self," that there is no permanent Self or soul. It means we have no fixed Self. It doesn't mean that we have no Self or that it doesn't exist, simply that it is impermanent. It essentially means that everything is constantly changing within our physical body. Thoughts, feelings, emotions, and millions of biochemical processes are changing. Nothing is static in us. In Buddhism, "I" consists of five aggregates, namely -- body, feeling, perception, mental formations (emotions) and consciousness. If we examine these five constituents, we see we have no ultimate control over any of them. Moreover, their properties are not associated with the Self. All the aggregates of being are not "mine." If 'I' has no control over any of the aggregates, then obviously there is no CEO in my body.

Figure 8.1: For happy and healthy life, we need to create a harmonious relationship among body, mind, inner self and the soul.

If we observe ourselves for some period, we see in our mind whenever we make any choice or decision that conflicting ideas emerge. Like when we switch on our TV, immediately conflict arises as to which channel we should watch. One part of self is saying I should see the news channel ; some other part of self is insisting I must enjoy some entertainment channel because I am tired and need relaxation. Suppose I decide I should catch up on the news. Now a new conflicting situation arises as to which channel. Which of my three favourite channels will I choose? Likewise, our mind harbours multiple states having varying degrees of conflict with one another. Hence, self consists of numerous conflicting drives, which continue to compete with one another.

Since there is no CEO or conscious Self in our body, many parts of selves strive to catch our attention and dominate. This is why our mind is usually in a somewhat unstable and conflicted position. Take another example : *I am very fond of eating sugary desserts like ice cream after dinner. Almost daily, my mind is in a conflicting situation. One part of self always insists that unhealthy treats be avoided after dinner. However, other part argues that nothing would happen if I were to take ice cream today – just this once, and in moderation. Every day the same situation arises.* It's a typical case of conflict between short-sighted self and long-term self. Each one of us comes across such conflicting desires. At those moments, "I" keep on struggling to make a balanced choice. Since there is no in-charge of Me inside, we keep on facing such dilemmas all the time.

There is a theory of modular mind, which states that our mind has a number of modules that are acting separately at the same time. There is no part of self that controls or coordinates these modules. They don't report to any authority stationed in our brain/mind. When we are in conflicting situations, different modules are active and trying to dominate the others. Noted American journalist and science author Robert Wright explains : *"Your mind is composed of lots of specialized modules—modules for sizing up situations and reacting to them—and it's the interplay among these modules that shapes your behaviour. And much of this interplay happens without conscious awareness on your part... This model also helps make sense of some of life's great internal conflicts, such as whether to cheat on your spouse, whether to take addictive drugs, and whether to eat another powdered-sugar doughnut."*

Our mind is quite often full of contradictions, conflicts, and inconsistencies because there is no controlling self in us. So-called conscious self almost always thinks it's in charge of us. However, the fact is the conscious self is not some all-powerful executive authority controlling our mind and its various modules that are experiencing conflicting drives. The self is not real, hence illusory in nature. But there are ways to make conscious-self strong and decisive. That can be done through the practice of mindfulness meditation.

8.1 Our body is mind and Mind is body: we are nothing but a psychosomatic structure of flesh and bones

In ancient times, there was a widely held belief of mind and body influencing each other in an intimate manner. However, the situation changed when philosopher and mathematician René Descartes (1596 – 1650) who is regarded as the father of modern philosophy, postulated the theory of mind-body separation (dualism). He defines the only certain and irrefutable belief as "I think, therefore I am." This theory states that mind and body are two distinct entities. It is opposed to the notion that identifies mind with the brain. He argued that the nature of mind (thinking part) is completely different from that of the body (non-thinking part) and therefore it is possible for one to exist without the other. This argument gave rise to the contentious problem of mind-body causal interaction: how can the body's sense organs cause sensations in the mind when their natures are completely different and apart?

Thus began the debate over the immaterial mind and the material body: Are they distinct entities or are they intimately connected entities? Descartes' theory challenged the very fundamental notion based on our ancient wisdom that mind and body are inseparable. Now, according to Descartes, both these realms – immaterial/nonphysical (mind) and material/physical (body) -- are separate and can't influence one another. Over the centuries thereafter, scientists, philosophers, and thinkers continued to agree on that notion. Even now in our contemporary world, this theory has not been completely discredited, despite mounting evidence to the contrary produced by medical scientists and researchers.

If we observe carefully, we can feel how emotions like anger, aggression, hatred, etc., instantly generate sensations in our physical body. When we get angry, it's very common for our heart rate and respiration to increase, accompanied by heat in the neck and face. As the adrenal glands flood the body with stress hormones, such as adrenaline and cortisol, the skin is likely to perspire. Likewise, when we experience chronic stress, many bio-chemicals are secreted and flood the bloodstream. These chemicals, known as neurotransmitters, prepare the body to deal with perceived or real danger in many ways, such as raising blood pressure to ensure faster speed and response time.

The mind-body connection postulates that our mind and body influence each other in a bi-directional manner. In other words, just as our physical body affects the mind, so too is the mind capable of making significant effects on our body. Studies have demonstrated that our thoughts affect neurotransmitters, the chemical messengers that enable the brain to communicate not only with different parts of itself, but also with the nervous system. Neurotransmitters control virtually all important functions of the body, from emotions to digestion to excretion. In this way, our thoughts directly influence our body through neurotransmitters.

Among the neurotransmitters that act as messengers between brain and body are neuropeptides. Their job is to transmit signals throughout the body. Neuropeptides are a naturally occurring group of compounds in our body. They comprise its most basic communication network. These chemicals connecting emotions and receptors are present in all cells of our body. When someone is happy, sad, or disgusted, specific types of neuropeptides carry those particular emotions to every area of the body. Reflecting the changes in our emotional state, neuropeptides are constantly changing their shape. Therefore, *when our emotional and mental state is out of balance, neuropeptides may induce physical symptoms.*

Since neuropeptides and their receptors also live in the body, the mind is in the body, just as it is in the brain. Biochemical messengers play a major role in shaping our lives. More than 200 chemical messengers have, so far, been identified, as well as six major neurotransmitters such as dopamine and serotonin. Every neurotransmitter affects our body in many ways. For instance, serotonin impacts both emotions and movements. It is a natural mood stabilizer and helps in sleeping and digesting.

Figure 8.1A: Our body, mind and inner self/spirit are all parts of one holistic entity.

Every thought we experience causes neurochemical changes, many of which are significant. For instance, when we help others, we get a surge of dopamine, the "reward" neurotransmitter. That is the physical reason we get a happy feeling when we unconditionally help others the mind-body connection can also be clearly explained through the example of chronic stress. As we all know, stressful conditions can lead to a host of illnesses, including some critical ones. It's very difficult for most people experiencing stress to identify its physical effects/manifestation in the form of early symptoms of illnesses. Stress arises when prevailing conditions become more difficult than one can handle. It is an automatic response to any stimulus or condition that requires us to adjust.

When stress persists for a long time and in acute form, it is termed "chronic." Many people, unaware of the mind-body connection, are unable to determine the extent to which their physical symptoms (like headache, stomach-ache, heart palpitations and, in the long run, type 2 diabetes and obesity) are provoked by chronic stress. Modern science has revalidated our ancient wisdom that mind, body, and soul are all one. Mind and body are so deeply and intimately intertwined that the term mind-body is widely used. The impact of thoughts on our body is instant, but in most instances, their impact is so slow or miniscule that it's not possible for most of us to notice. That's why the majority of us still cling to the belief that "mind and body are separate entities."

8.2 Our thoughts are linked to immune system – The thoughts create most of the mental and physical illnesses

Most of us have given thought to the popular truism that "Our thoughts create our reality." Though this may sound odd to some, it's a scientifically proven fact. The tenor of thoughts that flow through our mind has profound bearing on our mental and physical health and well-being. Suppose we are stuck in heavy traffic and we have to attend a very important meeting with some senior government official. Stressful thoughts of getting delayed and its likely implications generate immediate feelings in the body. If mental stress persists for an extended period, it becomes chronic in nature. Chronic stress will sooner or later create many physical problems such as headache, weight gain/obesity and diabetes.

How exactly do thoughts affect the body? How could our thoughts make us sick or happy? are some of the recurring questions that many people struggle with. The answer is very simple. When we suffer from chronic stress, cortisol hormone is secreted in greater quantity. It's released by adrenal glands, which are situated above both kidneys. Under normal circumstances, cortisol is essential as it helps our body to deal with stressful conditions. However, when cortisol levels become high over a longer period of time, it starts becoming harmful. If we engage negative and stressful thoughts for a long time, many health-related issues may arise because of decreased immunity. There is a direct link between chronic stress and impaired immune function. "Stress hormone" cortisol suppresses our body's immune system. Once immunity is low, we become susceptible to infectious and other diseases.

It has been confirmed through innumerable studies that negative and toxic thoughts lead to mental stress and related mental diseases, such as depression and anxiety. As previously discussed, the mind is highly geared to negativity. While it's often restless, "satisfactoriness" is the mind's default setting. We also tend to overthink, either worrying about something or ruminating about some past event. This too makes us highly susceptible to negative and distressing thoughts. Such thoughts are very "sticky" and difficult to get rid of. Unless we are skilled in the art of managing our thoughts well, we are prone to many diseases due to low immunity. *The source of many lifestyle diseases lies in our inability to handle our thoughts and feelings.*

Figure 8.2: There is a direct relationship between our thoughts, stress and immune system. Most of the diseases are the outcome of our weak immune system.

Emotions have a profound effect on our health. This happens due to low immunity, occasioned by life-snuffing thoughts and behaviours. It has been established that our emotions directly affect our immune response. In fact, negative moods may change the way in which the immune system functions. Pioneering work done in this field by Dr Candace Pert, an eminent American neuroscientist and pharmacologist who extensively researched neuropeptides, inspired Dr Pert to refer to them as "molecules of emotion." Pert describes the mysterious energy connecting body to mind and emotions as the free flow of information carried by the biochemistry of emotion -- i.e., peptides and their receptors.

As previously described, neuropeptides are small protein-like molecules used by neurons (billions of cells forming dense networks in the brain) to communicate with each other. They are neuronal signalling molecules that influence the activity of the brain in specific ways. Different neuropeptides are involved in a wide range of brain functions, including metabolism, reproduction, social learning, and memory. The strong link between emotional responses and the biochemical change they produce, specifically in the immune system, forms the basis of the nascent field known as psychoneuroimmunology (PNI). PNI explores the links between mind and body in regard to the immune system. The immune cells communicate directly with the brain, and vice versa, via neuropeptides. Cells in the immune system are responsive to all the neuropeptides that are triggered by our thoughts and emotions.

When we emotion, neuropeptides travel throughout our body and influence the functioning of various types of body cells. Neuropeptides change their own configuration, like a chameleon, due to thoughts and emotions. According to Dr Pert, depending upon the thoughts and emotions, specific neuropeptides are made in the brain and nervous system, white blood cells, reproductive cells, digestive system, and heart. They form a two-way network between psyche and soma, mind and body. The complex communication network between cells, neurotransmitters, neuropeptides, hormones, the immune system, blood, and nerves enables the body-mind to work as one healthy balanced person.

Among the most common health disorders are depression, anxiety, eating disorders, and substance abuse. Tens of millions of people suffer from these disorders around the world. In India, an estimated 56 million people are dealing with depression, and 38 million from anxiety disorders, according to a report by the World Health Organisation. We have a serious mental health crisis in India. Likewise, millions of people suffer from lifestyle diseases such as obesity, diabetes, cancer, heart and lung disease. All these mental and physical illnesses originate from our inability to manage our thoughts well.

The main causes of lifestyle diseases are lack of physical exercise, bad eating habits, chronic stress, and substance abuse. Most of the diseases start with low immunity, when our inner fighting system against bacteria, viruses, and other microorganisms is weak. *As we have seen, our thoughts and emotions affect our immunity level. If we learn to witness and control our thoughts, emotions, and thinking patterns, we can surely manage our immunity.* Mental disciplines like mindfulness and meditation can also help us to improve our ability to handle thoughts in healthy manner. Every time when we get trapped in negative and harmful thoughts, we should remember that if we allow these thoughts to persist for a longer time in our mind, they will sooner or later impact our physical health. We should never treat mind as a separate entity located inside our skull. Mind, body and self are all part of a single psychosomatic entity.

8.3 We get a feeling of euphoria and wellbeing after physical exercise. Endorphins – internal generation of morphine like chemicals

Whenever we do physical exercise like running or briskly walking, cycling, swimming, or a gym workout, we get feeling of well-being – sometimes even one of euphoria. We feel good and experience an elevated mood. Pain may even decrease after exhaustive exercise. The reason is the secretion of certain biochemical, endorphins, in our nervous system. Endorphins have profound effects on our mind and body. Endorphins have been suggested as modulators of the so-called "runner's high" that athletes sometimes experience with prolonged exercise. That's the reason doctors recommend aerobic and other physical exercises to patients suffering from depression. These are potent long-term antidepressants. Self-esteem, which becomes very low in such patients, also improves. These chemicals are also said to enhance our immune response.

Endorphins are produced by the central nervous system, which consists of a complex of nerve tissues in the brain and spinal cord. The two parts of the word endorphin -- *endo-* and *-orphin* -- are derived from the words *endogenous* and *morphine,* meaning, "a morphine-like substance originating from within the body." The principal function of endorphins is to act as analgesia, inhibiting the transmission of pain signals to higher brain centres; they also induce a feeling of euphoria very similar to that produced by morphine-like drugs. These chemicals are produced in the brain in response to a variety of stimuli. Stress and pain are the two most common triggers for release of endorphins.

We quite often feel sleepy after strong physical exercise like running or swimming. This feeling of sleepiness is again due to endorphins. They act as sedatives. Yogic breathing exercises like pranayama may have similar effects on us due to endorphin secretion. Likewise, certain foods like chocolate and chilli peppers are supposed to trigger the feeling of euphoria. Again, this is because of these chemicals secreted by our brain. *Though these endorphins can be released by many means, physical exercise is the best.* Eating chocolate, chillies, and spicy food, as well as laughing and having sex, are other natural ways to optimize secretion of endorphins. Depression and other mental problems often respond well to these natural therapies.

Depression and anxiety are among the most common mental illnesses all over the world. In many nations, they are reaching epidemic levels. Over 300 million people are estimated to suffer from depression, equivalent to 4.4% of the world's population. Although depression can and does affect people of all ages, from all walks of life, the risk of becoming depressed increases with poverty, unemployment, and life events such as the death of a loved one, a relationship breakup, physical illness, and problems caused by alcohol and drug use. At its worst, depression can lead to suicide. Nearly eight hundred thousand people die from suicide every year. It is the second-leading cause of death in the age group of 15 to 29. An additional 284 million people worldwide suffered from an anxiety disorder in 2017.

Figure 8.3: Physical exercises produce endorphins, the biochemical responsible for happy and pleasant feelings.

Numerous studies have established that symptoms of depression and anxiety often improve with exercise and other physical activities. Research shows that the psychological and physical benefits of exercise can also include improved mood. Regular exercise helps to alleviate the symptoms of virtually any mental disorder. Again, this is attributable to the release of endorphins, the "feel good" chemicals. Physical exercise may be safely used along with other treatments, such as medications and therapy, and may also be used alone.

One study has established that yoga and meditation can increase one's level of endorphins. People with depression and anxiety disorders often feel significant improvement through combining medication with the alternate ways of yoga, meditation, and physical exercises. When we exercise regularly, we tend to do so because it gives us an enormous boost. We feel more energetic throughout the day, sleep more soundly at night, and feel more relaxed and positive about ourselves. We can summarised by saying that *endorphins are a powerful producer of happy feelings. The best thing is that this biochemical can be produced within our own body.*

8.4 How to handle chronic pain conditions through alternative therapy – the time-tested ways to manage pain

We can't escape pain, both psychological and physical pain. Psychological or mental pain is universal, with humane and effective ways to address it. However, for physical pain, most of us immediately take the recourse of medicines that, in the developed world, are abundantly available.. The main problem in taking these medicines is their side effects and toxicity. Taking painkillers very frequently and for a long time can have detrimental effects on our health. Our tolerance to them gradually increases, and then we start upping the dosage or their frequency to cope with increasing pain. Since we are so vulnerable and sensitive to pain, especially when it is chronic, we may have no other viable option than to go for medicines often in dangerous and addictive doses.

Research has shown that more than one-third of people admit to taking more than the recommended dose of over-the-counter medicines for physical pain, thinking that taking an overdose will increase their effectiveness. Obviously, side effects become more likely. In many developed nations like the USA, there are pain management centres in hospitals and medical institutions for advising patients about non-pharmacological treatment options such as mindfulness therapy, homeopathy, chiropractic, and acupuncture. Studies and anecdotal reports give high grades to many of these therapies for chronic pain.

Sadly, the medical community is still not taking full advantage of alternative therapies that have been available to us for centuries.

The first imperative for one who suffers chronic pain is to know how to handle fear. Fear of pain increases its intensity. The more we are fearful of pain, the greater is our sensitivity to it. In May 2017, I underwent major surgery for replacement of my aortic valve (an abnormality present from birth) in Max Hospital, New Delhi. Of course, surgery is never a painful experience because the patient is under general anaesthesia. However, once the patient recovers from the anaesthesia, the real ordeal begins. When nurses start taking out tubes from different areas, as in my case from the chest, neck, and groin areas, the pain can be very bad. When the time came for my own tube-pulling, it occurred to me that if I could remove or greatly diminish my fear of pain the process would be comparatively tolerable. And it was! Since I have been a regular practitioner of Transcendental Meditation for the past 20 years, I knew the importance of being mindful under such circumstances.

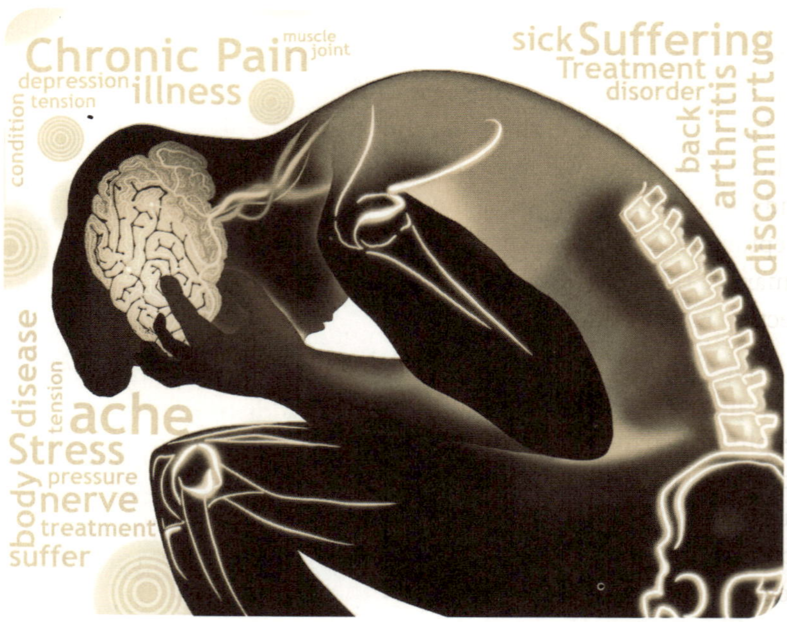

Figure 8.4: If we take care of fear of pain through the practice of mindfulness, intensity of chronic pain can be reduced.

My post-operative experience convinced me that the most effective nonmedicinal pain therapy is the way of mindfulness, being mindful and fearless of the sensations related to physical pain. Mindfulness, as we have seen, is basically the mental exercise of purposely paying attention in the present moment without judgment or interpretation. We need to observe whatever is happening around us without assigning any meaning. In other words, it's paying attention, nonjudgmentally, to thoughts, emotions, feelings, and bodily sensations, right there and then. Just observe the present moments. When we are mindful of the pain sensations, and we are free from any fear of pain, the intensity of pain is contained. There will not be any fearful conditions and anticipation of pain under mindfulness. It has been established by numerous research studies that mindfulness-based meditation can even help in effectively managing pain in patients suffering from chronic conditions like cancer .

Another very effective alternative therapy based on mindfulness is acceptance and commitment therapy (ACT). It's a behavioural therapy which has proven extremely beneficial in addressing a wide range of clinical conditions, including chronic pain. Primarily the aim of ACT is to lead a meaningful life while accepting and embracing the pain. Acceptance is a willingness to accept whatever is happening to us. We learn to accept painful feelings, thoughts, and sensations, allowing them to be there without struggling against them. In ACT, patients are taught to observe and accept the pain and associated feelings and sensations without resistance. When we resist pain or experience fear from it, pain conditions become more acute. Studies have confirmed that simple acceptance has great power to manage pain. Patients also need to learn to manage their distressing and unwanted thoughts and feelings through effective use of mindfulness.

In acceptance and commitment therapy, patients with chronic pain are required to learn two things. First, they should embrace or accept the physical pain conditions, including unpleasant thoughts, feelings, and sensations which are not under their control. They should neither struggle with the painful symptoms nor give them undue attention. Second, they must bring awareness to here-and-now experience, with openness. The aim is simply to let their thoughts come and go, and allow their feelings to be there, with attention focused on the present moment. This is how ACT results in abatement in symptoms associated with chronic pain conditions.

8.5 We can't effort to overlook gut bacteria , a crucial part of our mental and physical body.

It's surprising to know that the human body hosts a greater population of bacteria than its total number of cells. It is estimated that our gut contains about 100 trillion bacteria, nearly triple the 35 trillion cells in an average 67 kg body. Interestingly, there are about 20,000--25,000 genes in our body, while the microbes that are there in our gut have somewhere around 3.3 million genes. This strongly suggests that microbes constitute a vital part of our body. Much of the bacterial population is extremely important for numerous activities relating to digestion of food, and for making vitamins and neurotransmitters such as dopamine, serotonin, and GABA, all of which play a vital role in mood regulation.

In addition, healthy intestinal bacteria have been found to be essential for immune function. Apart from bacteria, within the intestines live a community of trillions of viruses, fungi, and protozoans which together constitute the gut microbiome. Our healthy microbiome is a diverse one, containing a wide variety of organisms living in our gut. It's a vast ecosystem weighing about 2 kg (about 5 lb), which is heavier than our brain.

Each one of us has a unique blend of microbes. No two individuals will have a same mix of bacteria. Our gut microbes are determined partly by our mother's microbes and partly by our eating habits and lifestyle. A large part of our microbes stays in the gut throughout life. They line our entire digestive system. Most live in the intestines and colon. More and more studies are establishing the role of gut microbes in our mental and physical health as well as our overall well-being. The connection between brain and gut is far more intimate and deep than previously understood.

It has been established that gut bacteria in healthy people are different from those suffering diseases. People with illnesses may house either too few or too many of a certain type of bacteria. Some strains of bacteria are healthy while others may be unhealthy or risky to our health. How we feel is reflected through our stomach. Recently, studies discovered that there are "mood microbes," or "psychobiotics" -- probiotics that are essential for our mental health. Probiotics are healthy gut flora. Some of us still remember that during our school days, our mothers used to feed us curd (known for its probiotic bacteria) before we left home for examinations. The main purpose for giving us curd was to lower our anxiety level.

Some studies have suggested that gut microbes directly affect stress and anxiety in such a way that alter our mood and behaviour both positively and negatively. This now gives a new meaning to the term gut feeling. Research also suggests that our gut bacteria are linked to many other diseases such as diabetes, obesity, depression, and heart disease. Just as we are what we think, "We are what we eat " is also true. The health of our gut bacteria depends largely on our food habits. A study indicates that over the course of days, a new diet can reshape the microbial community, and those changes are consistent and reversible.

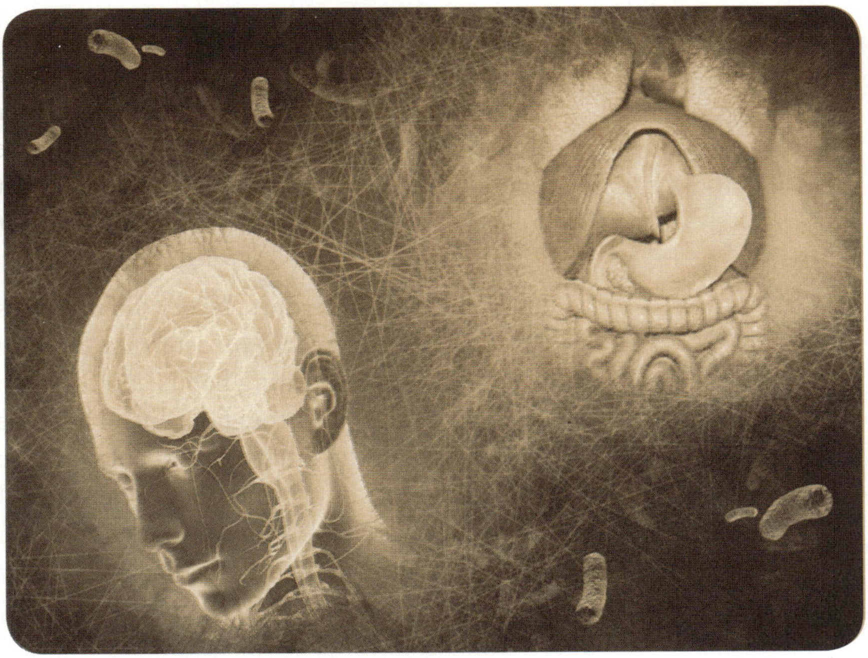

Figure 8.5: Gut bacterial plays a very important role in our emotional and physical health conditions.

When it comes to foods that help promote a healthy gut, we actually have two categories: probiotics and prebiotics. Prebiotics are non-digestible compounds found in the fibre of food such as onions, garlic, oats, asparagus, and bananas that promote the growth of beneficial microorganisms in the intestines. They serve as food for probiotics (the "good bacteria") as well as yeast. Unsurprisingly, yogurt is the best source of probiotics. Traditional buttermilk is another good probiotic food. Probiotics also help in converting fibre into short-chain fatty acids, synthesizing certain vitamins, and supporting the immune system.

On the other hand, excess alcohol and a diet high in saturated fat and animal protein have been shown to hurt gut microbes. To maintain a good balance of healthy flora, these foods should be avoided as much as possible. More and more people are now taking prebiotic and probiotic supplements to help improve their gut health. To ensure a healthy population of intestinal bacteria, the following five actions will be very helpful: 1. Eat a wide range of whole, plant-based foods ; 2. Include more fibre in your diet; 3. Avoid highly processed food; 4.Consume more probiotic and prebiotic foods ; and 5. Take a daily supplement of probiotics. Proactive steps such as these can go a long way toward saving us from many lifestyle diseases.

8.6 Body inflammation, a precursor to many chronic lifestyle diseases, is a key determinant for health .

When we experience pain and see redness and swelling in any part of the body, it means that inflammation is present. We can readily identify inflammation when it's external, but what about when it's internal, inside the body ? When some part of the body is inflamed, it means it's healing itself. It's a mechanism by which white blood cells (WBC) are trying to protect us from infection by foreign bodies such as bacteria and viruses. Like pain, is serves as an important protective mechanism. If there were no pain or inflammation, we would be unaware of the seriousness of the injury or infection. Our body is, in fact, continuously responding to foreign organisms. In other words, inflammation is among the processes by which the immune system recognizes and removes harmful invaders and begins the healing process.

What inflammation occurs, biochemicals are secreted from WBCs into the blood or the swollen/painful part. These chemicals not only protect that body part from bacteria and viruses but also increase blood flow to that area. That's why we see redness there. This protective mechanism also results in pain as nerves are stimulated. There are generally two types of inflammation: acute and chronic. Acute inflammation is a result of tissue damage; chronic inflammation is a slow, long-term inflammation lasting for a prolonged period of several months to years. The extent as well as the effects of chronic inflammation varies with the cause of the injury and the ability of the body to repair and overcome the damage.

Now various studies have established that inflammation of joints, arteries, and internal organs such as the brain and spinal cord is a major impediment to our health. When there is inflammation in internal organs, it means this condition may lead to a major or chronic disease like cancer, obesity, diabetes, coronary heart diseases, and chronic respiratory diseases. These are also referred to as chronic inflammatory diseases, and they are the leading causes of death in the world. The World Health Organization (WHO) ranks these chronic diseases as the greatest threats to our health. Their main symptoms are body pain, fatigue, insomnia, weight gain, gastrointestinal problems such as constipation and acidity, and mental disorders like depression and anxiety.

Worldwide, three out of five people (around 60%) die from chronic inflammatory diseases. These are all lifestyle diseases, having to do with how we live. And what are the main factors that cause chronic inflammation? There are five prime reasons - advanced age, unhealthy food choices, stress and sleep disorders, smoking, and obesity. First, as we age, we become more susceptible to chronic inflammation. Second, poor diet is an extremely common cause. When we consume excess amounts of refined sugar, trans fats, and saturated fats, we become very prone to inflammation. The food most rich in these ingredients lead to diabetes and obesity. Third, stress and sleep disorders are another very common feature of modern society. Stress has become almost a societal epidemic. Stress also leads to sleep apnea and insomnia.

Fourth, smoking is associated with lowering the production of anti-inflammatory chemicals and increasing inflammation throughout the body. In India, approximately 100 million people smoke the highly addictive bidi cigarettes, about 25 million smoke conventional cigarettes and about 10 million smokers die every year. Although there is a decline in the percentage of people smoking in India, a huge number of people still smoke. Lastly, overweight and obesity is another very important factor. This condition is measured by body mass index (BMI). It's a measure that takes into account an adult's weight and height to estimate body fat. Someone with a BMI of 26 to 27 is about 20% overweight, which is generally believed to carry moderate health risks. A BMI of 30 and higher is considered obese. There are many risks attached to this condition. Some studies show that BMI of an individual is directly related to the release of pro-inflammatory chemicals.

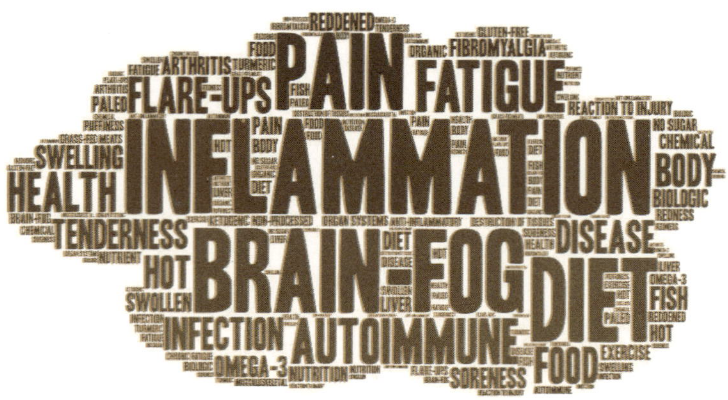

Figure 8.6: Body inflammation is the first sign of majority of the life style diseases. It's a vital determinant of health.

We are living in an era where more people are dying from obesity than from hunger. In fact, most of the world's population live in countries where overweight and obesity kills more people than underweight. Unhealthy lifestyle is one of the biggest challenges we are facing globally. Unhealthy diet, lack of exercise/sedentary lifestyle, environmental pollution, and lack of adequate sleep are the main culprits. In India, air population is another big challenge in most urban areas. Although more and more people are engaging in regular physical exercise, including morning walk, mental exercises like mindfulness meditation has still not become popular. Indian food is, in general, not very healthy. We use a great deal of sugar, spices, saturated and trans fat. Stress is also taking the shape of widespread sickness. The atmosphere in most workplaces is stressful.

The last but most important fact about inflammation is that while most people who suffer from these chronic inflammatory diseases take medicines and use other therapies to cure or contain them, they generally will not – or cannot – recognize the underlying cause of their diseases -- i.e., body inflammation. Most will readily take meds for their problems, but few will look into the causes behind internal inflammatory conditions. Coupled with mindfulness, an attempt to simplify and streamline working and living conditions would go a long way toward a happier and healthier society.

OOO

9

Transform Life by Learning to Manage Our Thoughts

It's well said that we ourselves are the sole creators of "heaven" and "hell" during our lifetime. These are not the imaginary places where we go after death. We create and experience the conditions ourselves. Our life can be hellish or as enjoyable as heaven, depending on how we manage our mind. Mind can be the best master or the worst servant. Outer reality is nothing but the reflection of our inner world. If we are happy and content, the outer world is full of joy and happiness. On the other hand, if the mind is depressed, sad, or distressed, then the outer reality is hostile. People out there are perceived as unfriendly, having the feeling of animosity toward us. The world "out there" is a human construct. We construct and perceive images and models of reality inside our mind. Our beliefs about the world around us, based upon our personal conditioning, feelings, emotions, and state of mind, all determine the reality we create inside our mind. There is no objective or "true" reality out there.

As we have seen in an earlier chapter, there are certain inherent characteristic features of mind such as automatic generation of thoughts, mind-wandering (when we don't focus our attention on anything), negativity bias, and cognitive biases. There are extremely powerful levels -- the subconscious and unconscious mind -- behind our conscious mind. The conscious part of mind is like the tip of an iceberg. In fact, a far stronger mind (nearly half a million times more powerful) works incessantly, and we are not even aware of it. Therefore, it's not easy for us to manage our thoughts. Negative thoughts are especially "sticky" and difficult to oust once they intrude into our head. As they become conscious, we unintentionally pay attention to them. Entertaining them, they increase in intensity and frequency, fuelling a "living hell." If we don't pay any attention to those thoughts, obviously they will leave our mind in little time.

Whether we worry and fret about something or are fearful and anxious, those repetitive and negative thoughts are reluctant to leave our head. Too often, our inner voice/ critic will keep on repeating self-critical thoughts. When we experience continuous bombardment of negative thoughts, unless we control them, they can potentially lead to mental illnesses. Mental illnesses like depression, anxiety, or attention deficit disorder invariably start with our inability to manage toxic and distressing thoughts. Then a time comes when those thoughts become uncontrollable. Even when we divert our attention or try to suppress them, they keep on disturbing us. In this chapter, an attempt is made to explain how we can manage thoughts when we face challenging situations. Negative thoughts are among the biggest obstacles we face on our life's journey.

9.1 "Whatever is going to happen will happen, whether we worry or not." How do we stop worrying and ruminating?

We all worry for one reason or another. Worrying is an inherent tendency of our mind as well as a constant problem with us. Worry refers to the thoughts and emotions of a negative nature, with fearful anticipation of poor outcomes. Most of us do have a number of concerns to worry about. As an emotion, it is experienced as anxiety or concern about a real or imagined fear or threat, often on personal matters such as health or workplace tensions. Most of us experience short-lived episodes of worry from time to time in our lives. Our brains are wired to worry first and think rationally later. It often becomes an automatic response to any perception of threat. Many of us will worry about virtually anything.

To a certain extent, worrying has positive effects because it prompts us to take precautionary measures or avoid risky behaviour. However, worrying often leads to distressing, negative, and often obsessive thoughts. Whenever there is a perception of danger, real or imagined, our mind keeps on deliberating and analysing until it's overburdened with negative thoughts. There will always be some imaginary or real perception of threat involved in our everyday life. And the more we focus on the issue giving us worry, the more we attract the same in one form or another. The mind tends to create worst-case scenarios based on any imaginary fear. *Unless we realise that worrying is a waste of time and energy and has deleterious effects on our health, we cannot fight against the mind's inclination to worry.*

Figure 9.1: ***Worrying is a total waste of time and mental energy – mostly we worry on things which eventually don't happen.***

Indeed, a number of studies have shown that worry not only puts strain on our mental health, but also on our physical health. Worrying in itself is not bad as long as it's controlled. It prods us to prepare better for a possibly difficult event or circumstance. But this is at the cost of our happiness. Very often, when our worrying won't quit, we experience difficulty in getting sleep, In the long run, worrying leads to many health-related issues. It even weakens our immune system. The problem with worrying is that it becomes a cycle of self-perpetuating negative thoughts. As we continue to worry, there is a steady flow of negative thoughts which we keep on repeating, with distressing variations, s until it becomes uncontrollable.

There is a famous saying that "whatever is going to happen will happen, whether we worry or not." Most of the time, it's merely a waste of time and mental energy. Fear of something tangible, or of the unknown with its attendant anxiety, are normal aspects of life. As long as our worries are limited and well managed, there is no problem. However, when we hold on to the same negative thoughts and fears, we fall into a vicious cycle. We invariably generate streams of associated thoughts. The scope of worry is thus enlarged.

All possible scenarios relating to the troubling subject run rampant through our mind.

The more we try to suppress those negative and toxic thoughts, the harder they become to control, Often we try to divert our mind to other activities, such as watching a movie, engaging in conversation with friends, or playing some game, etc., but that is of no help. Diversion of thoughts doesn't help in addressing the worrisome issue. Usually, the more we try to suppress negative thoughts, the more frequently those thoughts resurface. Absent the art of managing our worries, we then start worrying about worrying itself!

Helpful ways to manage or overcome worry are often suggested by psychologists, clergy, and writers of spiritual books. However, I am highlighting only two of the most effective of these methods. Probably the best strategy to stop worry and rumination is the one based in mindfulness, which involves non-judgmental awareness of present thoughts and emotions. We can reduce the frequency of episodes as well as their severity through mindfulness. We should remind ourselves of how many times in the past our fear was imaginary or unfounded. This will surely help in understanding the cause of fear in the case at hand.

One must stop periodically during the day for a few minutes and watch carefully how thoughts that generate worry are creating anxious feelings. Mere awareness of those thoughts and feelings can have profound effects on their intensity. *Negativity will decrease as we become more aware of what exactly is troubling us.*

The second effective method to stop worrying is to accept the situation as it is, and then move on. Worrying about worrying is also a dangerous trap. A 2005 study in the journal *Behaviour Research and Therapy* showed that people who naturally try to suppress their unwanted thoughts end up being more distressed by those thoughts. Under many circumstances, the strategy of acceptance is a far better tool to stop worrying.

When worrying becomes a common or even uncontrollable companion, patients are treated with cognitive behavioral therapy (CBT). It is a type of treatment that helps patients understands the thoughts and feelings that influence their behaviours. CBT is commonly used to treat a wide range of disorders, including depression and anxiety. The underlying concept behind CBT is that our thoughts and feelings play a crucial role in our behaviour. For example, let's say a person is worrying all the time about some irrational belief. Before delivering a speech to a small gathering, he is thinking/worrying that he is a worthless person and that people don't like him.

Quite often, worry is based on such obviously false beliefs. The essence of CBT is to help patients learn to change their emotions by changing their thoughts. There are several other tools to handle worrying. However, the most effective method is the practice of mindfulness, to improve one's self-awareness and make a habit of observing circumstances in a non-judgmental way. Mindfulness is discussed in greater detail in separate chapter of the book.

9.2 How to break the vicious cycle of continuous flow of distressing thoughts, the problem of overthinking?

Sit comfortably and close your eyes. Try to observe your breathing – the inhaling and exhaling. If your attention is distracted to some other thoughts or disturbance, bring your attention back to breathing. See how long you can comfortably observe your breathing. In most cases, you will get perturbed by the inflow of random thoughts. You can't sit comfortably and do this mental exercise. Some can't even close their eyes for two minutes. Why? The reason is overthinking, the flow of thoughts so forceful and continuous that the mind cannot relax for even two minutes. There is total identification of "I" with the thoughts. Such a situation is called "overthinking." The mind will not be quiet.

When we think too much, instead of actually doing what we would like to do, we merely think. It is just wastage of time and energy, and puts us in a vicious cycle of thinking and thinking over and over again. We can't be happy for very long in such a situation. It is the overthinking mind that makes us feel anxious and worried about the future. We also tend to ruminate on any past incident. For example, why did I make such a silly comment out of turn at that meeting? I could've avoided the embarrassment. Second, we worry about the future: something bad is going to happen. For instance, I will not be able to make a speech due to my language problem. All of my senior executives will be gathered at this event, and they'll surely notice.

This is how most of us, at some time or another, overthink. No one can escape from this mental characteristic. *As most of us are completely identified with our mind, we don't know when we overthink.* When we do, it's the stream of harmful and distressing thoughts that fill our mind. We hardly overthink on positive matters. We only ruminate or worry when we are trapped in unpleasant thoughts.

No one is perfect. Each one of us has some deficiency or other imperfection in their personality, behaviour, physical looks, and other attributes. Yet most of us give a great deal of attention to such real or imagined shortcoming, or any problem we encounter in our routine life. Psychologists have found that overthinking can be detrimental to our performance. Most of our pain comes from how we churn the negativity over and over again in our minds. The anxious brain is hypervigilant; always on the lookout for anything it perceives to be dangerous or worrisome. When we are depressed and anxious, we overthink.

When we keep on overthinking all the time, it invariably leads to a mental disorder such as depression and anxiety. These disorders, in turn, reinforce the overthinking. Under both conditions, we are deeply mired in distressing thoughts. Studies have shown that overthinking leads to serious emotional distress. When people can't escape from this condition, they often resort to unhealthy methods to cope with the problem. Many start abusing alcohol, some start or increase smoking, while others overeat. It becomes extremely difficult to enjoy sound sleep when our mind is disturbed. Studies confirm this, finding that rumination and worry lead to fewer hours of sleep and poorer sleep quality.

Figure 9.2: When we overthink, we keep of repeating the same of thoughts mostly negative and distressing over and over again

A recent UK study of more than 30,000 people showed that focusing on negative events (particularly including rumination and self-blame) can be the biggest predictor of some of today's most common mental health problems. When a negative thought arises in the mind, it has the tendency to attract more associated thoughts. When we think about dynamics that are harmful, fearful, or destructive, we are basically fuelling negative energy which lingers as memory in the brain cells/neurons – thus keeping the cycle going. Whenever the same set of thoughts is triggered, we get ourselves involved in the same loop of overthinking.

We therefore need to allow time to release the negative energy, and for that we must fully face what arises in the mind. This is achieved by a simple but very effective exercise of "relaxed awareness." We are required to watch the mind and observe the feelings in a non-judgmental, nonreactive, and, in a sense, detached way. Just sitting in a relaxed manner and acknowledging whatever arises in the mind is all it takes. After a few moments the negative energy, not given its usual fuel, will begin to dissipate, and we will see the pattern of negative thoughts start to break. As we stay in this space of relaxed awareness, intensity and frequency of negative thought will diminish.

Practicing mindfulness meditation is indeed an effective technique for controlling overthinking. Sages have often noted that the mind is like a monkey. It jumps from one group of thoughts to another, restless and sometimes even uncontrollable. On such occasions, we must exercise greater awareness in our observation of whatever thoughts are arising in consciousness. Once we become aware that such thoughts are disturbing our mind, we are better able to identify the core causes of overthinking. When we do this, from that moment on, the intensity and frequency of distressing thoughts will start to decline.

Most of the time, the main problem is that we are not aware that we are in overthinking mode due to strong identification with our mind. *We fail to realize that it's the mind that overthinks.* We sometimes get trapped in a cycle of negative thinking. Negative and distressing thoughts stick in our head and don't leave easily. Even if we try to divert our attention and busy ourselves with other things, the "stickiness of thoughts" may not allow those thoughts to loosen their grip. We then fall into overthinking mode. We continue repeating the same set of thoughts. Frequency and intensity of those repeated thoughts will not automatically abate. We can, however, break this cycle through awareness. Simple awareness of those recurring thoughts goes a long way toward limiting them. The best way to overcome overthinking is to learn the art of observing, accepting, and then letting our thoughts go. While it may initially seem difficult to practice, we can surely master this technique.

9.3 The best way to handle fear and anxiety is to confront them with a mindful attitude . There is a very interesting Zen story on fear, giving a powerful lesson about how to handle fear. The story goes like this:

"Once there was a young warrior. Her teacher told her that she had to do battle with fear. She didn't want to do that. It seemed too aggressive; it was scary; it seemed unfriendly. But

the teacher said she had to do it and gave her the instructions for the battle. The day arrived. The student warrior stood on one side, and fear stood on the other. The warrior was feeling very small, and fear was looking big and wrathful. They both had their weapons. The young warrior roused herself and went toward fear, prostrated three times, and asked, 'May I have permission to go into battle with you?' Fear said, 'Thank you for showing me so much respect that you ask permission.' Then the young warrior said, 'How can I defeat you?' Fear replied, 'My weapons are that I talk fast, and I get very close to your face. Then you get completely unnerved, and you do whatever I say. If you don't do what I tell you, I have no power. You can listen to me, and you can have respect for me. You can even be convinced by me. But if you don't do what I say, I have no power.' In that way, the student warrior learned how to defeat fear." – *Pema* Chödrön, an American Tibetan Buddhist nun and inspirational author

Fear and anxiety are among the most common and destructive of emotions. They are related and often coincide. Their symptoms may also overlap. The main difference between the two is that fear is a response to any specific threat, such as being at a great height, using an elevator, and traveling by air. The danger, whether real or imagined, is identifiable and feels definite and immediate. On the other hand, anxiety is a diffuse, unpleasant, and vague sense threat, ranging from mild apprehension to impending doom. Often anxiety follows from an unknown or poorly defined threat. Examples include everyday situations, such as having to attend some social function ("social anxiety "), addressing a large gathering, and writing a winsome resume.

Millions of people from all walks of life suffer anxiety disorders. In moderation, anxiety is fine, as it prods us on to work for favourable outcomes, as when we prepare for an interview or study for an exam. But when this feeling becomes acute, it morphs into a mental disorder. When anxiety is constant or overwhelming, worries and fears interfere with our relationships and work. This condition often becomes very acute and debilitating, leading to an anxiety or panic attack, and even to hospitalization. According to a WHO report, approximately 38 million people in India are suffering from anxiety. All across the globe, the prevalence of anxiety is rising sharply.

Generalized fear and anxiety disorders are a big challenge for all of humanity. Fear is deeply embedded in our collective psyche. For the earliest of humans (our primate ancestors) who lived as hunter-gatherers for nearly one hundred thousand generations, life-threatening danger was ever-present. From wild animals and even human predators to merciless weather, frightening living conditions led to the development of the "fear factor." The fear response expresses in a region of the brain called the amygdala, and though our lives are no longer in constant danger, the legacy of the amygdala remains active. Moreover, because we have been living in a relatively modern era for not even one hundred generations, there has not been enough time to evolve into less fearful, reactive humans. For the time being, unless we become more mindful, the tendency to fear and anxiety will remain hard-wired in our brains.

Figure 9.3: Fear from height is very common – the best way to handle fear is to confront it directly.

Overcoming fear and anxiety is an extremely challenging task. Rather than facing and confronting their fear, as in the Zen story above, more and more people are turning to medication to alleviate their symptoms. Fear is mostly imaginary, so we must understand that it's not going to harm us. Trying to gain entry, it will come very close to us, but does not have to touch us. Many try to avoid or escape the feeling of fear, but such avoidance means that fear is controlling our reactions. The trigger point of fear will remain active. If we have a fear of using an elevator, we should slowly and gradually try to use one. Take some close friends and then attempt using it for one level, then maybe more levels the next time. If, however, the fear is a full-blown phobia, medical supervision may be indicated. In any case, if we continue to sidestep our fears, they will only be reinforced further.

If we examine any situation relating to fear and anxiety, we find this message true and inspiring. The most effective way to handle fear and anxiety is to inculcate mindful attitude. This mind-set or attitude can be developed only through mindful living, which is explained in a separate subchapter. Practicing a mindful attitude allows us to give fear and anxiety close attention. This mind-set will yield a high degree of self-awareness. We must become aware of thoughts, emotions and feelings that are associated with fear and anxiety. When we bring awareness to that which calls our attention, instead of fighting or running away from fear, we can confront and weaken it. We must be willing to accept things as they are, rather than resisting and reacting to them. Gradually, as we practice a mindful attitude, the feeling of fear will disappear.

9.4 The inner voice – we all have an inner critique but we need to handle it carefully

Vinni Tayal, a businessman working in the national capital region (NCR) of India, is driving his car. He is in a hurry to reach his showroom because of some emergency. He is a law-abiding citizen who has never broken any traffic laws. However, on this particular day, he did break the law by running a red light. As luck would have it, he was stopped and asked to produce his driver's license, which, in his haste, he'd left at home. He was, as expected, fined but more importantly, he was delayed by 20 minutes. Right after the officer let him go, Vinni started as internal dialogue, asking himself, "Why did I go through that light?" and "You are a fool! Can't you wait for 30 seconds?" His distressing self-talk went on and on.

In another incident, a woman, Maya Raj, finds herself stuck in a traffic jam, getting late for an extremely important meeting. She is criticizing herself, wondering why she has taken a shortcut route knowing fully well of the usual traffic chaos on that route. She too is speaking to herself – harshly. Such incidents are not uncommon in our day-to-day lives.

We all are too familiar with the experience of silently speaking to ourselves. When we do something, stupid, forget to do something very important, or say something inappropriate or out of context, we are likely to follow up with scathing self-criticism. This common phenomenon is what psychologists call the "inner voice," and they have been studying it for a long time. For some, this voice speaks up occasionally. For others, the inner voice comes more frequently. Also known as internal monologue, it is a verbal stream of consciousness – thinking in words. It also refers to the nearly incessant banter one has with oneself. Much of what people consciously describe as "thinking about" may be thought of as an internal monologue, a conversation with oneself.

There is evidence that inner speech/voice and speaking out loud utilise similar brain mechanisms. Since it is a private act, it is difficult to study or conduct research on others. Inner voice is completely natural and healthy. It is a mixture of our positive, negative, and neutral thoughts. This internal dialogue can influence our feelings and behaviour. When our internal voice is negative, harsh, or self-criticizing, we can expect it to exacerbate our stress. In silent self-talk, we are our own judge and jury. *Many times, it amounts to a kind of mental torture.* Most often, the quality of our inner voice is influenced by our parents, friends, and others.

It often happens that we argue with ourselves on contentious issues, analysing them from different angles, evaluating the choices we made or are going to make. Our inner critic encourages us to see the world through a negative filter. The critical inner voice, a concept generated by clinical psychologist and author Robert Firestone, is developed early in life, especially after stressful and traumatic events. According to Dr Firestone's daughter, Dr Lisa Firestone, "*Attachment and early-life experiences have significant impact on our development and our adult relationships. Just as positive childhood experiences lead to confidence ability, and optimism, negative experiences foster low self-esteem, self-destructive behaviours, and pessimism.*" The critical inner voice is usually comprised of a stream of destructive thoughts toward ourselves and others.

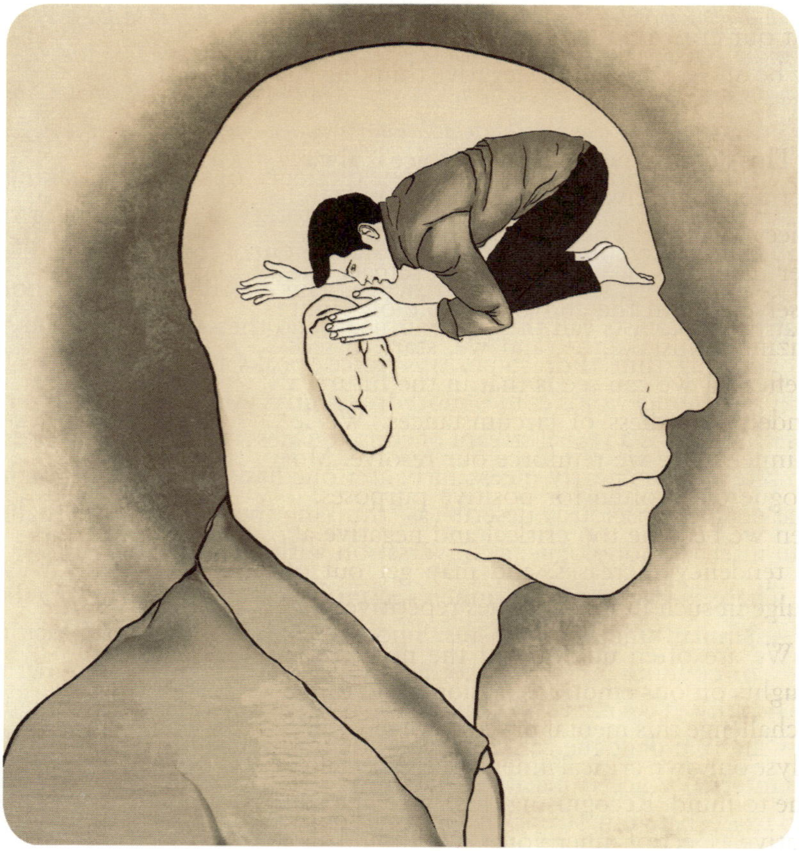

***Figure 9.4:* We often speak and argue to ourselves on contentious issues, the inner critique voice.**

Dr Firestone (Lisa's dad) further explains that *"Destructive thought processes influence us to make decisions that are against our interests and to take actions that negatively impact our lives. Unfortunately, our critical inner voice is so well integrated into our thinking that it not only affects how we act, but also how we are treated by others. If we shut ourselves up and refuse to be social, people may perceive us as timid or unfriendly. These actions not only influence us, but help shape our relationships."*

Our inner voice not only includes negative thoughts but also our beliefs and attitudes that affect our self-esteem. It sometimes encourages and strongly promotes self-defeating and self-destructive behaviours. This judgmental advisor also warns us about other people, facilitates cynical attitudes toward others, and is likely to paint a negative picture of the world. *Although most of us are aware of the machinations of this inner voice, many of our negative thoughts exist on an unconscious level.* At times, we may recognise what our critical inner voice is telling us, while on other occasions; we may be unclear about our negative thinking and simply accept it as being true.

This doesn't mean the inner voice is always negative in the sense that we criticize ourselves or passes judgments on the decisions, behaviour, or choices we make. There is a positive side to the inner voice too. Through inner dialogues, we analyse and evaluate the situation by speaking to ourselves. As in the above example of Vinni Tayal, immediately after realizing a mistake, he, and we, start to scold ourselves. The obvious benefit that we can see is that in the future, we will not recommit our blunder, regardless of circumstances. We learn lessons, and through the inner voice we reinforce our resolve. Most people do invoke inner dialogue quite often for positive purposes. The problem, however, is when we become too critical and negative about ourselves. Sometimes this tendency increases, and may get out of hand if we continue to indulge in such inner dialogues repetitively.

We are often unaware of the negative impact of such destructive thoughts on our emotions, actions, and the overall quality of our lives. To challenge this mental process, we have all the power to recognise and analyse our own critical inner voice, especially when destructive thoughts come to mind. Recognising this voice helps us to trace the origin of the negative aspect of inner voice. We should also learn to discern how and when these voices are triggered, and resist the temptation to get caught in a stream of negative thoughts.

Whenever we are caught by the critical voice, we should immediately become aware. Awareness is prerequisite to handling any problem. Once we're fully aware of a situation, dilution of the negative voice will begin. Weakening of those thoughts will automatically begin. Increased awareness will refine and broaden our sense of self, outshining this internal critic. The better we know ourselves, the better able we are to make conscious choices and decisions about our lives. We can reshape our self-perception and understand who we really are and what we really want in our lives.

OOO

10

Transform Life's Journey through Inner Governance

The ancient Greek motto "Know thyself" (often wrongly attributed to Socrates, who was merely elaborating on the idea) is an invitation to go within oneself, where all knowledge and wisdom lie. Socrates (469-399 B.C.) was a classical Greek philosopher known as one of the founders of Western philosophy. He is perhaps best known for his dictum: "The unexamined life is not worth living." In a world driven by material goods, comforts, glamour and social media, we may believe we no time to look inside. After all, we are busy people! If we ask ourselves if we truly know ourselves, our automatic response is likely to be a fully confident "Yes!" But is that really so?

The truth is that most of us do *not* know ourselves. Do we know the darker, or "shadow side" of ourselves? Everyone is aware of their positive side, sometimes even considering themselves better than others. (That belief proving, of course, that they are not better). Most of the time we do not try to go deeper, to understand the inners workings of our mind. We are largely ignorant. We do, however, strive mightily to gain knowledge about others and the outside world. Since early childhood we have been taught to be like that. There has seldom or never been any focus, at any stage, on self-knowledge, which, as Socrates knew, matters most in life. Through knowing ourselves, we are guided toward greater happiness, inner peace, and satisfaction. We can manage our thoughts and emotions with greater clarity and ease. Eventually, we come to see that the outside world that we perceive and interact with is merely a reflection of our own inner world, the mind.

Self-knowledge' – knowing oneself -- begins with self-inquiry. "Who am I?" would ideally be the first question that arises within us. With this comes the closely associated question, "What is the purpose and meaning of life?" Once we start deliberating on these questions, many related issues will arise, and the inward journey begins. We start seeing beyond the physical world we continuously experience. For instance, we are, most of the time, completely identified with our mind. We don't find any difference between "I" and the thoughts that come and go all the time. If we close our eyes and observe the mind carefully, we find space between the thoughts. As we spend more and more time observing our own mind and the thought process, we become increasingly self-aware. As self-awareness grows, managing the mind becomes easier. Likewise, we find ourselves paying attention to our own sensations and emotions, enabling us to be far more clear and intentional in our thoughts, words, and actions.

Ramana Maharshi (879-1950), an Indian sage and a proponent of Advaita Vedanta, advocated self-inquiry as a path to self-realization. As we know, most of time our thoughts revolve around "I," "me," and "my." For him, self-inquiry is constant attention to the inner awareness of "I am." This is the most efficient and direct way of discovering the unreality of the "I" thought. Ramana taught that identification with the "I" will disappear, leaving only self-awareness. The result is an "effortless awareness of being "commensurate with the decrease in" I thought.

The time will eventually come, according to Ramana Maharshi, when the thought of "I" never returns. This is what is known as Self-realization or liberation. The only way to make the mind cease its outward orientation is to turn inward. Initially, this seems difficult, but with experience, less effort is needed as the mind is drawn to the peace that comes from focusing on Inner Self. The more that the attention is directed inward, the more we realize our true nature and the better and more alive we feel.

In our contemporary world, huge emphasis is placed on physique, beauty, and overall appearance. Many people, therefore, love to spend their money, energy, and time on improving their looks. No doubt, physical health and a pleasant and approachable physical presentation are very important, but while pursuing this goal, some of us neglect other far more important aspects relating to our mind and its health.

Mental health can be strengthened by any strenuous physical exercise such as sports, aerobics, and dance. For mental exercises, the most tonic are meditation and mindfulness. In the recent past, thousands of research papers have confirmed the transformational changes that come with meditation. Even aging can be slowed to a great extent by the stress-reducing practice of meditation. People become happier and more peaceful when they meditate.

Meditation may best be described as a practice that leads us on an inward journey to greater awareness. When we meditate, we observe our mind and the incessant stream of thoughts that pass through it like clouds in the sky. We become serene and quiet. Even under challenging and tough circumstances, meditation gives us the clarity and resilience to overcome. If we are at peace with our mind and can allow our thoughts to come and go. Well, then we can surely become enlightened. As self-awareness grows, we become more mindful. Not only do we start knowing ourselves more deeply and intimately, but we also realize healthy self-love. Love, compassion, and empathy toward others increase apace. Life as a whole becomes more meaningful as our inner journey becomes deeper. Ultimately, this is what we all need most -- a meaningful and purposeful existence.

10.1 We need to listen to our Inner Self or the Soul as it guides us, especially through difficult phases of life.

Existence of Inner Self or Soul has long been a point of philosophical discussion, perhaps even in pre-historic times. In the absence of any scientific evidence, there has been merely speculation, like when we think about "life after life." Many say there is nothing even faintly like an inner self or soul; it's just a product of our imagination. In Hinduism there is a widespread belief in the Law of Karma, which says whatever happens to any person is the result of his/her past and present thoughts, words, and deeds. Birth after birth and death after death, the cycle of cause and effect continues. The theory of reincarnation and the Law of Karma both need the existence of a discrete soul. It's also believed that we generally miss its presence as we all are completely preoccupied in the material world. However, some scientists and thinkers feel that consciousness never dies, it can't be destroyed. So after death, the consciousness of a person will ascend to another realm. Concrete evidence is still awaited.

On the other hand, Inner Self or inner mind are terms we commonly use in a figurative sense. It's our true nature. We often make statements like "Listen to your inner self," or "Go within, to the deeper layers of your self," and "Journey inward if you want to know the real meaning of life." Most of us are not sure about the difference between mind and inner mind or self and Inner Self. Though we commonly refer to conflict between the Inner Self and the outer self, we usually add that we need to balance our outer self with our Inner Self. We see this balance as the prerequisite for both physical and mental health. We acknowledge the Inner Self as the main driving force in our life. It is, in fact, the source of our emotions, thoughts, decisions, perceptions, and choices.

If we observe our mind closely, we realise that it operates at two levels; hence, there are two entities within our head. On the outer level, we have what Buddha called the monkey mind or the thinking mind. It's an ego-driven mind. It is mostly restless, dissatisfied, indecisive, and busy as can be ("busy as a bee") in resolving conflicts, whether small or large, and immersed in thoughts relating to I, Me, and Mine. Then we find we have a deeper layer of mind that is the "observing mind," or inner mind. Suppose we are disturbed and experience a stream of negative thoughts pouring into our thinking mind. Sometimes we notice this clearly, calmly acknowledging, "Oh! I am disturbed by such and such." It means there is a part of mind that's observing the thinking mind, if we pay attention to it. However, the problem is that our thinking mind is usually so busy (and loud) in processing fast-changing data from the surrounding world that we overlook our inner mind, the observing/witnessing mind.

The thinking mind/ego-driven self and the Inner Self operate simultaneously and parallel in the mind. As we are totally identified with the thoughts that are appearing and disappearing in our consciousness, our whole spectrum of mental space is engaged. We hardly notice and involve our Inner Self. When the thinking mind dominates, we spend most of our time only partially aware of our surroundings. In those moments we are hardly aware of the Inner Self. Emotions, thoughts, and our selfhood intermingle, with no separation between them. On the other hand, our Inner Self is above and beyond personal identity, the ego aspect of "me." Inner Self is thought to be connected to the Divine Presence and Power, the Source, God (or whatever Supreme Being we choose to believe in). Our inner self is rooted in love. Choices made from this part of the mind are always in our best interest, and for the good of everyone around us.

In psychology, the process of introspection relies exclusively on observation of one's mental state, while in a spiritual context, it refers to the examination of one's Inner Self. It is closely related to self-reflection. Journeying inward, we can learn about our thinking and behaviour patterns through the Inner Self/observing mind. Becoming the conscious observer of this inner voice can be a game changer. So the greatest gift we can give to ourselves is the growing sense of self-awareness. The realization that there is an observer of the incessant chatter in our mind can be the liberating and empowering discovery of our life. By doing so, we get to observe the mind and its thoughts, that are coming in and out of our awareness. Self-observation can also help free ourselves from habitual behaviour and hard conditioning that so often impede our progress.

During difficult periods of life, it's only the Inner Self that can truly help us. It's our inner voice, from our heart, and not from the egoic mind. Our Inner Self is always in sync with our best interests. Since most of the time we don't hear our inner voice due to the cacophony of the materialistic world, there is no one to guide us. People often advise their disturbed friends to "Listen to your own inner voice." Many of us can recall at least one occasion during our lifetime when we were about to commit some big mistake, but were impelled to resist by the Inner Self. Fred Alan Wolf, an American theoretical physicist and world-renowned spiritual writer, said that "Humanity needs to listen until such time as the voice of inner self or the soul is heard throughout the universe as the only voice of love and compassion that has ever existed."

10.2 The Focused Purpose - without meaningful purpose, life is like a ship drifting wildly in the sea

We all tend to live in our own area of comfort and ease. Most of us get habituated to a routine and repetitive life. Every day during waking hours we keep on performing monotonous and repetitive tasks. Hundreds of times a day, we engage in behaviours that require little or no focused concentration on our parts. In the beginning, those tasks required our attention to learn them, but once we memorised them and became skilled, we ceased to pay attention. Things are now done on autopilot mode. We live our lives on a day-to-day basis, nothing new to do. When asked, most cannot recall the last time they did something new or original.

Figure 10.2: Purposeless and directionless life is like a ship in a wild sea

The biggest challenge before the majority of the population is to create some sort of purpose beyond their routine and repetitive life. Before we identify purpose and start working on same, we need to come out from our comfort zone. Until we step back from our complacency, we can't design our destiny. Effort is needed to so much as think of embracing change in our routine and easy going lives. For example, one man I know has been working for years as a manager in a public-sector bank near his home. Having received a promotion, he is required to get transferred to another city, which is 500 km away. To fulfil his long-standing destiny of becoming a general manager in that bank, he has a tough choice. He is required to go to another city and get settled there. He has, like many others in a similar situation, passed on his promotion and chosen to stay on the same job. He was not willing to come out from that comfort zone. He is happy in his own world of comforts.

To come out from our comfort zone is always a big challenge, primarily due to familiarity and sense of security and certainty. We feel emotionally secure while continuing to stay in that zone. We also have a fear of uncertainty. We are not sure what will happen when we leave that part of life. We are bound to feel some sort of anxiety for the future. Like the bank manager, uncertainty about a new job and its location prevents many from embracing the new and unknown. The very thing that's required to fulfil destiny is the willingness to embrace change that may or may not be pleasant. To design destiny, we should now identify the purpose required to fulfil it.

Life is the outcome of a series of actions and decisions we continue to make throughout our lifetime. In the normal course of a day, we're generally unaware that even a small decision can have wider implications in the future. A seemingly inadvertent action may lead us to altogether new territory. And just as likely, large decisions can take us nowhere. They may eventually prove counterproductive, or result in a fiasco. Despite that uncertainty, we all desire and work for a better future. We make plans for the future. Without purpose, we simply can't design our destiny. Those of us who identify their purpose and then work in that direction are already in the act of fulfilling that purpose or intent. Identifying our purpose and then working out the details to fulfilling it are prerequisite for the design of destiny. So the key in life is to identify purpose and to work on it so that your destiny will be in alignment with your purpose.

In the words of Thomas Carlyle, "A man without a goal is like a ship without a rudder." Drifting with the wind, no wind is favorable. *A purpose in our mind and the destination we intend to reach are two sides of the same coin.* Most of us, however, live our lives, most of the time, without any specific purpose. Many live a monotonous, repetitive, and addictive life – the life of "quiet desperation" identified by Thoreau. Following the same kind of routine is the pattern of their life. Life takes them where it wants to be, rather than they taking it where *they* wish to be. Given that this is so, how can these people design their destiny? If we have purpose, then our decisions, actions, and behavior can be targeted in that direction; otherwise, our journey is aimless drifting. Therefore, what we must do for a better future is to create a purpose, both short term as well as long term. Then we strive in that direction.

Figure 10.2A: A purpose in mind and the destination we intend to reach are two sides of the same coin.

The destiny is a future outcome of an event in our life. If we aim for any specific destination and then achieve that outcome, we succeed in designing our destiny. Otherwise, the destiny is an outcome of random events that continue to happen in the routine course of life. Choice is solely ours, and purpose is the intent. It can be for the benefit of any person, people, or thing. When we don't fulfil our intent, we fail to reach a destination or destiny we desire. So the desired result or outcome is our aim in both cases -- i.e., for fulfilling our purpose as well as our destiny. Purpose is intent while destiny is the destination that we intend to reach. Fulfilling our destiny means to achieve the desired purpose. Hence, the first thing we need to do is chart the course for fulfilling our destiny, the intended destination in the future. Then have a specific purpose that will inspire us along that path.

To achieve our purpose, we need to stay in focus until we achieve it. We can otherwise get distracted and sidetracked in other directions. We may be frustrated and discouraged by failures, setbacks, or delays. This is very common in our experiences. We enthusiastically start something afresh but abandon it along the way. We are mostly impatient as we await results without realizing that success often comes with a hefty dose of frustration, failure, or delays. As we start out, our purpose must be accompanied by a focused attention. All related decisions, choices, and actions along the way must be focused. Focused attention is prerequisite to designing our destiny.

Focus is required not only for actions and decisions that we make in pursuit of our purpose, but also to exclude undesired and unnecessary thoughts and actions. We need to check the distractions that are part and parcel of our everyday lives, noticing when they prevent us from being focused or attentive to the task at hand. Distractions come from both external as well as internal sources. *To stay focused in a world full of distractions is becoming one of our biggest challenges, especially for the younger generation in the modern world.* To remain focused or attentive is not an easy task. Our mind has an inherent tendency to wander whenever we are not making an effort to be attentive.

Mind-wandering seems to be the human brain's default mode of operation. The mind reverts to wandering mode unless it is engaged in some interesting or absorbing activity. When we drive, read, listen to elevator music, or engage in a boring conversation, our mind invariably wanders. When this happens, multiple thoughts float through our working memory, which is short-term memory used for temporarily storing and manipulating memory in an active, readily available state. The mind is actually focusing on open goals and unfulfilled intentions, which are generally numerous at any given point in time. According to researchers, people typically spend nearly half of their waking hours thinking about something other than what they are doing. Now the bigger question arises, which is how to address the issue of "monkey mind," and the distractions that claim it. These problems limit our efforts to identify and pursue destiny.

The reason so many people don't discover their purpose or realize their full potential is that they are constantly being distracted from their purpose. We don't concentrate and plan for the future in a focused manner. Besides, we also doubt about our ability to achieve what we desire. These doubts weaken our will power and determination required for focusing on the purpose for longer time. Presently when we are increasingly using digital technologies, the scope and extent of distraction is rising sharply. As a result attention span is gradually reducing. Therefore, we need to work harder for becoming more focused and attentive towards our targeted purpose. The solution lies in mindful living. .

10.3 Mindful Living We can overcome hindrances to our holistic growth through "mindful living."

Venketesh, a senior executive in central public-sector enterprise, is usually highly stressed while at work. He is impulsive and short-tempered. No one likes him because of his inconsiderate behaviour. He is diabetic and suffers other related health issues. One day while driving his car, he met with an accident because of his carelessness. He was deeply absorbed in his office problems. His relationship with his wife and daughter had also been deteriorating by the day. He was therefore losing control over his internal as well as external world. There are millions of stressed people like Venketesh. Because they lack the self-insight born of mindfulness, they can't manage their work, relationships, and personal life.

People with better control over their internal and external affairs can succeed more easily in determining their future outcomes and, in turn, their destiny. We can have great control over our career, social relationships, and lifestyle. We may not always have choice in selecting our career or job, but how we work in any organisation or cooperative setting depends largely on us. Nor do we usually have any choice in selecting our boss or workplace, but how we handle our boss (or bosses) depends solely on us. We may feel stuck in certain circumstances because of others, but how we react and respond to those conditions depends entirely on us.

After giving it some thought, most of us can recognize that the root of all our problems lies within the mind. Whether the problems are because of behaviour, relationships, poor health, or mental disorders, somewhere the cause lies within our mind. Most are ignorant or uneducated about the workings of their own mind. Since we are completely identified with our thoughts, we fail to see our mind as a separate entity. Unfortunately, this mind will generally not allow us to go deeper and explore its inner workings. It convinces us to stay in the comfort zone, discouraging us from venturing out to seek new opportunities and realizations. It resists change whenever such ideas come up.

The solution to many of the problems, if not all, relating to mind lies in being mindful and fully aware of what's happening in our surrounding environment. When we are mindful, we pay attention to the present moment. We act nonjudgmentally and in an open manner. We can't be in a state of mindlessness or impulsiveness if we are fully present in every moment. When we are mindful, we can observe our thoughts and feelings from an objective distance, without judging them.

Mindfulness and awareness are the foundations of mindful living. Both are crucial to greater control over the mind. Awareness is the state of being fully awake and aware. It's the understanding of what is happening, or what exists. We should try to calmly understand the nature, quality, and extent of any problem that comes our way, or is found inside of ourselves.

Figure 10.3: "Meaningful life - we all need to have some meaningful purpose beyond our own 'Self'

I People with a high level of self-awareness know themselves in depth -- their weaknesses and strengths, what motivates them and how they handle their emotions. Their self-awareness goes a long way toward directing their life in the desired direction. Such people are especially good at availing themselves of opportunities at the most opportune times. They have the ability to perceive, feel, and be conscious of the thoughts and feelings of themselves and others. Self-awareness provides the capability to look deeply into the mind.

Once we start living mindfully, we become increasingly aware of what is going on around us all the time. This is called meta-awareness, to be aware of awareness. When we are stressed or emotionally disturbed, we are able to regain equilibrium much faster if we live mindfully. In other words, we recover faster from virtually any disturbance. When we suffer from anxiety, stress, negative or depressing thoughts, the amygdala, our brain's integrative emotional centre, is especially active. When we practice mindfulness, the amygdala, in those moments, resumes normal function much faster. People become far more affectionate, kind, and empathetic in their relationships once they start living mindfully.

In order to exercise greater control, both internally and externally, we need to live mindfully. Attentive and focused on whatever is happening outside of us; it follows that we will act as the situation demands. In the "normal" course of events, we think and act from our habituated and conditioned mind. In the corporate world, mindful executives are capable of focusing more readily on pressing issues adapting to challenging situations, and seeing from a broader perspective. Mindful leaders of big organizations are most often attuned to the emotions and feelings of their subordinates. They are more compassionate and empathetic toward their workforce. In this way, mindful executives are more committed to happiness and the overall well-being of the organization.

We all travel a slippery slope and are susceptible to falls, even when we take all the care and precautions required. Those who prepare themselves well for such unforeseen events can pick themselves up quickly and rise to any challenge. *The greater the control exercised over mind and body, the faster we recover from such falls; the more self-aware and conscious we are the faster is the recovery.* The deep acceptance inherent to self-awareness smooths our transition to normalcy. Although we have little to no control over what happens due to outside forces/events, fast and quick recovery from difficulties is in our own power. We have the inbuilt resources to reshape our circumstances, leading to the destination we desire.

To be successful -- whether we are studying at any level or working in the private or governmental sector or as a househusband or housewife -- we need to be mindful of all that we do. We can be focused and attentive to our goals only when we are mindful. Other people can be directed and encouraged in a more effective manner when we respond mindfully. Overall, our chances of achieving what we intend or desire increase when we think and act mindfully. We become more loving and compassionate with others. Mindful living can act as a catalyst in designing our destiny. We can enjoy richer experiences with mindful living. Several time-tested recommendations as to how to live mindfully are discussed separately in relevant chapters.

10.4 Through the practice of mindfulness-based meditation, we can bring about transformative changes in our physical and mental life.

Meditation is currently one of the most powerful wellness trends in the world. It's growing exponentially across many nations, including the USA and India. Since the benefits of meditation have been validated by scientific studies across the globe, very large numbers of people are turning to it in droves. Meditation along with yoga, two ancient practices, is now officially the most popular alternative health practice in the United States. According to the survey conducted in 2017, nearly 14.2% people practiced meditation as contrast to just 4% in 2012. The corresponding figures of Indians practicing various forms of meditation are not available. Meditation is thriving, and has become a billion-dollar industry in US.

People are now realizing that mindfulness meditation is the best tool to train their minds. Meditation studios, brands, and apps are popping up worldwide. Along with a healthy diet and exercise, meditation is being recognised as one of the three pillars of well-being. As the way the mindfulness meditation grows ever more popular, a solid backing of research studies conducted worldwide keeps pace. Otherwise, this practice would not have spread so rapidly. Today there are more than 4,000 research studies, according to US National Library of Medicine, pubmed.com, on the subject. About 25 papers were published each year in the 1990s, whereas over 400 were published in 2016. In fact, many studies of meta-analysis are coming up corroborating the results of various research projects.

A listing of meditation's benefits on both physical and mental health, validated by research studies, would become voluminous. Therefore, only certain critical areas are being touched upon here. When we meditate, we practice moment-to-moment awareness while observing whatever happens around us. It's like any other physical exercise. The result is that our mind gradually becomes more focused and attentive. As we become more aware, our meta-awareness (awareness of awareness) increases. We become nonreactive, responding appropriately to situations as the need arises. We then start observing ourselves from a distance. It's a big positive change that happens when we meditate. We begin to make more conscious choices and decisions because of increased self-awareness and attention to the present moment. Once we begin to live mindfully and are attentive to whatever is happening around us, many pleasant changes in our mind and body start manifesting.

When we are not attentive and focused, our mind is wandering in many directions. Nearly half of the time, we are not concentrating or focusing on the task at hand; it means we are on default mode. At that time, in the brain, the default mode network (DMN) is active. It's a network of interacting brain regions. These areas can be detected easily through functional MRI, due to higher activity in the network. When the brain is at rest, DMN is active. This is in fact the thinking brain. When we practice meditation, our DMN becomes quieter and less active. In other words, our thinking mind is under check. We gradually inculcate the habit of becoming more and more nonreactive and nonjudgmental. This can truly be called "becoming awakened" or, in the words of philosopher Gurdjieff, "waking up." We can experience inner peace and serenity in a stressful world.

Whatever may be our core purpose in life, we all want to live a healthy and happy one for the longest possible time. No one wants to die prematurely. What is happening now is that more people are dying from lifestyle diseases. Research has shown that through regular practice of mindfulness meditation, we can slow down our aging process. According to one estimate, a person of 30 years of age who does regular meditation for the next five years can expect a biological age of 23 at the age of 35 ; his non-meditating counterpart will show, on average, a biological age of 36 years. Such difference in biological age can be observed in real life situations. So for a longer and much healthier life, meditation can be the best and easiest option available. The reason behind slow aging is primarily taking care of mental stress, which most of us experience.

Figure 10.4: We are bring many transformation changes in our physical and mental health through the practice of meditation

The relationship between the slowing down of aging and reduction in psychological stress has been established by researchers. Stress leads to the shortening of telomeres (the protective caps at the tip of chromosomes), which is considered the main marker for aging. In a trailblazing study conducted by scientists Elissa Epel and Elizabeth Blackburn of the University of California, it was found that stressed mothers of seriously ill children had shorter telomeres. Both scientists later got a Nobel Prize for this study. In this way, a direct connection between chronic stress and aging was established. The relationship between mindfulness meditation and mental stress and anxiety has also been confirmed through numerous studies.

With meditation, we have far greater control over our emotions. Meditation prompts changes in the emotion-processing part of the brain, the amygdala. Through this practice, depressing, distressing, and other negative thoughts are under check. We will not be overwhelmed by those thoughts because they will not be able to stay in the brain for very long. Their "stickiness" has gone. When the metaphorical thief finds nothing of value in a house, he will exit that house at his earliest opportunity. Likewise, negative thoughts that are not entertained have no incentive to stay. The resulting sense of peace and well-being pervades in every area of life. Under stressful and unpleasant conditions, regular practitioners can lead a peaceful life. Even when disturbed by upsetting events, they recover very fast, and with greater self-control.

As we have seen, meditation can transform one's life with far more self-awareness, focused attention and clarity. Through these attributes, we can live mindfully. With better control over our inner life, we certainly can live life on our own terms. Clarity and control are also the conditions in which a strong sense of compassion and empathy take root, which can give meaning to our life. Studies have established that through meditation, we can become more compassionate and empathetic toward others. We understand their feelings and point of view with greater clarity and understanding. Living mindfully, with warm feelings of love and compassion, also improves our immune system. Overall mental and physical health improves significantly with regular practice of meditation. Numerous studies have shown remarkable structural and functional changes in the brain of practitioners. The only requirement for beginning meditation is to break the mental inertia and come out from the comfort zone.

10.5 Learn to meditate – simply start observing the present moments

Meditating is an extremely simple mental exercise, but in practice people find it very difficult to continue. What is generally seen is people enthusiastically starting it but quitting after a few sessions or a few days, due to a variety of reasons. Most common is lack of patience and perseverance. During initial sessions, they find it difficult to observe breathing for an expended time. Though gradually, this "observation" becomes more and more easy, students tend to lose patience. Those who succeed in the first few days sit quietly for an uninterrupted 10 to 15 minutes, then they generally start practicing meditation regularly. Moreover, they, in between, start seeing its impact on their mind and body. By following the steps listed, anyone can learn meditation.

One can meditate even while walking, sitting, or lying on the ground, but the most recommended posture is sitting quietly, with spine straight, in peaceful surroundings.

Sit on a cushion on the floor, or on a chair, with a straight and unsupported back. Pay close attention to the movement of the breath. Breathing in, be aware that you are breathing in, and how it feels. Breathing out, be aware that you are breathing out.

Feel the coolness of air going in, and the warmth of the air coming out from the nostrils.

Continue this simple process for the length of your meditation practice, constantly redirecting the attention back to the breath.

Figure 10.5: There are many easy ways to practice mindfulness based meditation.

While we meditate, we are, as to be expected, distracted by surrounding sounds, physical sensations, and the irrepressible arising of thoughts. Whenever this happens, gently recognise that you have been distracted, and bring the attention back to the breathing. Just observe whatever is happening in a non-judgmental manner while observing and watching the breathing.

This is the essence of breathing-based mindfulness meditation.

In Transcendental Meditation, ™ instead of breathing, we pay attention to a mantra. TM is one of the most important and worldwide popular meditation techniques. Introduced way back in 1955 by Maharishi Mahesh Yogi (1918-2008), the technique is again very simple. One has only to inwardly repeat, silently, in the mind, a continuous mantra or word that is pleasing to the mind in order to achieve a restful state. TM gives our mind an inward direction. It helps us to turn the attention within, and once that is accomplished, the mind starts to settle down.

Another very popular meditation in India is Vipassana meditation, which is taught in various centres set up throughout India and abroad by the late S.N. Goenka. In Vipassana, meditators are asked to practice, for the first few days, breathing-based meditation, as explained earlier. After that, they need to observe their thoughts and bodily sensations in a non-judgmental way. This meditation is considered far tougher than TM and mindfulness meditation, but is very effective.

As we have seen, in meditation we are, while sitting quietly and comfortably, present to observe our breath or bodily sensations, or to repeat mantra with closed eyes. The idea is not to do anything intentionally, just experience the present moments. We are not required to react or respond to thoughts arising in our mind, but simply to observe and let them go. Whether we attend to the breath (mindfulness meditation) or mantra (TM) or bodily sensations and thoughts (Vipassana meditation), attention is distracted and our mind automatically goes in a different direction. Better yet, it simply rests. It is very difficult to hold our attention on breath, mantra, or the coming and going of physical sensations and thoughts, continuously for even 20 seconds. Random thoughts are certain to arise. Regardless of the nature of the distraction, we may then gently bring our attention back to the breath or mantra. We keep on repeating this process while meditating. *Focus, un-focus, and then focus again goes on without resistance. When we do this, the mental faculty gets trained and we become more and more focused.* As we become more focused, mind's wandering lessens, and we become happier. .. or less unhappy. This is the simple science behind meditation.

In the same way that we practice mindfulness meditation, we can practice mindfulness in our daily activities – for instance, while eating, walking, and talking. In mindfulness meditation, the idea is to pay attention to whatever is going on in the present moment, simply to be aware of what is happening. If we are speaking, we must pay attention to the words we speak, and attentively listen to what the other person is saying. If we are walking, we should be aware of surrounding sights and sounds, our body movements, such as feet touching the ground, and the flow of the breath.

10.6 Myths and misconceptions surrounding meditation – That's the reason meditation is not getting very popular

Over the past decade, there has been a tremendous growth in mindfulness meditation in many parts of the world, especially in the USA. It has become a billion-dollar industry ($ 1.1 billion in 2017) in America, where the number of meditation practitioners has recently grown from 4% to 15%. Large numbers of CEOs and Fortune 500 companies have introduced it to their employees, primarily to increase productivity and reduce stress levels. Educational institutions as well as hospitals and medical universities have adopted mindfulness in a big way. For pain therapy and stress reduction, this programme has been officially taken up for their patients. More than 1000 apps are currently available for teaching and practicing meditation.

It's clear from the above that meditation has become a widespread movement in the USA. Though the corresponding figures are not available for India, it's certain that a far smaller percentage of Indians are engaged regularly in meditation. Isn't that surprising? Maharishi Mahesh Yogi, way back in 1975, introduced Transcendental Meditation ™ in the USA, making it popular among a large population. India is a land of origin of meditation practice. The oldest documented evidence of meditation practice is found on the Indian subcontinent, from approximately 5,000 to 3,500 BCE, where wall art shows people seated in meditative postures. Many kinds of meditation practices began and developed in India. Unfortunately, the number of meditation practitioners in India has not grown to the extent that many countries are now witnessing.

The reasons why meditation practice is not becoming a widespread movement in India as it is in many other parts of the world are the beliefs and myths that are attached to it. First, people are not convinced in their heart that just sitting silently can stop the movement of thoughts in their mind. Failed meditators the world over conclude after a few minutes (or even days) of effort that it's not possible to disregard their thoughts. They don't realize that to manage one's thoughts requires time and effort. Sitting for just a few minutes will not reduce the flow of thoughts into their mind. Very often, people start learning or practicing meditation when they are mentally stressed or disturbed. At trying times, it's undoubtedly more difficult to practice meditation. *Agitated, our "monkey mind" is far more restless; it requires rigorous efforts to calm it. Many people in sheer frustration discontinue practicing meditation.*

Figure 10.6: There are certain misconceptions among us, which don't let us to practice meditation.

Another related belief that people often harbour is that it takes years to get benefits or desired results from meditation. To the contrary, studies have confirmed that within a few days, people start getting results. Mind starts feeling relaxed. We feel more focused and attentive after even two weeks of practice. When people think it would take months and even years to get desired results, they obviously are hesitant to go for meditation. Time constraint is another excuse people often use to rationalize their reluctance. No doubt we are busy people, even if we actually have plenty of time available for meditation. People don't know how to manage their time effectively. Meditation even improves the skill of time management. Since with meditation, one becomes more focused in all matters, more spare time is freed up for productive use.

More importantly, some people perceive meditation as a practice meant for spiritual people, who have little to no interest in worldly affairs. Especially among older people, this belief is very prevalent. They feel once we start meditating, we will lose interest in our family, relationships, and society at large. They often believe that meditation is meant for people like monks, living at high altitudes, having no interest in the outside world. They are oblivious to the fact that mindfulness-based meditation can be practiced whenever we have time, even while travelling, walking, and simply relaxing. It's not necessary to practice it during the early hours of the day. That notion of practicing meditation at dawn is no longer valid.

Lastly, in India, a variety of meditation practices are currently in vogue. Many spiritual leaders are promoting their own "designer" meditation. Some of them are not mindfulness-based practices. For instance, practitioners may be required to "concentrate" on some object, or even on a point between their eyes (the *tisra til,* or third eye). Unfortunately, there are no studies or research to corroborate the benefits of practicing these newer approaches to meditation. Despite that, hundreds of thousands of followers are regularly meditating along "new & improved" lines. That's why when followers don't observe quick and easy results, they discontinue the practice. In this way, meditation as a whole is discredited. Those who believe they have failed will obviously have second thoughts before they restart meditation.

10.7 Controlled and deep breathing can helps us in managing our mind/body – the art of Pranayama

Breathing is the most natural thing in our life. We breathe on an average 12-15 times in a minute, which translates to about 20,000 times a day. Since it's so natural to breathe, we are often unaware of it. Most of us don't breathe correctly, and it's shallow breathing most of the time. We don't take the full breaths we're capable of, and that can have wide ramifications on our work and well-being. Our intake of oxygen is therefore less than optimal, with most of it not reaching the lower part of our lungs. This is important, because many small blood vessels responsible for carrying oxygen to cells are located in the lowest portion of the lungs. When these areas don't get adequate oxygen, we tire easily and can feel short of breath.

The way we breathe directly affects every organ, system, and function of our body. Our health and well-being depend on it. In fact, breathing is also related to our emotions. When we are angry or stressed or fearful, our breathing is especially shallow. To improve health, happiness, and overall well-being, paying attention to breathing is essential. Breathing exercises work well for relaxation and handling mental stress. Proper deep breathing also increases our self-awareness and ability to concentrate and focus. We become more mindful. Spending as little as 20 minutes a day on deep breathing exercises can bring many positive changes to our overall health.

Figure 10.7: Through controlled and deep breathing, we can improve our immune system and thereby overall health

Most of us have noticed that when we take deep breaths, we feel relaxed. We are also advised to take a few deep breaths when we feel angry. When people say "take a deep breath" at a time of acute stress or anger, it's not merely a cliché but has a sound medical basis. Deep breathing increases the supply of oxygen to our brain and stimulates the parasympathetic nervous system, which promotes relaxation and calmness. Breathing techniques help us feel connected to our body as they remove awareness from any negativity. So the mind gets quiet. The best way to feel relaxed, especially under stressful conditions, is to do breathing exercises. It's a quick and easy remedy also for anxiety. Proper breathing technique acts on anxiety by automatically slowing the heart rate and lowering or stabilizing blood pressure. The effect on anxiety is almost instant.

Most of the time, we breathe shallowly, in a way that limits the diaphragm's range of movement. So the lowest part of the lungs doesn't get the full amount of oxygenated air. That can make us feel short of breath and anxious. By way of deep breathing exercises, oxygen intake increases, causing greater circulation of the blood. Significantly more oxygen reaches the internal organs. *Breathing correctly in a controlled fashion also helps strengthen the immune system, which in turn improves our overall health.* Enhanced too is our capacity to concentrate and be attentive to whatever is at hand. Many lifestyle diseases can be managed and controlled by regular practice of yoga, breathing exercises, and meditation.

The art of controlling and regulating the breath apparently began in prehistoric times, when yogis practiced pranayama to improve their health. In fact, Buddha also advocated breath-centered meditation to realize enlightenment. In our own times, as science started conducting studies on breathing exercises and publishing the results, the art of pranayama started becoming popular. In India, pranayama is a household word and millions of people do yoga along with pranayama in an integrated fashion. Thousands of studies in recent times have established the benefits of practicing pranayama.

Pranayama, most commonly known as the practice of deep breathing, derives from the Sanskrit words *prāna,* meaning breath or life force, and *āyāma*, which means extension or expansion. Yoga masters/gurus describe pranayama as the skill of controlling and regulating the inhalation, exhalation, and retention of breath. During pranayama, the attention of mind is focused on the breathing process. There are many types of pranayama in which inhalation and exhalation are repeated at regular intervals. However, the duration of withholding of breath and the duration of inhalation and exhalation vary from one exercise to another.

Deep breathing also goes by the names of diaphragmatic breathing, abdominal breathing, belly breathing, and paced respiration. When we breathe slowly and deeply, the air coming in through our nose fully fills our lungs, and the lower belly rises. Whether it's called belly breathing, abdominal breathing or diaphragmatic breathing, the idea is simple. When we take a deep breath, the diaphragm moves down to allow the lungs to expand with oxygen. A significantly larger amount of oxygen than is gathered from chest-breathing is then available for delivery to the bloodstream. On the exhale, the diaphragm moves close to the lungs and carbon dioxide is expelled.

There is a pranayama technique called 4-7-8 developed by Harvard-trained physician Andrew Weil. This technique is designed to bring the body into a state of deep relaxation. Here breath is held for a period of time which allows our body to replenish its oxygen. This breathing exercise gives our internal organs and tissues a much-needed oxygen boost. Sitting or lying in a relaxed position, we inhale to the count of 1, 2, 3, and 4 (for four seconds). Then we hold our breath while counting from 1 to 7. The held breath (for seven seconds) is the most critical part of this practice. Finally, we exhale air while counting from 1 to 8. The exercise is repeated for four full breaths. Dr Weil has even described it as a "natural tranquilizer for the nervous system." This exercise is recommended for deep relaxation, sound sleep, and to handle stress and anxiety. It is said to be as good as practicing mindfulness meditation.

10.8 In this world of social media obsession, Learn to avoid FOMO and pursue JOMO.

Technology is reshaping the world in many ways. Within the broad reach of "tech development," numerous revolutions are taking place, affecting our lives in different ways. If we compare our lives with the life we were leading a decade back, it's clear to see that most major aspects have become easier, more comfortable, and more secure. Various gadgets, connected to the Internet, are changing the way we work, communicate, study, exercise, play, and behave. Technology is making a huge impact on our education, health, working environment, medicine, lifestyle, entertainment and travelling. In these unambiguous ways, the world is becoming a friendlier place. But is technology making us happier and more joyful in this digital age? There is no easy answer. It is yes and no at the same time. Potentially, we can become more happy and joyful if we learn to use technology rightly and judiciously, which is to say, for the greater good of all. If not, there is no end to the problems it can cause.

The greatest impact it is having on our lives comes from the virtually unlimited information we are suddenly privy to. Information from the Internet used for entertainment, education, and greater understanding in all areas is transforming our lives. According to one report, "Over 2.5 quintillion bytes of data are created every single day, and it's only going to grow from there. By 2020, it's estimated that for every person on earth, 1.7 MB of data will be created every second." It's a mind-boggling statistic, difficult to grasp. *Of the world's 7.7 billion population,* there are 3.48 billion users of social media in 2019, with the worldwide total growing by 288 million (9 percent) since this time last year. Imagine, WhatsApp users share more than 1 billion videos daily! What a temptation and range of choices we have for those videos and texts on these platforms ! Many of us feel overburdened and conflicted when bombarded by material that is so very difficult to resist. Whatever spare time we earlier had is now going to social media, watching and sharing information in various forms.

Figure 10.8: The joy of missing out (JOMO): while busy on digital screen they are missing out their precious and joyful moments.

When we are busy on digital media, we are intentionally or unintentionally under the spell of FOMO (fear of missing out). We don't want to miss anything, especially the news and presumed fun that our friends are having. There is an obsessive desire to check and see text messages and videos, whenever there is a notification sound. Even when notification is off, a powerful urge still compels many to check their mobile at short intervals. The younger generation, particularly in Western society, is especially vulnerable to this addiction. There is a neurological basis behind this urge. We get addicted to social media by way of dopamine, which is a neurotransmitter, a chemical released by neurons, the nerve cells that send signals to other nerve cells. Dopamine causes us to desire, seek out, search, find, and then seek some more. The neural circuitry driving this process is no different from that which holds slot machine users in their seats, and keeps cocaine users in thrall to their habit. Whenever we post a message on, say, Facebook or Twitter, we seek the reward of "likes," or responses of any kind.

In nutshell, FOMO is real and has become an epidemic because of social media. Unchecked, the dangers of FOMO become apparent. Hours spent on social media can even affect one's mental health. Attention span is reduced from the continuous temptations and rapid-fire pace of digital distractions. We are becoming attention deficient. Because of this obsession with social media, people of all age brackets are suffering from mental disorders like depression and anxiety. The younger generation, especially high school and college students, are the most affected. Researchers are even recommending that social media addiction should be treated as a disease.

Is there an antidote to this digital addiction? Social media is fine, even nurturing, when used in a balanced way. Obviously, it's a rich source of all kinds of valuable information. It can encourage and facilitate meaningful relationships between close friends. We can inform, amuse, motivate and inspire others via our videos or text messages. We can share our moments of adventure, joy and sorrow with close friends. Likewise, we can use social media for the greater good of society by way of fundraisers and service opportunities. However, far too many, on the prowl for "likes," use it mostly to seek attention and instant gratification.

As more and more time is spent on social media, we miss out on real-life interaction and the authentic joy that only it can offer. Caught in a neural feedback loop of reward-seeking, the bright awareness of the present moment is lost. We have Danish psychologist Svend Brinkmann to thank for the term JOMO -- Joy of Missing Out. Brinkmann wrote a book of the same title, *The Joy of Missing Out: The Art of Self-Restraint in an Age of Excess.* Brinkmann argues that the biggest barrier to JOMO is the personal and cultural problem of FOMO. If we want to live a life that is sustainable for both ourselves and the planet, all of us need to learn the art of self-restraint, and limit our desires to "have it all."

The fundamental point that we all need to understand is that true meaning and happiness are to be found in real-time interactions, against which cyber connection is a pale imitation. Suppose a person had a long-held desire to watch a world cup. One fine morning his close friend somehow manages to acquire a few tickets, and then there he is, now watching a real-time game with real flesh-and-blood buddies. The person finds himself experiencing intense elation and happiness throughout the match. He did not plan or text or connives or works for his joy. It was the natural and spontaneous present-moment outcome of his friendships and love of sports.

Our ultimate aim is to enjoy life to the fullest. Quite simply, we enjoy life through experiencing happy and joyful moments. Such feelings can be enjoyed only when we are fully present in those moments.. We need to be intentional with our time. Instead of anxiously responding to FOMO on social media, we must learn to be receptive to experiences that give us, as well as others, the feeling of joy and happiness.

10.9 Avoid the emerging sickness of busyness by learning the art of doing nothing .

Most of us love to be busy. We enjoy being *very* busy, even if it adversely affects our health. Some have no alternative other than to be too busy because it's linked to their livelihood. This is true especially for the economically weaker sector of society. However, for many others, frenetic activity is a sign of success or being rich and famous. How busy one wishes to be in their work and play is generally under their control. Many are overly busy only because of poor time management. They enjoy – or are more often oblivious to -- wasting or mismanaging their time. They want others to perceive them as busy people who are much in demand; they do *not* wish to give the impression of laziness or unimportance. If many people are waiting outside a clinic, people may not be able to see a famous and successful doctor. Of course this is mainly in the context of India. *Oh, I have no time; too busy even to die; I haven't gone on vocation in five years; I don't take leave from my office, are some of the common phrases we often hear from others.*

Figure 10.9: The Art of Doing Nothing, not even in 'thinking mode' - Dutch people earmark certain time to practice it in their busy schedule.

We are living in a highly materialistic world where the yardstick for success measures the wealth we have, the status we've achieved, and the power we enjoy in society. Somehow we take busyness as a positive personal attribute and symbol of leading a good life. It's linked with our personal development and self-worth. Simply being busy is not a problem, but when busyness expresses as chronic stress, it becomes a serious issue. There is a direct relationship between busyness and stress. At a certain threshold, outer busyness is felt inwardly as chronic stress. There is little difference between active life, busy life and stressful life. All overlap.

When we suffer from chronic stress or chronic busyness, many symptoms starts appearing. Under mild conditions, we experience fatigue, irritability, irregular sleep, headache, and disturbances in bowel function. However, when we experience chronic stress, we can potentially suffer from many mental and physical problems, ranging from heart disease and cancer to disorders of the digestive and immune system. The list is exhaustive. Studies have shown that premature or early death is more likely when stress is ongoing. Most of the time, people will not realize that the problems they have started experiencing in their body are due to chronic stress conditions. Suppose someone is gaining weight or having a rise in their sugar level. Chances are that person may be under chronic stress. Unfortunately, doctors tend to prescribe medication for those illnesses rather than advising the person to manage stress.

Managing stress is not an easy thing; it calls for a change in our mind-set. We should first be convinced that excessive busyness is detrimental to our health. Chronic stress is nothing but busyness beyond our tolerance limit. Without self-awareness, it's extremely difficult to handle such a situation. But with proper time management and prioritisation of work, we can handle busyness to a great extent. We must better recognize the need for and the importance of tasks at hand. More importantly, we must learn to do less, or even at times to do nothing. Doing nothing is far more difficult than doing something. When we have other things to do, even if they are unproductive or wasteful, doing nothing becomes all the more difficult a task. Sitting all alone in a room and observing our own stream of thoughts or our breathing is a dreadful prospect or experience for some people. Many are afraid of facing their own thoughts. So to avoid such situations, we keep ourselves busy, unaware of the difference between busyness and chronic stress.

"Doing nothing" doesn't mean that we sit quietly in a room and go into contemplative mode. We are not required to think or start analysing or imagining things. What we *do* need is to go beyond the incessant stream of thoughts. We should observe our thoughts, let them come and go. Just be aware of those thoughts. We shouldn't pass judgment on them, nor assign any meaning to them; all that's needed is plain awareness of thoughts. This is nothing but mindfulness meditation. Not only do we grow increasingly aware of ourselves, but in so doing we become more adept at managing our stress level. The best thing that we can do is to start practicing mindfulness in our day-to-day life. When we become focused, attentive, and start living more in the present, our stress will automatically decrease.

In the Netherlands, the Dutch people practice a lifestyle concept called *Niksen,* which means doing nothing. *Niksen* is promoting the art of really switching off, doing nothing, and taking time for oneself. It literally means "doing nothing," or to be idle or to do something without any utility. During mindfulness meditation, we are required to observe our own stream of thoughts and be present in the moments at hand. However, in the Netherlands, *Niksen* enthusiasts take time out to sit quietly and observe the surrounding environment. They might listen to music or lose themselves in thought; a long walk in their neighbourhood or a pretty forest is a popular choice. People can simply relax in a dark room. Now growing popular in other parts of the world, *Niksen* has proven to be an effective remedy for stress and anxiety.

11

Life's Journey – learning lessons while undertaking life's journey for our holistic development

Life is nothing but learning lessons till the end of our life. During the journey we undertake, we often come across moments when we have meaningful lessons to be learnt. If we don't learn then those lessons may be repeated in future other we pay a cost for not learning those lessons. Sometimes lessons are hidden, we need to decipher while on other occasions they may be explicit and clear. Either way, life is filled with lessons. During our life's journey we experience pain and suffering, joys and sorrows, celebrations and tragedies, hardships and heartaches. Every segment of our journey has something or the other to learn. There are challenges and opportunities we come across on many stages of our life. The journey is always interesting with uncertainties on many occasions. Sometimes a small and insignificant event can have wider ramifications on our life, it future course. This is called butterfly effect. According to this theory, a very small in initial conditions can have a significantly different outcome. Same theory applies in our life.

If we really want to live a meaningful life, then learning lessons is an extremely essential part of life. If we chose to live in the self-created comfort zone, doing the same kind of repetitive and habitual work then it's a different story. Otherwise to achieve a meaningful purpose or create a destiny we desire, we need to learn lessons. Learning lessons help us in achieving bigger objective in life. Not only we can avoid mistakes or failures but also we come across opportunities which we would otherwise miss. It also make us prepared better for facing challenges that we come across during the course of life's journey. *In fact, failures and setbacks contain bigger lessons for us to learn.* Very often, failures precede success. If we miss to learn lessons from the failure, then getting success on next occasion becomes more difficult and challenging.

Another important aspect of our life journey is that we come across people who play a very significant role in our life. May such people are destined to meet us for some bigger purpose, which we generally realize later. These are also known as meaningful coincidences, which we may experience during our lifetime. Those people give us meaningful lessons and help us in undertaking our journey. They may change the future course of journey. Otherwise, ours is like a train journey where people board and then left after accompanying us for certain stations. However, some of the people will continue to travel with us for most part of the journey. At any junction of our journey, if we look back and see what we have so far learnt based on our experiences, then we all have lessons and learnings that can be shared with others.

11.1 Accept the life as it is presented to us

Life is a dazzling collection of experiences of all kinds. Our life oscillates between extreme suffering on one end and blissful moments on the other end. Most of the time, we are nearer to the mid-line, leading a routine and repetitive life with its ups and downs. It's extremely difficult to be perfectly happy for a long time because of the complex nature of our mind. It becomes restless for one reason or another. Suffering can be very severe and usually persists longer than happiness. People suffer for days and months, because they don't know how to get to the heart of their problems. When a situation is "unsolvable," meaning beyond our control, what do we do? Should we keep on struggling and reacting to the problem and continue to suffer?

No one is immune to trying times, such as those we meet with serious accident, the loss of a loved one, sudden business failure, heavy financial loss, or any other miseries. Despite our best efforts, we simply cannot avoid eventualities in life. If we resist such situations, suffering is invariably aggravated. Finding and applying a solution to the problem would of course be the first option. When there is no immediate solution, we can change our perception of it; that is the other option. If we can neither solve the problem nor change our perception of it, then all that's left is to accept the situation as it is. It helps to remember the adage, "What we resist, persists." Suppose someone's leg is amputated after a severe accident, then the only options are to, first, wholeheartedly accept the situation and then, if available, find the best-possible prosthetic.

In most situations, the options are to either resist or accept the unfortunate event or experience. Take the very simple situation of, say, expecting to be late for an important engagement due to a traffic jam. The choices before us are clear: Either we start scolding the driver or cursing the traffic chaos or criticising the local traffic police for not making adequate provisions, or we may accept the traffic jam as something not in anyone's control. Either we waste our energy in reacting to persons and/or circumstances, thereby perpetuating them, or we see things from a bigger perspective and accept what's presented. Clearly, the choice lies with us.

Now let's take another example: a middle-level executive is working in a company where his boss frequently puts him down, irrespective of his performance, in front of his colleagues. In such delicate circumstances, when one's job is on the line, it's a difficult choice whether to accept the situation as it is, or not. If that executive confronts his boss, then he may lose his job; otherwise, he will have to compromise his self-respect. It's therefore important that we shouldn't accept a trying situation in all cases. "Acceptance" of the unacceptable can't be practiced. On such occasions, it helps to remember the Serenity Prayer: *God, grant me the serenity to accept the things I cannot change, the courage to change the things I can, and wisdom to know the difference. Here, beauty lies in our ability to be receptive and flexible in adapting ourselves to changed circumstances.* We should accept challenges wholeheartedly and learn from these experiences when our plans fall through.

Reluctant to accept our own failures or mistakes, we generally try to rationalize or justify them. That's just human nature. Acceptance is quite difficult on such occasions. However, the fact is, no mistake or failure is without a hidden lesson. We must accept responsibility unconditionally for any outcome/result of our actions. Receptivity and acceptance of changing circumstances is key to success. Looking at case studies of many extremely successful personalities, we realize that their initial journey was not free from failures. Such people have the ability to accept their failures, snap back fast from setbacks, and carry on!

Acceptance means we can turn our distressing and angry ruminations into equanimity and progressive thoughts. On such occasions it helps to embrace thoughts like: Whatever I could do, I did; now I can't do anything further or Whatever has happened, has happened; now I must move on. An attitude of acceptance can neutralize unpleasant experiences. Otherwise, there is no limit to the tail-chasing ruminations over the events that have taken place. There is a movement in psychology known as positive psychology that stresses the power of acceptance. Based on this, some therapies, including an Acceptance and Commitment Therapy (ACT), have been introduced. ACT is commonly used in reducing the symptoms of depression, anxiety, obsessive-compulsive disorder (OCD), and psychoses. It also helps in tackling chronic stress.

Through ACT, patients are taught to practice mindfulness, to be aware and observe present moments in a non-judgmental way so that they can accept and tolerate negative thoughts and feelings. In most of these abnormal mental conditions, sufferers are badly trapped in negative and distressing thoughts. People fail to control the incessant stream of harmful thoughts. If we are able to practice acceptance and mindfulness through ACT, we can overcome the problem of negativity associated with stress and mental illnesses.

With the power of acceptance, we can overcome almost every challenge. What really matters in life is the wisdom and resilient that we bring to bear on difficult situations. Resilience impels us forward during tough times. If we don't accept the situation as it is, we may get energetically stuck in those circumstances, and that may jeopardise our journey. Most of the time, rigid mind-set and attitude lock us in to those trying times. Therefore, to redesign our life's journey, we need to inculcate the habit of acceptance.

11.2 3 extremely hard things to do, but once we succeed; we can surely transform our life

Most of us do not change significantly throughout our lifetime. We tend to stay and enjoy life in our comfort zones, where we feel secure. Disturbing the status quo is always a difficult move, due to fear of the unknown. And that's why leading a conditioned and repetitive life is an easy option for most of us. Even when conditions are not optimal for growth, we love to resist change, rather than making an attempt to transform our thinking and our lives. Unless we grow and evolve to a higher level, we may never experience life's deeper satisfactions. Without basic contentment, happiness will always be a distant dream. To evolve progressively in life, we should continue to adapt to changing situations. However, we are required to make consistent efforts to change ourselves, to face and confront the rigidity in our thinking and behaviour. The following suggestions for growth are extremely hard to implement, but if we succeed, our life will surely be transformed.

To detach from our mind and thoughts : Each one of us is deeply identified with his or her mind. We feel that our mind, body, and inner self is a single entity. This identification is complete in most of us. To distinguish one's mind from its steady stream of thoughts is a nearly impossible task. When we feel "uptight" in any way, and match that feeling with related thoughts about what's gone wrong, we are trapped in a negative loop. The more we try to distract our attention away from our mind, the more we are attracted to the same set of compelling thoughts. In fact, on many such occasions, the frequency and intensity of the negative thoughts increase. This happens to all who do not learn the art of managing their mind. And, as previously discussed, we must also contend with a strong inclination toward negative thoughts as opposed to positive ones.

Unless we know how to observe our thoughts and feelings nonjudgmentally, we continue to suffer from a stream of negative thoughts. This simple observation can be achieved through the practice of mindfulness and meditation. Because of our modern lifestyle, meditation may strike us as a difficult or time-consuming task. After all, we are "busy people" with no time to sit quietly with closed eyes – doing nothing! – while watching our thoughts. There are many myths and misconceptions associated with meditation that may stop us from starting the practice afresh. Precisely for these reasons, relatively few people, especially in India, practice meditation. Absent meditation, it is much more difficult to detach ourselves from our mind. But just 20 minutes a day of this very simple practice can definitely bring numerous transformational changes to our mental and physical health.

To change our habitual and conditioned behaviour : Since most of us continue to repeat the same thoughts and actions throughout our waking hours, we tend to become habitual. If nothing else, the familiarity of a fixed modus operandi helps us to carry out routine tasks with ease. Very little effort, attention, or energy is required for these everyday actions.. Our habitual and conditioned behaviour starts in early childhood, when parents taught us to do things for the first time. Those learnings are deeply embedded in our subconscious mind, after which we generally don't attempt to challenge them. Our belief system as well as behaviour remains generally fixed. Since parents are the role models for their children, people often continue to emulate their parents' ways and retain their values right into adulthood. Our behaviour becomes as automatic, conditioned, and as subconscious as pedalling a bicycle.

Figure 11.2: It's extremely difficult to change our habitual and highly conditioned behaviour, a serious impediment to our growth.

For those who somehow consider themselves better than others, there is even less interest in changing habitual behaviour. Every day, the same sets of thoughts are recycled, as life becomes more and more habitual. When offered an opportunity to change, or to see something in a different light, such people like to say that they are "all set" -- set in their own secure and comfy prison. Responses to any given circumstance become static and predictable. Such a life becomes easy, effortless, and, seemingly, secure. However, this is a serious impediment to mental and spiritual growth. To change any strongly conditioned and habitual behaviour is an extremely wrenching and time-consuming task. Many prefer to remain imprisoned in their self-created zone of comfort and ease. Success in changing habits and behaviour patterns opens the way to transformative changes.

To practice the power of acceptance: One of the main causes of suffering in life is resistance to change. We resist and react to any change that brings disruption to our life. No one is immune to unwelcome changes. Impermanence is the only constant in life. There are situations that we come across in life where nothing can be done. Circumstances can be so perplexing or tragic that nothing is left for us to do but accept the situation as it is. Let's say that Arjun met with an accident that was someone else's fault and his leg had to be amputated. One option for him would be to keep on suffering the unfairness of it all -- "Why me?" Although nothing could be done once the tragedy had taken place, his bitterness toward the perpetrator and the surgeon – and life itself -- could remain. The second option would be to accept what has happened to him and move on with his life. The latter option is of course the only way to cope with the situation and escape much of the suffering. However, it's not an easy thing to practice acceptance. Acceptance is not resignation or failure on our part; it's simply accepting and allowing a situation to be as it is.

There is a famous quote from Carl Jung, the legendary Swiss psychiatrist and psychoanalyst : "What we resist persists" and, he added, "will grow in size." Most of us do feel at least a few deficiencies in ourselves. Ideally, we will accept what we presently are. We must not regret, or feel ashamed if something is lacking in us. However, we can always make efforts to improve our character and personality -- which are entirely in our hands. If someone is born with an intractable or unchangeable deficiency, he or she has to live with it. One must accept reality. Too often we mistake acceptance for weakness or surrender, when it is actually a sign of great strength. When we can accept life as it's presented to us, we can be sure that we are growing in spirit.

It's always a challenge to bring about major changes in one's life. Since we are all inclined toward a comfortable life with the least disturbance possible, we generally resist big changes. Too risky! Yet if one can succeed at the above three challenges, however difficult they may be, they can transform their lives.

11.3 3 harsh realities of life: the earlier we learn them, the better our life's journey

It's well said that life is certainly not arranged for one to be happy. We can never be perfectly happy, and when we are, we know that it probably won't last. Conversely, if we don't know how to handle our mind, we can keep on suffering for months or years at a time. On any small pretext, we can become severely stressed. If we fail to manage our mind, instead letting things go out from our control, it can lead to thoughts of, or actual, suicide. Once people are trapped in their own vicious cycle of toxic and distressing thoughts, it becomes extremely difficult to break out of that cycle.

India is the most depressed and also among the unhappiest countries in the world. Nearly half of the working population is mentally stressed. Millions suffer from anxiety. The reasons are multifold, but the main reason is that we don't know how to care for and manage our mind. We attach more importance to physical rather than mental exercises like meditation. We must also learn from our experiences, which give us valuable lessons. The following are the hard realities that we should learn for our spiritual growth.

We are imperfect and insecure humans: Humans have evolved from apelike primitives though the process of evolution. For more than two million years, humans lived as hunter-gatherers. For more than 95,000 generations, according to evolutionary biologists, they were hunting animals and collecting plants, fruits, and seeds for their food. They were also protecting themselves from predators and extremely harsh environmental conditions while trying to deal with illness and disease. Therefore, fear and aggression got embedded in their collective psyche. Now in the modern world, though living conditions have come up a notch or two, the same part of the brain so easily triggered by fear and aroused to aggression – the amygdala -- remains active.

Figure 11.3: We are inherently very insecure and vulnerable people.

We are modern humans with a partially primitive brain. This is the reason we are so fearful and anxious. Mentally fragile, we tend to become angry (and even violent) at the slightest provocation. Unless we make consistent efforts, it's difficult to manage our mind and thoughts. Mind is negatively biased as well, as it wanders randomly when unfocused and inattentive.. Even a small negative event or interaction with others can feel distressing. Our thinking is also flawed as we suffer from many cognitive biases, as explained earlier in this book. Because of all these qualities, we humans are imperfect and insecure. This reality we must acknowledge and realize as we continue along life's journey.

We can never be perfectly happy : while there may be many things we want to achieve in life; the ultimate purpose is to be happy and live life to the fullest. However, many of us don't set our priorities with this goal in mind. Almost all of us strive to be successful in life rather than realizing happiness. We are led to believe that if we possess wealth and comforts, happiness will automatically come. And when we do become wealthy, most of us are inclined to chase after even more pleasure and emotional gratification. In the process of seeking so-called happiness, we tend to create bigger desires. After just a few months of new-car ownership, a desire may arise for an even better one. If we buy a lovely home, it's almost inevitable that an even lovelier one may soon be in in our sights.

Satisfaction and contentment never come from the pursuit of wealth, material goods, or pleasure. We tend to forget this basic fact. Money of course is needed for happiness, but only to a certain extent. Then it becomes neutral, and further pursuit of it is counterproductive. Rather than seeking happiness in the outside world by way of possessions and indulgence in pleasures, we need to look inside our mind. We must learn to manage our mind if we want happiness. This we mostly don't do. That's why we can never be perfectly happy : we don't set our priorities straight and more importantly; we look for happiness in the outside world.

True reality of the world is beyond our reach: Each one of us perceives reality in our own unique way. Through our senses, we receive sensory stimuli that are interpreted by our brain and stored as internal models of reality. Unique to each individual, these mental constructs, and all their assumptions, are shaped by our educational, social, and political background, and resulting belief systems. Therefore, there is no way by which we can know the objective reality of this world. Now fake news and "alternative facts" through social media are further aggravating this problem. Across the world, reality is being distorted and manipulated by social media. We must, in any case, remember that what we think we know about the presumed truth may not be based on truthful and objective information.

11.4 We must learn at least 7 great lessons for our life's journey

Life offers us endless opportunities to learn lessons from our experiences, right up to our dying day. Our ability to learn from our surrounding environment as well as from those with whom we interact is critical. Unless we can learn from our failures and mistakes, we can't grow mentally and spiritually. Wisdom comes from experiences that carry meaningful messages required for life's journey. The following are the lessons one must learn to lead a happy and meaningful life.

Impermanence – the ultimate reality of life: The most fundamental aspect of all existence is impermanence. The concept of impermanence (anicca) forms the bedrock of the Buddha's teachings. Reality is never static. For instance, in our physical bodies, billions of cells die and are replaced by fresh cells every day. Most parts of our body are changed in about 10 years. Likewise, everything in the universe is in a constant state of flux. Our life's conditions are also changing all the time. However, we generally don't notice it. Whenever there is change leading to disruption in our life, we resist. We don't accept changes easily if they are not suitable and favourable for us. When we resist or react automatically to them, suffering starts. This is one of the biggest causes of suffering in our life.

Our life's journey is like a rollercoaster ride with ups and downs: No one escapes the inevitable vicissitudes of life. Even small and insignificant incidents can morph into major events. This is called the butterfly effect. The idea is that a small change can make much bigger changes happen. Every day our newspapers are filled with stories of accidents and unusual happenings. People lose their lives through no fault of their own. Our behaviour, thinking, and the way we take action are all highly complex, their outcomes not often in our hands. We decide one thing and something else may very well happen. No one – not even kings and queens – can expect life to be a magic carpet ride.

Ego is the biggest impediment to our spiritual growth : Ego is self-image that we have built over time; it's another name for self. We create our self-image by all the labels that people pin on us. There is a very strong sense of self-identification: "THIS is what I am." Ego, as we age, may become greedy, fearful, limited, and increasingly self-centred. All of our emotional and psychological problems arise from this largely false idea of ourselves. Many people keep on accumulating material things in order to satisfy their ego, which, by its very nature, tends to inflate if not held in check. In this process, we also forget our true nature. However, for creating a deeper sense of satisfaction and happiness, we need to "dissolve" – or at least tame! -- our ego. Until this happens, it's almost impossible to grow spiritually .

We are what we tell ourselves, each moment of the day: Lord Buddha very rightly asserted that "We are nothing but thoughts." We are what we think about ourselves and the world around us. Thoughts lead to choices, which in turn become our actions and fodder for further thoughts. Then our actions make our destiny. There is no reality beyond our mind and the thoughts that are generated throughout the day. The outer world is the mirror of the inner world, and vice versa. If we entertain positive thoughts and block or defuse distressing and toxic ones, we are happy persons. Heaven and hell are nothing more than the constructs of terrified minds. Therefore, it's imperative that we observe what kinds of thoughts we harbour from moment to moment. Ultimately these very thoughts will determine our future, our destiny.

Invest in yourself : Maximum possible returns are to be expected when we make a strong investment in ourselves. Whether this investment takes the form of money, energy, and/or time, it's the best choice. Whatever the purpose or purposes of our life may be, they cannot be realized unless we grow in life. Even more important than physical development is our mental and spiritual growth. Without it, life becomes stagnant, even robotic Obviously, such a life offers little to no satisfaction and is sometimes characterized as a "living death." Therefore, whenever and wherever possible, we should invest in ourselves, so that we may continue to grow.

Life is a solo journey ; barring a few friends and family members, no one travels with us : Each one of us is generally lost in his or her own *very busy* world. We are perpetually "on the go," pursuing our goals and passions. In our highly materialistic world, there can be stiff competition among ourselves for available resources. "Success," however one defines it, is often the prime motive. Many see success in terms of having more money and power, higher status in society, and more creature comforts. However, we humans are social animals, interacting and sharing with others all the time. In this digital age, we are connected with large numbers of "friends" on social media. However – and perhaps as a partial consequence --- true person-to-person, caring friendships appear to be becoming more rare. Studies (and personal observations) show that people -- especially those of the younger and elder generations -- are becoming lonelier in modern society.

Figure 11.4: We all undertake solo journey but in the modern age, we are getting more and more disconnected from others.

We learn best from our own experiences, especially failure. We can't learn the hard lessons necessary for growth unless we experience failures and commit mistakes in life. Failure is an essential part of learning. Life generously offers a series of lessons that we keep on learning and assimilating. Our lifetime experience is a cocktail of failures and successes, suffering and joy, ups and downs. Studies have established that our best learning comes not from our classes in school, but from real-life experiences and failures. In their "85% rule," researchers use that percentage to account for the things we learn through experiences. They further suggest that people who fail 15% of the time learn the fastest. Though it's difficult to generalize, it's true in most cases that our greatest learning and personal growth comes through failure. We can then plan more wisely and meticulously. When we stumble under pressure, we become attuned to our weaknesses. Unless we are "brought up short," we don't seriously pay attention to our weaker areas. Behind every defeat and mistake we experience, there is something important to learn.

12

Moving Toward the End of Life's Journey

Every one dies but most of us are afraid of it. We don't even want to discuss it with our close family members and friends. We want to live longer but we don't want to take the steps required for longevity. It's a difficult situation, through which most of us pass. However, most of us don't fear death as much as we fear the process of dying, especially the uncertainty surrounding death. We all want to die gracefully and peacefully. If we are certain of dying in a peaceful way, then that fear is substantially less. What is really dreadful about death is the suffering and pain that is associated with the process of dying. Therefore we are fearful of death because of uncertainty, physical and emotional pain, and the loss of everything and everyone we have loved in life. The anxiety that's caused by thoughts of ceasing to be is called death anxiety.. We also experience the fear of being harmed in life. It's the most fundamental companion to death anxiety.

As time moves along, we all start seeing gradual changes in our physical body. We don't become old at any specific age. Aging is highly subjective and its nature and speed vary from one individual to the next. One is our own age, purely the years, months, and days we have so far lived. This is known as chronological age. Another marker is our biological age. It refers to physiological changes in the body that commonly occur as we age. Then comes psychological age, which is based on how we feel, act, and behave. A 70-year-old may feel as if he or she is 80 years old or perhaps just 50 years of age, depending on the way that persons feels and acts. Our feelings and attitudes toward aging have significant impact on the process of aging itself. We have tremendous power over the speed of our own aging. We can accelerate as well as slow down the process of aging. There are proven ways to retard aging. Health experts have prescribed many effective approaches, on the basis of recent research, that can slow down our aging.

Interestingly, as we age, time appears to be moving faster than it did before. When we are young, we continue to experience new things in life, facing fresh delights and novel challenges. As we make our way into adulthood, there may also be a struggle for better living conditions. At that time, comparatively speaking, time moves slowly. On the other hand, when we get older, we mostly experience repetitive and habitual life, doing the same things again and again. At that stage, time, unbroken by nuance, seems to move much faster. Older people tend to say they "don't know where the time has gone." Time really does move fast when there's nothing much to distinguish Monday from Friday. So how can we slow down our perception of time when we get old? The answer lies in experiencing, thinking about and learning new things at that older age. By visiting new places, starting new projects, learning new languages, reading books and magazines, and playing mind games like Sudoku, we can make our life more interesting and creative.

As we get older, most of us slowly and reluctantly start accepting the inevitability of death. Our only wish for those final days is to die gracefully, without pain and suffering. We don't want to experience uncertainty about death. One study shows that when people face imminent death, they start accepting it and focusing on the positive because they know they don't have much time left. Absent soul-searching and acceptance, most people are uncomfortable in talking about their death. This is also the reason why very few write a will, designating distribution of their assets after they die. The only way to accept death and the process of dying is through mindfulness. The greater the self-awareness and mindful living, the more easily we can accept death and prepare well for the last leg of our life's journey.

12.1 Time is all in the mind . It seems to run faster as we get older, but we can slow it down.

The time displays on our clocks and the time we all experience is different. Each one of us experiences time in our own unique way. Though time is objective, our experience of it is subjective. Most of us have surely noticed that time seems to speed up as we age. Now numerous studies have confirmed this experience. Time appears to be moving much faster than it did in our childhood and young adulthood when, for instance, a single summer felt like a year.. Depending on one's outlook and experience, the days, months, and years appear to offer either less or more time than usual. Even irrespective of age, we often experience time subjectively. When we are bored or in painful situations, time moves slowly. On the other hand, for one who is watching an entertaining film or engaged in interesting conversation, the time flies. In the words of Albert Einstein, "Put your hand on a hot stove for a minute, and it seems like an hour. Sit with a pretty girl for an hour, and it seems like a minute. That's relativity."

Researchers have not, thus far, been able to pinpoint the exact reason or reasons why the perception of time changes so radically as we age. While there are many theories, it remains a mysterious phenomenon. In 2005, two German researchers at Ludwig Maximilian University of Munich conducted a very important study on time perception. Around 500 participants, ages 14 to 94 years, took part in the study. They were asked to fill out questionnaires relating to their perception of the passage of time. Possible answers ranged from "very slowly" to "very fast." Results support the popular consensus that the passage of time seems to accelerate with age.

One convincing explanation of this old/young difference in time perception is that when we are getting old, our life often becomes highly repetitive, routine, and habitual. As there are hardly any new and unfamiliar experiences, the brain is not processing new information. Life remains by and large the same day after day – its hours smudged in sameness. On the other hand, when we are in childhood or later as adults, are brains are almost constantly processing fresh new experiences. The person is seeing things for the first time, witnessing new places, meeting new people, learning new ideas, concepts, and skills. Therefore, the researcher explained, "As a result, our early years tend to be relatively overrepresented in our autobiographical memory and, on reflection, seem to have lasted longer." (*Scientific American: 'Why* Does Time Seem to Speed Up with Age?" July 2016) As we grow older, most people are now mostly on default mode, thinking and experiencing the same things again and again, with few significant or challenging changes in routine life. This makes the time seem to run faster. We will then always be surprised when the next Diwali season or Christmas comes up so soon after the last one. How quickly the new festival time has arrived!

Figure 12.1: Time runs faster as we age due to doing more of habitual, repetitive and monotonous tasks during the day.

Many of us also start to feel "settled" once we enter our late forties or early fifties. Our children may leave the nest for college or job, get married, start a family...and life becomes comparatively comfortable and settled as the struggle period is, for the most part, over. At this point, many find themselves "mellowing out" - and feeling more satisfied with life. This tends to be especially true when one reaches retirement from active service or a profession, and life becomes more routine and habitual. The same routine in the morning -- going for a walk, practicing yoga, reading newspapers, checking email, having breakfast followed by the afternoon leg of similarly regular activities. This goes on and on. Barring new experiences, now much fewer in number (such as marriages, graduations, visiting children abroad, the birth of grandchildren, etc.),life moves along on expected lines. No newness in life. No new memories are excitedly added. Life speeds up and now starts sprinting to the finish line. And then alas! It's New Year's Eve again!

Recently, a study concluded that "Physics is the reason time seems to fly when you're grown." According to Adrian Bejan, the J.A. Jones Distinguished Professor of Mechanical Engineering at Duke University, ''the present is different from the past because the mental viewing has changed, not because somebody's clock rings. Days seemed to last longer in your youth because the young mind receives more images during one day than the same mind in old age." He further explains that 'the fact that adults have fewer new experiences than children contributes to the appearance that time is moving faster. Therefore as we get older time becomes slower because no new experiences and so no processing of images.

Now the question arises as to whether we can slow down the pace of time as we get older? Yes, we can do it by being open to trying and experiencing new things in life. For starters, we can minimize our routines. Start reading books of interest, visit new places, make new friends, start playing a new sport such as golf or pickleball (excellent choices for older people), and engage in mental games like Sudoku. What we are required to do is break down the walls of your comfort zone, come out from the areas of comfort and ease and start venturing into new fields, develop new habits, and learn new skills. All these activities will definitely help anybody to escape the sense of loneliness and vulnerability. Secondly, they will go a long way toward sidestepping age-related mental diseases like dementia and, most importantly, help you to lead a healthy and fulfilling life.

12.2 Learn to slow down the aging process! We can surely do it to a great extent.

We are all programmed to die one day. How many tomorrows each one of us will see, no crystal ball can tell. People can survive for decades with terminal diseases. In the world, a little over 53,000 people die every day, and about two-thirds die of age-related diseases. In developed nations, nearly 90% of people, due to improved medical facilities and greater awareness of health, die of conditions and complications related to the natural aging process. Our average lifespan is determined both by vulnerability to accidents, and geriatric or lifestyle conditions such as cardiac diseases, cancer, diabetes, obesity, and lung diseases. Thanks to improved living conditions and medical interventions, people can now slow the aging process. We can better treat some of the leading causes of death, impacting how long we live. Longevity and healthcare are intimately linked. Some see death, while inevitable, as a condition to be indefinitely avoided.

There are many effective ways by which we can manage our aging speed. Depending upon our lifestyle choices, in a single decade we can age by fifteen years or just seven years. Obviously, some age much faster than others. Many age-related physical symptoms become very prominent in some people while in others they appear quite later. As we age, many start witnessing increased fatigue, weakened bones, and ill health ; we start observing wrinkles, age spots, and sagging skin. Aging is an outcome of complex changes in our normal biological functions.

There are many reasons why we age. However, three well-established triggers of the aging process are, first, shortening of telomeres, the tip at each end of chromosomes in our cells ; second, deterioration of the mechanism that repairs damage to DNA;; and lastly, accumulation of free radicals in the body. When cells divide chromosomes are replicated and each daughter cell inherits an identical pair. Chromosomes are thread-like very minute structures located inside the nucleus of cells. Each chromosome is made of protein and a single molecule of deoxyribonucleic acid (DNA).

Telomeres make sure that the DNA gets copied properly when cells divide. Each time a cell copies itself, the DNA stays the same but the telomeres get shorter. A time comes when telomeres get too short to do their job, causing our cells to age and stop functioning properly. Therefore, telomeres act as the aging clock in every cell. Once telomere length reaches a particular cut-off point, the cell can no longer divide and eventually it dies. How telomeres work and why some people age faster than others still needs to be answered by scientists. Further, as we age, the environment and normal cellular processes cause damage to our genes. This damage compounds over the course of life and is known to accelerate aging. Regarding free radical theory, many of the changes that occur as our bodies' age are caused by free radicals. Damage to DNA, protein cross-linking, and some other changes are attributed to free radicals. Over time, this damage accumulates, resulting in aging.

Death and the process of dying is one of the most fascinating areas of research. Many institutions across the world are studying this subject to delay and possibly even defeat this process. Death will be "optional" within just 25 years, and the aging process will be "reversible," according to two genetic engineers, José Luis Cordeiro and David Wood. Their book, *The Death of Death,* asserts that "immortality is a real and scientific possibility that could come much earlier than originally thought. Humans will die only in accidents, never of natural causes or illness, by around the year 2045." They further maintain that "Old age starts to be classified as an 'illness' so that publicly funded research into its 'cure' can extend." Cordeiro, who is based at MIT in the USA, says he has "chosen not to die" and that in 30 years' time, he will be "younger" than he is today. There is no denying the possibility that that time may come sooner, rather than later.

Figure 12.2: Leading an active life through regular physical exercise is the best way to slow down the aging process

That we have tremendous power to slow down our aging process is not commonly known. Many variables that influence how long we live can be altered. In this age of social media, plenty of videos go viral every day in which 90-plus people are dancing, running marathons, and many other activities which we generally don't expect at that age. The actions we can take to increase our odds of a longer and more satisfying lifetime are really quite simple. Every day, new research is published on how to slow down aging.

The first and the foremost requirement for longevity is that we remain active throughout life. One undisputed fact about the modern lifestyle is that we humans are becoming less and less active. The majority still don't move or walk sufficiently during the day. Insufficient physical activity is a leading risk for many lifestyle diseases, such as diabetes, heart and lung diseases, and cancer, and has a negative effect on mental health and quality of life.

In fact, people in India are among the world's laziest, taking an average of 4297 steps in a day, compared to the world average of about 5,000 steps. Out of 46 countries, India's rank is 39th. For a healthy life, we should take at least 10,000 steps a day. Most of the workday, as we know, is spent sitting for up to 8-9 hours a day -- highly harmful for our health. Recently, the World Health Organisation (WHO) released a report ranking countries based on how physically active their citizens are. Surprisingly, India ranked 117 in the list of 168 nations, with 34% of our population being far too sedentary. Medical science agrees: there is no substitute for physical exercise for those seeking a long and healthy life. Also weighing in on longevity-friendly measures, Harvard Medical School, USA, outlines the following five mandatory actions (other than the obvious avoidance of smoking):

1. Regular physical and mental exercise/activities daily
2. Eat a healthy diet rich in whole grains, vegetables and fruits, and substitute healthier monounsaturated and polyunsaturated fats for unhealthy saturated fats and trans fats. Also eat less! Studies have confirmed that eating less helps reduce signs of aging .
3. Maintain a healthy weight and body shape.
4. Challenge your mind. Keep learning and trying new activities (to limit cognitive decline).

A Johns Hopkins-led study of 6,200 men and women over years found that those who adopted four smart behaviours reduced their chance of death from all causes within that time frame by an astounding 80 percent. How to live longer? Here are those four factors, all within our control:

1. Although your best plan to live longer is to adopt all four lifestyle factors, if you had to choose one, the researchers say, this is it -- avoid smoking.
2. The healthiest people in the study maintained a body mass index (BMI)—a ratio of height to weight that measures body mass -- of less than 25.
3. Aim for about 30 minutes of activity a day most days of the week. Try breaking it into three 10-minute bouts of activity per day – a 10-minute walk in the morning, another at lunch, and a stroll after dinner.

The study found that the healthiest people followed a Mediterranean-style diet. That means a diet rich in fresh fruits and vegetables, tree nuts with healthy oils, fish (and less red meats), whole-grain carbs and olive oil for cooking.

Over and above all, meditation also helps in slowing the aging process. As we have seen earlier, the shortening of telomeres is the main physical reason behind aging, and one of the main reasons behind this shortening is mental stress. Numerous studies have established that meditation practice helps reduce mental stress to a great extent. Stress is one of the greatest contributors to lifestyle diseases, the most outstanding being obesity, diabetes, and cardiovascular ills.

12.3 The fear of death and dying: We must learn to die gracefully and peacefully

'I exist, therefore I die' is a statement from Descartes of universal truth. Death is the certainty that no one can doubt. When and how we die are equally uncertain. One can guess, but no one can know about their own death. As long as we live, we live with fear of death and dying. When we are driving or crossing the street, fear of death is ever in the background. Obviously, it's why we are careful and vigilant. Not only at the individual level is this fear of inevitable death, but also in the collective psyche. Fear of pain associated with dying is far more powerful than the fear of death itself. We all want to live long and then die peacefully. This is perhaps the strongest desire we all have in common. All our actions and choices are directed toward the goal of long and abundant life.

No one dies because of aging. There is almost always a natural cause of death when we die, even in very old age, such as diseases or infections. Major causes of natural deaths are heart attacks and heart diseases, diabetes, diarrheal disorders, respiratory/lung diseases, cancer, Alzheimer's and other kinds of dementia. According to World Health Organization statistics from 2015, the top 10 killers, many of which are lifestyle-related, account for 51.4% of all deaths globally. Ischemic heart disease and heart attack/stroke are the world's biggest killers. Such deaths are, for the most part, painful and traumatic. On the other hand, many succumb to a silent heart attack, while sleeping. Among the worst, "ways to go," certain kinds of cancer can be the most painful of all.

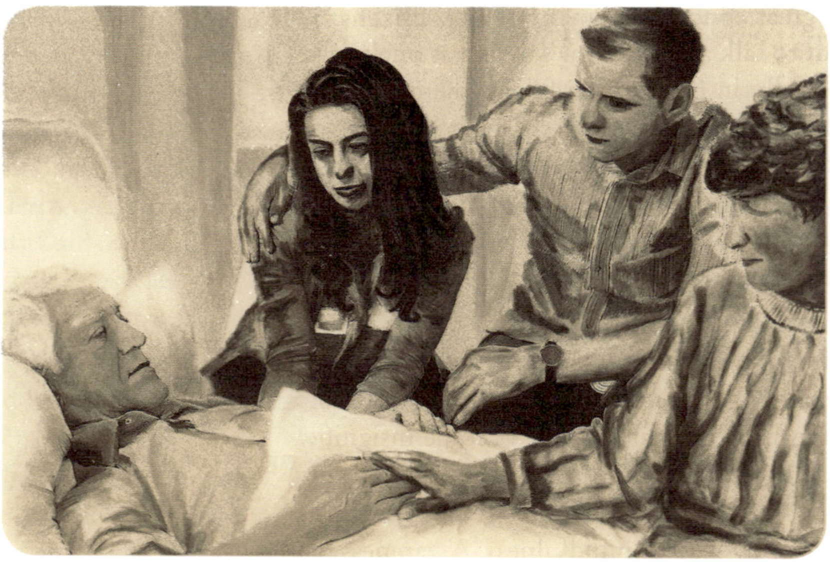

Figure 12.3: We all want to die gracefully especially when our close family members and friends are with us

We all want to experience a "good death" after living to the fullest. Looking into what constitutes a successful or good death, an important study by researchers at the University of California, San Diego School of Medicine, came up with some answers. The study identified 11 core themes of a good death: preferences for a specific dying process, pain-free status, religiosity/spiritualty, emotional well-being, life completion, treatment preferences, dignity, family, quality of life, relationship with healthcare provider, and "other."

The top three themes across all stakeholder groups were preferences for a specific dying process (94% of reports), pain-free status (81%), and emotional well-being (64%). People want to die not only peacefully, but with some measure of control. No one wants to suffer pain, which is the biggest fear of all, To eliminate suffering, euthanasia (the painless killing of a patient suffering from an incurable and painful disease, or in an irreversible coma) or palliative care (specialized medical care for people living with a serious illness) are becoming popular worldwide.

The top concerns for aged people facing imminent death are first, that their death be painless ; second, that they not become a burden on others ; and thirdly, that they are not alone near or at their death. Loneliness is a great concern for many senior citizens. Sadly, most people do not want to talk about death. To discuss one's own death is generally taboo, especially in India. Even family members and close friends of terminal patients don't dare to discuss this delicate subject. The fact is, by not acknowledging and discussing death, we cause more harm to ourselves. Our quality of life would be improved considerably if only we could embrace death gracefully. We must take death and dying as a natural phenomenon in life, and work on removing our inhibitions.

Being mindful of death can have a positive impact on our health and well-being. Our whole perspective on life will change when we keep the inevitability of death at the back of our minds. Our worries and fearful ruminations will become insignificant. We will always keep meaningful goals in mind. Quality of life improves if we think about death for at least a few moments before we start each day. This can be possible by way of mindfulness. Awareness of death will lead to greater self-awareness and more power of acceptance. This then opens the heart to more compassion and empathy for others.

Facing our own death when it becomes a certainty, as happens in cases of advanced cancer, is greatly eased by the practice of mindfulness. It can also be extremely helpful in alleviating pain. Rather than resisting and automatically reacting to pain, people can, through mindfulness, be aware of pain and accept it nonjudgmentally. In addition to strong pain- relieving medications and palliative care, mindfulness can be a very effective approach to preparing patients for death. Through mindfulness, one can accept death more gracefully and peacefully. Of course, mindful acceptance does not completely remove the suffering, but it can reduce the pain and fear of death. Through acceptance, not only can we calmly acknowledge the onset of death, but also the feelings and thoughts associated with death.

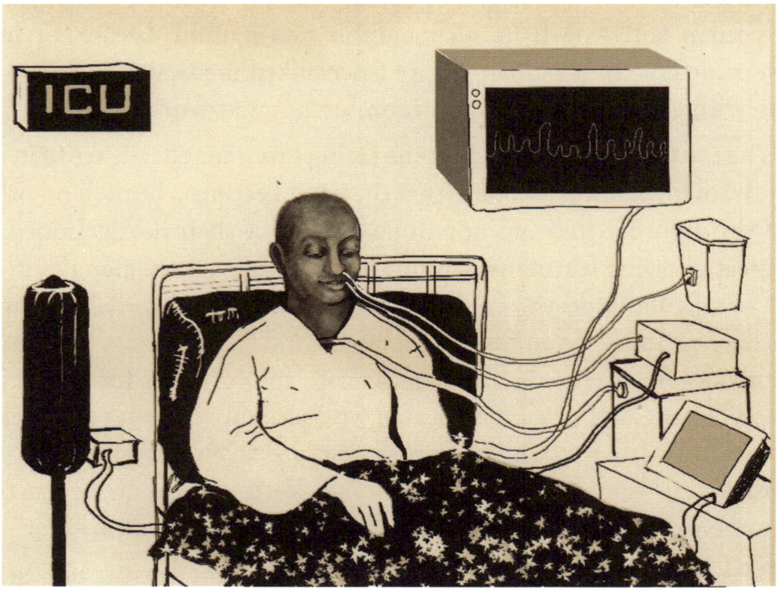

Figure 12.3A: Through the practice of mindfulness, we can accept death more peacefully.

There is also a Buddhist meditation practice called Maranasati, which uses various visualization and contemplation techniques to meditate on the nature of death. This is also known as mindfulness of death or death awareness. When we forget that we will die, we tend to lead a habitual and complacent life. We may even start doing things that we don't really approve of or wish for ourselves. Through this meditation practice, we become more aware and accepting of death as a natural ending to our life. In Maranasati, practitioners learn to accept impermanence and suffering, while also becoming more closely and intimately aware of death.

OOO

AWAKENING THE THINKING MIND
BALVINDER KUMAR

Welcome to the
Book Release Function
'Awakening the Thinking Mind'
BY BALVINDER KUMAR
In presence of Chief Guest
SHRI NARENDRA SINGH TOMAR
Hon'ble Union Minister of Rural Development, Panchayati Raj, Drinking Water & Sanitation

AWAKENING THE THINKING MIND

AWAKENING THE THINKING MIND
SPIRITUAL JOURNEY

AWAKENING THE THINKING MIND